A TASTE OF AM[

Since abandoning her career as a Fleet Street news reporter to have her family, Clare Walker's life has revolved around food of one sort or another, be it home cooking, professional catering or food retailing. During her eight years at home with two children she researched, recipe-tested and wrote two cookery books. The first, *The Home Gardener's Cookbook*, which she produced with co-author Gill Coleman, was published by Penguin in 1980. *A Taste of American Cooking* was compiled during her two-and-a-half year stay in New York City, when she also co-founded a new community newspaper, the *Main Street Wire*. On returning to Britain in 1981, Clare returned to full-time journalism, joining the weekly magazine *Caterer and Hotelkeeper*, of which she became deputy editor in 1983. That job brought her into contact with Britain's top hoteliers and famous chefs such as Anton Mosimann, Prue Leith and others. In August 1985 she moved into another food area – this time consumer retailing when she took on the editorship of another weekly trade journal, *Super Marketing*.

Clare Walker is married to Iain Walker, assistant editor of the *Mail on Sunday*. They have two children and live in Surrey.

Keryn Christiansen grew up in Perth, Western Australia, where she went to the medical school of the University of Western Australia to gain her Bachelor of Medicine and Bachelor of Surgery degree. By the time she and her husband went to New York, she was a registrar in microbiology at the Royal Perth Hospital. On her return, she resumed her career and became a specialist in clinical microbiology before becoming a consultant. Dr Christiansen's love of cooking began only after she married – before that she happily admits to not being able to cook a thing. Now, however, she is an expert and experimental cook.

A
Taste of
AMERICAN
Cooking

Clare Walker
with Keryn Christiansen

PENGUIN BOOKS

Penguin Books Ltd, Harmondsworth, Middlesex, England
Viking Penguin Inc., 40 West 23rd Street, New York, New York 10010, U.S.A.
Penguin Books Australia Ltd, Ringwood, Victoria, Australia
Penguin Books Canada Limited, 2801 John Street, Markham, Ontario, Canada L3R 1B4
Penguin Books (N.Z.) Ltd, 182–190 Wairau Road, Auckland 10, New Zealand

First published 1986

Made and printed in Great Britain by
Cox & Wyman Ltd, Reading
Filmset in Ehrhardt (Linotron 202) by
Rowland Phototypesetting Ltd,
Bury St Edmunds, Suffolk

This book is dedicated to my mother,
Barbara Good

CONTENTS

PREFACE

I first met Keryn Christiansen beneath the large collection of national flags that edge the gardens of the United Nations building in New York. It was an auspicious place to begin a partnership which would eventually involve us in the cuisines of so many of those countries. At that time I had already embarked on my research for this book, and Keryn was soon to be occupied with her work as a Research Fellow in Infectious Diseases at New York's most prominent cancer centre. Our joint involvement in the book, however, did not begin until many months later.

My admiration for Keryn as a cook had been growing steadily the more I dined with her. She deftly boned the miniature chickens known in America as 'Cornish hens' with a skill that amply demonstrated the adroitness of her doctor's hands: she was as adept with the kitchen knife as she was with the scalpel! But that was not all that recommended Keryn as an ideal partner in my project. We shared the advantages of being able to see America with the fresh eyes of newcomers, of wanting to learn more about the native cuisine, and of enjoying the opportunity to experiment with new foods and new recipes.

Once our partnership was launched, our early morning coffee sessions began, during which we worked out together our menus for the following days, discussing what had been a success and why the odd disaster had ended up in 'the trash can'. One such example was the pioneer's 'vinegar pie', which proved that desperate people will eat anything! Fortunately, in this affluent day and age, we do not have to resort to such measures!

We also shared experimental cooking sessions together, trying out new dishes on our two families. Keryn became very popular in her department at the Sloan Kettering Memorial Hospital, where her American colleagues were regularly called upon to sample her culinary experiments and to pass critical judgement on their authenticity.

Once our friends, neighbours and colleagues became interested in our work, people started to hand over to us unusual or traditional cookbooks to help in our research, or home-made dishes for us to sample like Pennsylvanian sand tarts or pot pie, Jewish chicken soup, Norwegian meatballs. Everywhere we went we quizzed Americans on their background and their cooking heritage. Nothing was ever taken for granted. We conducted straw polls among our American acquaintances to find out the answers to things that puzzled us – for example, nowhere could we find out how 'popovers' are served. We soon learned that some people like them for breakfast with butter, while others serve them like their British counterpart, Yorkshire pudding, with roast beef.

Thanks to my partnership with Keryn, this book was completed, and as a result of the friendship which grew with the size of the manuscript, this is more than a cookbook – it is a collection of fond memories. For all that, I owe Keryn Christiansen a great debt of gratitude.

C.W.

ACKNOWLEDGEMENTS

Our major debt of gratitude goes to our two families, particularly husbands Iain and Frank, who willingly ate everything put in front of them – and not everything was initially a success! Their constructive criticisms and advice, coupled with their staunch support and encouragement, helped us greatly in the compilation of this book. The four children, Kirsty, Andrew, Elaine and Brad, have between them eaten their way through most of this book, usually without complaint, for which we thank them.

To all our American friends and colleagues who gave us their help, we will always be grateful for their support and friendship. Special thanks go from Clare to Karen Purritz, Lynette Chattanow, her parents Mr and Mrs Youndt, Nanchang Redfern, Ailsa Brown and many others from Roosevelt Island, New York. Keryn would also like to thank her colleagues Ed Bernard, Dr Nancy Collins and Helen Rigopoulos.

We would also like to acknowledge the help and cooperation of Howard Mitcham, who has allowed us to reproduce some of the entertaining ways he used to prepare shellfish.

Finally, our thanks to Annie Lee for sympathetically editing our book and to Eleo Gordon for publishing it.

Clare Walker *and* Keryn Christiansen
April 1986

MEASUREMENT EQUIVALENTS

LIQUID MEASUREMENT
—————EQUIVALENTS—————

These have been the most difficult to balance accurately. The following is as accurate a conversion table as we could draw up. The term 'scant' means 'slightly short of or less than', and the term 'generous' means 'slightly more than'. These terms are less awkward to handle than dealing with difficult fractions of a pint, for example ⅖ pint, which are not normally given on measuring utensils.

Fluid Ounces	Non-American Pints	Metric
2 fl oz	3 tbsps (¹⁄₁₀ pint)	60 ml
3 fl oz	5 tbsps (⅛ pint)	90 ml
4 fl oz	6 tbsps (scant ¼ pint)	120 ml
5 fl oz	exactly ¼ pint	150 ml
6 fl oz	generous ¼ pint	180 ml
8 fl oz	scant ½ pint (⅖ pint)	240 ml
10 fl oz	exactly ½ pint	300 ml
12 fl oz	generous ½ pint	360 ml
14 fl oz	scant ¾ pint	420 ml
16 fl oz	generous ¾ pint	480 ml
18 fl oz	scant pint	540 ml
20 fl oz	exactly 1 pint	600 ml
24 fl oz	scant 1¼ pints	730 ml
28 fl oz	scant 1½ pints	860 ml
32 fl oz	exactly 1¾ pints	1 litre (1000 ml)
40 fl oz	exactly 2 pints	1¼ litres
48 fl oz	scant 2½ pints	1½ litres

——FLOUR MEASUREMENT EQUIVALENTS——

Imperial	Metric
1 oz	25 g
1½ oz	40 g
2 oz	50 g
3 oz	75 g
4 oz	100–125 g
5 oz	150 g
6 oz	175 g
7 oz	200 g
8 oz	250 g
10 oz	300 g
12 oz	350 g
14 oz	400 g
1 lb	500 g
1¼ lb	600 g
1½ lb	¾ kg
1¾ lb	850 g
2 lb	1 kg
2½ lb	1.15 kg
3 lb	1.35 kg

——SUGAR MEASUREMENT EQUIVALENTS——

Imperial	Metric
1 oz	25 g
2 oz	50 g
2½ oz	65 g
3 oz	75 g
4 oz	100–125 g
5 oz	150 g
6 oz	175 g
7 oz	200 g
8 oz	250 g
12 oz	350 g
1 lb	500 g
1¼ lb	600 g
1½ lb	¾ kg
2 lb	1 kg

——BUTTER MEASUREMENT EQUIVALENTS——

Imperial	Metric
½ oz (large knob)	15 g
1 oz	25 g
1½ oz	40 g
2 oz	50 g
2½ oz	65 g
2¾ oz	70 g
3 oz	75 g
4 oz	100–125 g
6 oz	175 g
8 oz	250 g
12 oz	350 g
1 lb	500 g

——SPOON MEASUREMENTS——

The levelled metric capacities of the spoon measurements used throughout this book are:

⅛ tsp	=	0.6 ml
¼ tsp	=	1.2 ml
½ tsp	=	2.5 ml
1 tsp	=	5 ml
½ tbsp	=	7.5 ml
1 tbsp (1½ tsps)	=	15 ml

NOTE: All spoon measures given in this book are *level* unless otherwise stated.

——MEASUREMENTS OF LENGTH——

Centimetres	Inches
½	¼
1	½
3	1
5	2
8	3
10	4

13	5
15	6
18	7
20	8
23	9
25	10

TEMPERATURE EQUIVALENTS FOR
——OVEN THERMOSTAT MARKINGS——

Centigrade	Fahrenheit	Gas mark	Heat of oven
110°C	225°F	¼	Very cool
130°C	250°F	½	Very cool
140°C	275°F	1	Cool
150°C	300°F	2	Cool
160°C	325°F	3	Moderate
180°C	350°F	4	Moderate
190°C	375°F	5	Fairly hot
200°C	400°F	6	Fairly hot
220°C	425°F	7	Hot
230°C	450°F	8	Very hot
240°C	475°F	9	Very hot

NOTE: All recipes in this book are cooked *on the centre shelf* of the oven unless otherwise stated.

GLOSSARY OR EQUIVALENTS

American	English
all-purpose flour	plain (no raising agents) flour
cake flour	finer flour for cake-making
cornstarch	cornflour
baking soda	bicarbonate of soda
granulated sugar	caster sugar
superfine sugar	even finer caster sugar
confectioners' sugar	icing sugar
molasses	treacle
biscuits	scones
cookies	biscuits
popovers	individual Yorkshire puddings
muffins	cake-like buns
coffee cakes	cakes for eating with coffee
napoleons	custard slices
Long Johns	long-shaped doughnuts
candies	sweets
light cream	single cream
heavy cream	double cream
half and half	top of the milk
lemonade	lemon squash
Seven-Up/Sprite	lemonade
popsicles	iced lollies
white raisins	sultanas
candied peel	mixed peel
zucchini or green squash	courgettes
rutabaga	swede

squashes	vegetable marrows
scrod	cod under 3 lb in weight
sole	flounder (or dabs)

INTRODUCTION

The cookery of the United States of America is *potentially* one of the best in the world. Now such a sweeping statement is bound to cause a great deal of surprise and controversy, for, to the average non-American, American cuisine has failed to gain any reputation at all abroad, and whatever reputation it does have is too often unfavourable.

We have to admit that we both arrived in America armed with the same misconceptions – though our preconceived notions of the culinary desert that awaited us here were soon shattered. When my husband, Iain, first suggested that I should spend our short-term posting to New York investigating American cookery for a book, I told him it would be rather a slim volume!

I could be forgiven my ignorance. What little the outside world knows of American cooking is largely restricted to the not-so-haute cuisine of the hamburger, hot dog, plain grilled (broiled) steak and 'mom's' apple pie and ice-cream. Too often these items are relegated even further down the scale of cookery excellence by their awful presentation abroad. For example, the thin pre-packaged meat mixtures which are usually passed off in Britain in particular as 'hamburgers' or 'beefburgers' are poor imitations of the fat 'quarter-pounders' of ground beef that constitute a real hamburger. The hot dog, devoid of an array of relishes or hot sauerkraut, is indeed a pathetic offering.

It is undeniable that the fast food industry in America *is* phenomenal. Every American town, no matter how small, has its convenience food outlet, and in urban zones as dense as New York there is virtually one on every block. However, if you never look beyond the fast-food craze, you will never discover the real culinary heritage of this extraordinary country. Every year millions of tourists pour into America – the start of the 1980s saw a record estimated 21.6 million holidaymakers visiting the USA. To those who care to look further than the hamburger chains and pizza parlours, there is the chance to experience and enjoy the widely varied cuisine of this cosmopolitan country. For it is here that our real interest lies, and here that we found more than enough material to fill this book.

We discovered and fell in love with sourdough cookery; went overboard for the marvellous New England chowders and the satisfying gumbos of New Orleans; became addicted to the famous New York cheesecake; brunched on red flannel hash, eggs Benedict, English and American muffins, and of course pancakes and waffles heavily laced with rich maple syrup. We invested in electric ice-cream machines and attempted to rival the local ice-cream parlours with their dazzling array of flavours. We shopped in Chinatown for woks, chopsticks, rice bowls, fresh beancurd and beansprouts, and other unusual ingredients. We bought a pasta machine and churned out delicate home-made noodles, spaghetti, linguine and cannelloni.

These were some of the pleasures we learned to enjoy in America. And now it is our hope that this book will convey to you, the reader, some of the thrill of these discoveries. We hope to show you that America *does* have a cuisine of its own, which is far richer and more exciting than most people imagine, and more truly international than any other cuisine in the world.

But before we proceed further, one word of warning: if you are expecting to find a collection of the world's most exotic recipes in this book, you may be disappointed. That is not to say that Americans do not cook and enjoy gourmet dishes, for many do; or that this book is devoid of such recipes, for it is not – the fish and shellfish chapter is full of what we in Britain might regard as extravagant dishes. What this book reflects is the ordinary day-to-day cooking of the average American. As Craig Claiborne, the much respected food critic of the *New York Times*, once commented in his column: 'There is no national cuisine here. Many of our great dishes are wholly regional – the gumbos and crawfish dishes of Louisiana, the Mexican-inspired foods of the Southwest, to name a few. Most American dishes – from grits and chili to clam chowder – are coarse, unpretentious and unsophisticated.'

Regrettably, we have been forced to part with some famous and traditional recipes because of the difficulty of obtaining, or the prohibitive cost of, some ingredients: sautéed and fried soft-shell crabs, crawfish pie, chipped or frizzled beef, etc.

Our aim in writing this book is to interpret American cooking specifically for British, European and Australian cooks, who we hope will be surprised by the variety of dishes so popular in the United States of America. It is not a general cookbook, but an opportunity to sample a taste of America. Through it we may explode some of the myths and misunderstandings about American cooking which foreigners have cherished for so long, and which have become so prevalent that many Americans have ended up believing them too.

We hope to prove that our opening statement was not a wild or ill-considered remark. The key word is, of course, '*potentially*', for it is undeniable that whatever promise American cooking holds has yet to be realized.

So why should we try to argue that this cuisine *could* be one of the finest in the world? And why do we believe that Americans are more interested in food and cookery than is commonly believed? There are a number of important points to be considered here:

(1) No society on earth is as cosmopolitan as the United States of America. The large-scale immigration of so many nationalities into this country during the first 300 years (but more particularly the last 100 years) of its existence has naturally influenced its cuisine. Each new influx of people has brought a new style of cooking techniques and a new collection of recipes, some of which have gradually become absorbed into the American way of life and its culinary heritage: it is possible for American cuisine to benefit from the best of all worlds.

Most people still believe that American cooking is solidly rooted in English traditions, but other influences are particularly notice-able to the outsider: the native heritage from the 'red' Indians; French (New Orleans); German (Pennsylvania 'Dutch' or Deutsch as it should really be); Scandinavians; Italians; Irish (so strongly represented in cities like Boston and New York); Chinese (with their famous Chinatowns of San Francisco and New York); Japanese (a relatively new influence in food); and Mexican. Other ethnic and religious groups have also had a marked effect on American cuisine: the Jewish people (who are an integral part of New York life); the Cajuns and Creoles of Louisiana; and the Shakers of New England and Ohio. Finally, there is the slight influence of 'soul food', the cooking of American blacks, which is based heavily on the recipes of the southern slaves.

(2)   No other country, to our knowledge, can rival the United States for its all-the-year-round availability of fresh produce, for example the fruits and vegetables which thrive in the balmy, winter-free climates of California and Florida. It is possible to wade through the winter snowdrifts of New York to buy a basket of strawberries for no more than they would cost during the re-nowned English strawberry season. Fresh salad produce is avail-able all the year round to satiate the incredible American appetite for salads. What is questionable, though, is the quality of this produce, which has lost something in flavour to the stampede of mass production. (If you wish to examine this problem in greater detail we would recommend *The Taste of America* by John L. Hess and Karen Hess, published in America by Penguin Books, which is a scathing attack on the American food industry and American eating habits. It is not our intention to cover ground already tackled so thoroughly in *The Taste of America*, but instead to present a more optimistic picture of American cookery.)

We are hopeful that the day will dawn when Americans refuse to tolerate this sacrifice to progress any longer. There are already optimistic signs that this is happening with the recent introduction of green markets in New York City, giving the supermarket-dependent residents a chance to buy fresh fruits and vegetables from the farmer himself. As increasing millions of Americans are travelling abroad annually, they are discovering the delights of the tasty tomato and will rebel more against its woolly-tasting coun-terpart. Then, and only then, can American cuisine begin to reach its full potential.

(3)   Nowhere in the world is it possible to buy a larger or more comprehensive selection of kitchen gadgetry and labour-saving devices. There are few dishes, no matter how complicated, that cannot be re-created with relative ease by the well-equipped

American cook. Many tools and gadgets have been adapted to electricity. For example, America is the home of the electric wok (that most useful of Chinese cooking utensils) and the electric waffle-maker, almost making the old-style waffle iron redundant, except to the purists. You can buy electric popcorn machines, peanut-butter-making machines and, of course, every variety of the indispensable food processor. Entire books are devoted solely to listing the extensive range of kitchen items available in America, to their uses and to their recipes, for example, *The Cook's Catalogue* and *The International Cook's Catalogue* (Beard Glazer Wolf Ltd); *The Cook's Store – How to Buy and Use Gourmet Gadgets* (Fireside); and *The Whole Kitchen Catalog* (compiled by the editors of Consumer Guide).

(4) A baffling array of cookbooks covers every conceivable subject and ethnic cuisine, with dozens of books specializing in one item alone, for example, beans, honey, ice-cream, hamburgers. The selection is astounding, threatening the avid cookbook collector with potential bankruptcy! We knew of one place in Connecticut which stocked over 2,000 different cookery titles. One cookbook, compiled by the magazine *Better Homes and Gardens* (Bantam Paperbacks), is the single best selling book in America (excluding the Bible and Webster's Dictionary), with over 20 million sales. All this demonstrates to us that Americans *are* interested in cooking, and it is safe to assume that they are not just interested in reading about food, but are also practising what they learn in their own kitchen. Some cynics have suggested that there is a new snobbery about food and the knowledge of food, and that many cookbooks are only bought for show. Our experience of living among Americans belies this.

Another interesting development is the increasing success of cookery magazines and cookery schools and courses. The most popular magazines at the time of writing are *Bon Appetit*, *Cuisine* and *Gourmet*. Although their circulation figures are comparatively small in relation to the huge American population (for example, *Bon Appetit*, the market leader, was selling just over one million copies per issue in the early 1980s), the cookery world is experiencing something of a boom, with new magazines being launched to try to take advantage of the upsurge of American interest in cooking – an interest which has also led to the establishment of more cookery schools and courses. A survey in 1981 of such facilities in New York City reviewed nearly fifty part-time courses.

(5)   One of the fascinating results of our research has been the amazing, amusing and interesting folklore and history attached to so many traditional American recipes, for example, hush puppies (page 192), anadama bread (page 179), pumpernickel bread (page 178), Caesar salad (page 138), and the gumbos of New Orleans (pages 38–42). Such folklore demonstrates Americans' interest in their food and its origins.

Consider also the raging controversy which surrounds the ingredients of some recipes, for example, Manhattan clam chowder and New England clam chowder (a dispute which went as far as the Maine State Legislature!) and Indian pudding. Pride in local dishes can be so fierce that several states will argue over a recipe's origin. For instance, Brunswick stew (page 110) is claimed by Virginia, North Carolina and Georgia as their own. Who could argue in view of this that Americans are not interested in food?

(6)   When many developed countries have so quickly forgotten the old-fashioned ways of preserving foods with the advent of refrigeration and modern canning processes, it is somewhat surprising to discover in the world's most industrially advanced country that you can still find real corned beef (tougher cuts of beef preserved in salt, water and sometimes spices like mustard seed); salt pork (belly of pork or fat back preserved in salt); salt cod (a speciality of New England coastal states); lox (salted salmon); smoked turkey; jerky – sometimes called chipped or frizzled beef (dried strips of beef or originally buffalo meat which is becoming popular again and is still carried in cowboys' saddle packs); and a great variety of dried fruits such as apple slices (see schnitz und kneppe on page 95), prunes, peaches, papaya, pineapple and apricots.

An excellent example of how old methods of food preparation survive is the increasing popularity of sourdough cookery – San Francisco being the best place to sample sourdough bread and sourdough French bread (see pages 182, 183).

(7)   A Gallup Poll conducted in the early 1980s for the National Gardening Association in America showed that a staggering

thirteen billion dollars worth of food is being cultivated in American 'backyards' or home gardens. One obvious conclusion from this statistic is that a good many people are going to a lot of trouble and expense to sample the delicious flavour of fresh-picked produce, which contrasts with the popular image of the American housewife continually opening up a can of this, a packet of that, or popping a TV dinner in the microwave oven.

(8)   One final, unarguable point in our case: while other famous cuisines, like those of France and China, have evolved over thousands of years, American cuisine is, by sharp contrast, in its early infancy. As James Beard, one of America's most famous cooks and food writers, put it: 'After all, France created French cuisine over centuries and I daresay some of it was purely experimental cookery . . . We are barely beginning to sift down into a cuisine of our own.'

Beard also wrote: 'Whereas eight years ago people sneered at the notion that there was such a thing as an American cuisine, today more and more people are forced to agree that we have developed one of the more interesting cuisines of the world. It stresses the products of the soil, native traditions and the gradual integration of many ethnic forms into what is now American cooking.'

We believe that all these factors point to the possible greatness of American cookery. The internationally based heritage is there, the raw materials are available, and the knowledge and interest are there. One day when all are successfully combined on a national scale, the world's leading cooks had better guard their culinary laurels, for American cuisine will have finally matured.

C.W.

SOUPS

——MANHATTAN CLAM CHOWDER——
Serves 6–8

This soup has stirred up a raging controversy along the east coast of America. The villain of the piece is the tomato, whose presence in Manhattan chowder (or Long Island chowder as it is sometimes called) outrages New Englanders who believe that their chowder is the authentic recipe. (The soup originated with the French fishermen of New England and their '*la chaudière*' – the colourful tradition of boiling their fish scraps and vegetables in iron pots at the quayside.) At one time the dispute between the two sides reached the august heights of the Maine State Legislature, where a bill was introduced proposing to outlaw the use of tomatoes in clam chowder!

Unfortunately the quahog or hard-shelled clam always used in this chowder is not readily available in most other countries, although the French do cultivate special beds of clams. Other molluscs, for example mussels, oysters or cockles, may be substituted.

100 g	salt pork or bacon	4 oz
24	fresh quahogs or hard-shelled clams	24
	or	
350 g	tinned or bottled baby clams	12 oz
1½ litres	boiling water	2½ pints
1	medium onion, finely diced	1

2	large stalks celery, finely diced	2
350 g	tomatoes, skinned and chopped	12 oz
2 dsps	fresh parsley, chopped	2 dsps
	or	
1 dsp	dried parsley	1 dsp
1	bay leaf	1
1 tsp	Worcestershire sauce	1 tsp
	pinch of cayenne	
400–500 g	large potatoes	14–16 oz

Rinse the salt pork to remove excess salt and pat dry. Cut the pork or bacon into dice, and fry in a heavy pan until the fat runs and the pieces are becoming crisp. Drain, leaving the fat in the pan and reserving the pork.

Scrub the clams well and place in a large saucepan with the boiling water. Boil until the shells open – about 5–10 minutes (see note below). Remove the opened shells from the pan and reserve the clam liquor. Take out the clam flesh from the shell and chop it roughly. Strain the reserved liquor through a double layer of muslin or cheesecloth to remove any sand particles, etc. If using tinned clams, rinse the clams in their liquor, chop them, and strain the liquor as above.

Add the onion and celery to the pork or bacon fat and sauté until softened – about 5 minutes. Return the salt pork, chopped clams and strained clam liquor to the pan with the tomatoes, parsley, bay leaf, Worcestershire sauce and cayenne. Cover the pan and simmer over a low heat for 3–4 hours. Half an hour before the end of cooking, peel and dice the potatoes and add them to the pot. When ready to serve, check the seasoning of the chowder and serve hot. Small oyster crackers (miniature salted crackers) are a popular addition to the soup.

NOTE: A clam is dead when the shell stays opened. Do not buy shells that are already open and which do not snap shut when tapped. Most clams will open in boiling water after 5 minutes. Those that have remained shut after 10 minutes in the water may be forced open using the tip of a strong knife or an oyster knife.

———NEW ENGLAND CLAM CHOWDER———
Serves 6–8

Clam digging was a new and unexpectedly enjoyable experience –
even the children could enjoy prodding around the tidal muds
searching for soft-shelled clams. But finding the hard-shelled
quahogs traditionally made into clam chowders required the
adults to wade waist deep during low tide to rake the bottom of the
sea bed. A half-moon shaped rake, a floating basket and a lot of
patience are all that is necessary to ensure that the clam-digger
will enjoy a good and relatively cheap meal. Substitute other
molluscs, for example mussels or cockles, for the clams.

24	*fresh quahogs or hard-shelled clams*	24
	or	
350 g	*tinned baby clams*	12 oz
100 g	*salt pork or bacon, diced*	4 oz
2	*medium onions, peeled and finely chopped*	2
6	*medium potatoes, peeled and diced*	6
1/2 tsp	*salt*	1/2 tsp
	freshly ground pepper	
730 ml	*milk*	scant 1 1/4 pints
240 ml	*cream*	scant 1/2 pint
2 tbsps	*melted butter*	2 tbsps

Scrub the clam shells well and boil as detailed on page 28 until
they open. Chop the clams and strain any of their liquor with the
clam water through a double layer of cheesecloth or muslin. If
using tinned clams, rinse the clams in their liquor, chop them, and
strain the liquor as above.

Fry the diced salt pork or bacon in a large saucepan until brown
and crisp. Drain and place on kitchen paper. Sauté the chopped
onions in the pork fat until softened, then add the diced potatoes,
salt and pepper to taste, and sauté for 10 minutes.

Return the chopped clams to the pan with the strained clam
liquor and enough water to cover, and cook for 20 minutes with a
lid on the pan. Add the fried salt pork or bacon to the soup.

Heat the milk and cream together, but do not boil, and add to the chowder. Finally, add the melted butter, test for seasoning, and serve hot with small oyster crackers (miniature salted crackers).

——CHICKEN CHOWDER——
Serves 8–10

1–1¼ kg	chicken plus giblets	*2–3 lb*
1¼ litres	water	*2 pints*
100 g	salt pork or bacon, diced	*4 oz*
1	medium onion, peeled and diced	*1*
2	stalks celery, diced	*2*
300 g	potatoes (2 medium), peeled and diced	*10 oz*
240 ml	milk	*scant ½ pint*
1 tbsp	fresh parsley, chopped	*1 tbsp*
120 ml	single cream	*scant ¼ pint*
	salt and pepper to taste	

Put the chicken and giblets in a large saucepan with the water. Bring to the boil, then cover the pan and simmer for 1–1½ hours, depending on the size of the bird. Remove the chicken and discard the giblets; strain the chicken stock and reserve. When the chicken is cool enough to handle, remove the flesh, dice and reserve. Discard the bones and skin.

Fry the diced salt pork or bacon in a large pan until it is crisp and some of the fat has been extracted. Drain from the pan and reserve. Sauté the onion and celery in the pork or bacon fat for about 5 minutes, then add the diced potato and cook for a further 2 minutes. Add the chicken stock and chicken pieces, cover the pan, and simmer for about 20 minutes until the vegetables are tender. Stir in the milk, diced salt pork or bacon and parsley and return to the boil. Remove from the heat, stir in the cream, season to taste with salt and pepper and serve hot.

———CORN CHOWDER———
Serves 6–8

15 g	*butter*	*large knob*
100 g	*salt pork or bacon, diced*	*4 oz*
2	*medium onions, diced*	*2*
3	*medium potatoes, peeled and diced*	*3*
480 ml	*chicken stock*	*generous 3/4 pint*
3–4	*sweetcorn cobs, to yield 350 g (12 oz) kernels*	*3–4*
1 litre	*milk*	*1 3/4 pints*
240 ml	*double cream*	*scant 1/2 pint*
	salt and pepper to taste	

Heat the butter in a large saucepan and fry the diced salt pork or bacon until crisp. Remove from the pan and reserve. Add the diced onions to the fat and sauté gently until golden – about 5 minutes. Add the diced potatoes and the chicken stock, cover the pan, and cook for 15–20 minutes until the potatoes are soft.

Strip the kernels from the corn cobs (see pages 120–21), add to the pan, and cook for a further 5–10 minutes until the corn is tender. Finally, stir in the milk and cream, season to taste with salt and pepper, and re-heat the soup without boiling. Serve hot with the reserved salt pork or bacon pieces scattered over the top of the soup.

———BOUILLABAISSE———
Serves about 8

Although this famous fish dish originated in the French seaport of Marseilles, it has become a popular recipe in American coastal areas where it is adapted for the use of whatever catches are abundant in the local waters. The name originates, so rumour has it, from a Marseilles fisherman's two commands for its preparation: *bouilli* (boil – usually for exactly 15 minutes) and *baisse* (stop).

————For the stock————

500 g	fish trimmings	1 lb
2 litres	water	3½ pints
1	medium onion, peeled and chopped	1
2	cloves garlic, peeled and chopped	2
12	peppercorns	12
1 tsp	salt	1 tsp
1	bay leaf	1
2–3	stalks fresh parsley	2–3
½	lemon, sliced	½
¼ tsp	celery seeds (optional)	¼ tsp

————For the bouillabaisse————

3 tbsps	olive oil	3 tbsps
1	small onion, peeled and chopped	1
2	cloves garlic, peeled and chopped	2
500 g	tomatoes, skinned and chopped	1 lb
2 tbsps	fresh parsley, chopped	2 tbsps
1	bay leaf	1
	cayenne to taste	
½ tsp	salt	½ tsp
175 g	fresh prawns	6 oz
12	mussels	12
175 g	scallops, shelled	6 oz
¾ kg	white fish fillets (e.g. cod, haddock, halibut)	1½ lb
3	slices lemon	3
	large pinch saffron	
240 ml	white wine	scant ½ pint

————For the garlic bread————

100 g	butter	4 oz

| 4 | *cloves garlic, peeled and finely chopped* | 4 |
| *12–16* | *slices French bread* | *12–16* |

a large skillet or frying pan

Put all the stock ingredients into a large pan. Bring to the boil, then cover the pan and simmer for 45–50 minutes. Strain the stock and reserve.

Heat the oil in a large pan and sauté the onion and garlic for about 3 minutes to soften. Add the tomatoes, parsley, bay leaf, cayenne, salt and reserved fish stock.

Chop the heads off the prawns. Scrub the mussels and remove the black 'beards'. Chop the scallops into bite-sized pieces. Cut the fish fillets into medium pieces. Add the shellfish and fish pieces to the pan with the lemon slices, saffron and wine. Bring to the boil, cook for 15 minutes, then remove from the heat.

Meanwhile, prepare the garlic bread. Heat the butter in the skillet or frying pan, add the garlic, and sauté for 2–3 minutes. Brush the garlic butter over both sides of the slices of French bread. Fry the bread slices in the skillet or pan until browned on both sides. Serve the bouillabaisse over the garlic bread in large, warm soup bowls.

MADAME BEGUE'S* CREOLE
——BOUILLABAISSE——
Serves 6

(From Howard Mitcham's *Creole Gumbo and All That Jazz* (Addison-Wesley, Reading, Massachusetts, 1978) – adapted to our usual recipe format)

As with many other French dishes, the Creoles of Louisiana adopted and adapted this Marseilles soup/stew and made it their own. Unlike the traditional French bouillabaisse, the Creoles do not use 'trash fish' (the ugly, unmarketable catches) and do not add different kinds of shellfish.

Redfish is a lean fish found almost exclusively in Gulf coastal waters. Other lean fish may be substituted, for example flounder, plaice, sole, lemon sole and turbot.

* Madame Begue was 'one of the finest Creole cooks in New Orleans' during the middle to late 1800s.

——The stock——

	fish heads, tails and bones from the fish (see below)	
1 litre	*water*	*1 3/4 pints*

——The dry marinade——

1 tbsp	*dried parsley flakes*	*1 tbsp*
1/4 tsp	*powdered thyme*	*1/4 tsp*
1/4 tsp	*basil*	*1/4 tsp*
1/4 tsp	*powdered bay leaf*	*1/4 tsp*
1/2 tsp	*ground allspice*	*1/2 tsp*
1/4 tsp	*cayenne*	*1/4 tsp*
2 tsps	*fresh garlic, finely minced (chopped)*	*2 tsps*
1/2 tsp	*freshly ground black pepper*	*1/2 tsp*
1 tsp	*salt*	*1 tsp*

——The fish——

3/4 kg	*red snapper fillets, skinless (about 6)*	*1 1/2 lb*
3/4 kg	*redfish or other lean, white fish fillets, skinless (about 6)*	*1 1/2 lb*

——The garlic bread——

6	*cloves garlic, peeled*	*6*
2 tbsps	*olive oil*	*2 tbsps*
12	*thin slices French bread*	*12*
	extra olive oil for frying	

——The bouillabaisse——

3 tbsps	*olive oil*	*3 tbsps*
1	*large onion, peeled and finely chopped*	*1*
2 tbsps	*flour*	*2 tbsps*
2	*cloves garlic, peeled and minced (chopped)*	*2*

240 ml	dry white wine	scant 1/2 pint
480 ml	fish stock (see above)	generous 3/4 pint
500 g	tin tomatoes, chopped	1 lb
1/2 tsp	powdered saffron	1/2 tsp
	salt and freshly ground black pepper	
	fresh parsley, chopped	

a large skillet or frying pan

'If you don't have a skillet large enough to hold the 12 pieces of fish, you'll have to cook them in shifts.

'Make a simple stock by placing the heads, tails, and bones of the fish in a saucepan with a quart or more of water. Boil for 30 minutes and strain through triple cheesecloth. You need only 2 cups.

'Rub the dry marinade thoroughly into each side of the fish fillets. Set them aside.

'Make garlic bread in advance as follows: Put 6 cloves of garlic through a garlic press [or finely chop], and mix the pulp with 2 tablespoons of olive oil. Cut 12 thin slices of French bread, and brush on one side with the garlic-oil mixture. Fry the bread on both sides in olive oil until golden brown. Set aside and keep warm.

'Now to cook the fish, place a quarter cup of olive oil in the large skillet [or frying pan] and heat it. Turn the heat low. Sprinkle the finely chopped onion in the pan. Place the fish fillets in the skillet on top of the onion, and cook gently for 5 minutes. Turn them over with a spatula and cook 5 minutes more. Remove the fish pieces, place on a platter, and keep warm. Add the flour to the skillet and blend well with the olive oil and onion, making sure it's free of all lumps. Stir in the minced garlic. Add the dry white wine, the fish stock, and the tomatoes. Cook for 15 minutes until the mixture thickens a little. Stir in the saffron, and season to taste with salt and freshly ground black pepper. Return the fish fillets to the sauce, and "bouilli!" (boil) for 5 minutes, then "baisse!" (stop).

'Put 2 slices of fried bread on the bottom of each of 6 preheated soup bowls. Place one slice of red snapper on one slice of bread and a slice of redfish on the other. Ladle the sauce over the fish, sprinkle with chopped parsley, and serve at once.

'When you see what a hard job it is to make this brew, you'll understand why Antoine's [one of New Orleans' most famous restaurants] makes you order it 24 hours in advance.'

GARBANZO (CHICK PEA) SOUP
Serves 6–8

250 g	dried chick peas, soaked overnight to give 500 g (1 lb) drained peas	*8 oz*
1½ litres	stock or water	*2½ pints*
250 g	bacon, diced	*8 oz*
1	medium onion, peeled and chopped	*1*
1–2	cloves garlic, peeled and crushed	*1–2*
1 tbsp	chili powder	*1 tbsp*
250 g	tinned tomatoes, roughly chopped	*8 oz*
	salt to taste	
	fried croûtons (optional)	

a skillet or heavy frying pan

Drain the soaked chick peas and place in a large saucepan with the stock or water. Bring to the boil, then reduce the heat to a simmer.

Meanwhile, fry the diced bacon in a skillet or frying pan until crisp. Remove from the pan and pour off any excess fat. Sauté the chopped onion and crushed garlic in the bacon fat until softened – about 5 minutes. Add the chili powder and fry for a further 2 minutes. Finally, add the tomatoes, the bacon and salt to taste. Transfer the pan's contents to the chick peas and stock, cover the pot, and cook gently for 1½–1¾ hours until the peas are tender.

NOTE: Traditionally this soup is served as it is. Presumably the peasants of Mexico where this soup originated did not possess liquidizers. However, we found the soup was improved by being puréed and as such may be served with fried croûtons and a sprinkling of chili powder in the centre of each bowl. Tinned chick peas may also be used.

——JEWISH CHICKEN SOUP——
Serves 6–8

This is one of the best known of all Jewish recipes and is often called 'Mom's chicken soup' or 'Jewish penicillin' because it is a favourite meal to serve to invalids who have little appetite for anything stronger.

2–2¼ kg	*uncooked chicken plus giblets*	*4–5 lb*
1	*beef knuckle bone, split*	1
4	*stalks celery with leaves, sliced*	4
4	*large carrots, peeled and halved*	4
2	*large onions, peeled and quartered*	2
	fresh dill, chopped	
	salt and pepper to taste	
	sprigs fresh parsley, chopped	
	matzo balls (see below)	

a 7–8 litre (12 pints) cooking pot

Cut the chicken into quarters and put them with the giblets, beef bone, celery, carrots, onions, dill and seasonings into a large cooking pot. Cover with water, bring to the boil, then cover the pan and simmer gently for 2 hours.

Strain the stock from the pan and skim off the fat. Discard the giblets, the beef bone and the skin and bones from the chicken. Return the stock, chicken flesh and vegetables to the pot. Add more water if necessary. Add the chopped parsley, check the seasoning, and serve hot with matzo balls.

——MATZO BALLS (KNAIDLACH)——
Makes about 15

Jewish cooks love to put lots of extras into their soups like matzo balls, mandlens and home-made noodles. Matzo meal is the crushed crumbs from the unleavened matzo bread made of flour and water.

2	*eggs, separated*	2
3 tbsps	*chicken fat*	*3 tbsps*
100 g	*matzo meal*	*4 oz*
1/2 tsp	*salt*	*1/2 tsp*
1/4 tsp	*ground ginger (optional)*	*1/4 tsp*
	Jewish chicken soup (see	
	previous recipe)	

Beat the egg yolks with the chicken fat to combine. Mix together the matzo meal, salt and ground ginger, if using. Gradually add 120 ml (scant 1/4 pint) of the hot soup to the egg and fat mixture, then beat the mixture into the matzo meal, beating until smooth.

Whisk the egg whites until stiff and fold into the dough. Refrigerate for 1 hour.

Form the dough into small balls about the size of a walnut. Drop the balls into the boiling Jewish chicken soup, cover the pan and boil for 25 minutes. Serve hot.

——GUMBO FILÉ——
Serves 8–10

Gumbos are possibly the most famous of all New Orleans dishes. Virtually anything can be added to a gumbo, so feel free to improvise as much as you like. However, if you wish to create a genuine gumbo you should pay some attention to the making of the roux and devote at least half an hour to its preparation. Gumbo lovers may find it less time-consuming to follow the example of many New Orleans cooks, who prepare large batches of roux at one time and freeze the remainder in small packets for later use. In New Orleans you may even buy packets of ready-made 'Creole gumbo mix', including the roux.

It is the roux that gives the gumbo its distinctive flavour. As Howard Mitcham put it: 'When the Creole-Cajun and black cooks of New Orleans took hold of the delicate French roux, they whammed it and whacked it until it became something alive, strong and vibrant, a perfect backdrop for cooking the seafood, game and vegetables that were available in the region.'

Filé (ground sassafras leaves) is the thickening agent introduced by the Choctaw Indians for this soup/stew, which contrasts with an okra gumbo where the vegetable is used to thicken the stock. If you cannot buy filé powder, convert this recipe to an okra gumbo by adding 500 g (1 lb) of sliced okra with the herbs, or thicken with a *beurre manié* – equal amounts of butter and flour blended together.

1¼ kg	chicken, cut into pieces	3 lb
250 g	smoked or spicy sausage, e.g. Spanish chorizos or German frankfurters, chopped	8 oz
1 tsp	salt	1 tsp
500 g	prawns	1 lb
100 g	butter	4 oz
50 g	flour	2 oz
2	large onions, peeled and chopped	2
2	cloves garlic, peeled and crushed	2
2 tbsps	fresh parsley, chopped	2 tbsps
½ tsp	dried thyme	½ tsp
2	bay leaves	2
¼ tsp	cayenne	¼ tsp
	freshly ground black pepper	
100 g	ham, chopped	4 oz
4–5	tomatoes, skinned and chopped	4–5
18	oysters or mussels and their liquor	18
2 tbsps	filé powder (ground sassafras leaves)	2 tbsps

———To serve———

steamed or boiled rice

Put the chicken pieces in a large pan with the chopped sausage.

Cover with water, add the salt, and boil for 45 minutes. Strain the chicken and sausage from the stock and reserve both meat and stock. Remove the chicken flesh from the bones, dice it and reserve.

Wash the prawns, cover with water in a large pan, add a little salt and boil for 5 minutes. Drain the prawns from the pan, peel off the shells and heads, and reserve the prawn flesh. Return the shells and heads to the prawn broth, boil vigorously for 15 minutes, then strain the prawn liquor into the chicken stock.

To make the roux, melt the butter in a heavy skillet or pan over a low heat. Add the flour and stir it in until the mixture is creamy and free from lumps. Turn down the heat very low and continue to stir for about 25–30 minutes. When a roux reaches its climax and is done, it begins to brown very rapidly, so take care not to burn it.

When the roux is browned, add the onion and garlic and cook slowly for 5–7 minutes until soft. Stir in the parsley, thyme, bay leaves, cayenne and pepper to taste.

Put the roux and vegetable mixture in a large pan with the sausage, chicken, chopped ham and tomatoes, and cover generously with the chicken and prawn broth (making up the liquid with extra chicken stock or water if necessary). Simmer gently for 1 hour.

Scrub the oysters or mussels, open, and add the oyster or mussel flesh and liquor to the gumbo with the reserved prawns. Cook for 10 minutes longer.

Test for seasoning, remembering that the salt is also an important part of a good gumbo. Do not be timid in adding more salt, as an insipid gumbo is considered to be a disaster. Turn off the heat and leave the gumbo to stand for 5 minutes. Finally, add the filé powder and stir well. *Do not* be tempted to add the filé powder while the soup is boiling or it will become stringy and unpalatable.

Serve the gumbo in preheated soup bowls with a little steamed or boiled rice in the bottom of each bowl.

——SEAFOOD GUMBO——
Serves 10–12

This gumbo uses okra as a thickening agent in place of the filé powder used in the previous recipe.

50 g	butter	2 oz
25 g	flour	1 oz
2	medium onions, peeled and chopped	2
2	cloves garlic, peeled and chopped	2
3	spring onions, chopped	3
1	small green pepper (optional), de-seeded and cut into strips	1
500 g	fresh okra, topped and tailed and cut into 3–4 pieces	1 lb
500 g	tomatoes, skinned and chopped	1 lb
1	bay leaf	1
1/2 tsp	ground thyme	1/2 tsp
2 tbsps	fresh parsley, chopped	2 tbsps
1/2 tsp	cayenne	1/2 tsp
1–1 1/2 tsps	salt	1–1 1/2 tsps
12–18	oysters	12–18
500 g	prawns (shrimp), uncooked	1 lb
1–2	crabs, still in their shells, cooked	1–2
	or	
500 g	lump crabmeat	1 lb
1 1/2 litres	fish stock (including oyster liquor and prawn stock, if any)	scant 2 1/2 pints
1 tbsp	Worcestershire sauce	1 tbsp
	boiled or steamed rice	

a 4–5 litre (7–8 pint) pot or pan

Melt the butter in the pan, add the flour and blend well. Cook over a medium heat, stirring frequently, for about 15 minutes, by which time the roux will be darkly browned.

Add the onions, garlic, spring onions, and green pepper if

desired. Cook for a further 4–5 minutes, then add the okra, tomatoes, bay leaf, thyme, parsley, cayenne and salt, and reduce the heat to low while preparing the shellfish.

Scrub the oysters and open the shells with an oyster knife or other strong knife, saving all the oyster liquor in the shells. Remove the oysters from the shells and strain the liquor through double layers of cheesecloth or muslin.

The prawns may be cooked in the gumbo in their shells, or you may pre-cook them in boiling water until the shells turn pink, strain and reserve the stock, and shell the fish before adding to the gumbo. (As a matter of personal preference, I like the prawns cooked in the gumbo in their shells – it seems to add to my enjoyment of the meal.)

To prepare the crabs, remove the top shells and take out the gills. Cut off the face portion. Rinse the crabs to clean. Break off the claws and legs and cut the body portion into two pieces.

Combine the oyster liquor, prawn stock (if any) and extra fish stock to make up to 1½ litres (scant 2½ pints) in all, and add to the gumbo.

Bring to the boil and simmer for 1 hour. Add the crab pieces and cook for a further 5 minutes. Add the lump crabmeat (if not using whole crabs), the prawns, and the shelled oysters. Cook for a further 5 minutes, check the seasoning, and serve over rice in large, warmed soup bowls.

NOTE: As pointed out in the gumbo filé recipe (page 38), a real New Orleans gumbo should be peppery and fairly salty. If, however, you prefer less spicy foods, reduce the cayenne to ¼ teaspoon.

————VICHYSSOISE————
Serves 6

Despite the French name of this delicious chilled soup, Vichyssoise was created in New York at the Ritz Carlton Hotel by its French chef, Louis Diat. The soup, first made in 1910, was named in honour of the chef's home town of Vichy in France.

4	leeks	4
40 g	butter	1 1/2 oz
500 g	potatoes, peeled and diced	1 lb
1 1/4 litres	chicken broth or stock	2 pints
2 tsps	salt	2 tsps
1	bay leaf	1
1/4 tsp	cayenne or freshly ground pepper	1/4 tsp
1/4 tsp	grated nutmeg	1/4 tsp
480 ml	double cream	generous 3/4 pint
	fresh chives or parsley, finely chopped	

Wash the leeks well and slice finely. Heat the butter in a large pan and sauté the leeks until soft – about 5 minutes. Add the potatoes, chicken stock, salt and bay leaf and simmer, covered, until the potatoes are tender – about 20 minutes. Remove the bay leaf and add the cayenne or pepper and the nutmeg. Purée the soup in a blender or through a sieve until smooth. Return to the pan, add the cream and heat through without boiling. This soup is traditionally served chilled, so chill well before serving with finely chopped chives or parsley to garnish.

NOTE: It is also delicious served hot.

——PHILADELPHIA PEPPER POT——
Serves 10–12

The famous story surrounding this soup concerns General Washington's attempt to perk up the flagging morale of his starving troops during the War of Independence. The army was stationed at Valley Forge in Pennsylvania in 1777–8 when Washington summoned the head chef and ordered him to create a great dish to inspire the soldiers. The chef only had scraps, peppercorns and some tripe, but the resulting soup was reputedly a great success.

Whether this tale is true or not, this soup has always been a Philadelphian classic and used to be sold in the streets of the city by vendors.

I	*veal shin or knuckle*	I
3 litres	*water*	5 pints
3	*sprigs parsley*	3
I	*bay leaf*	I
I	*sprig thyme*	I
	or	
I tsp	*dried thyme*	I tsp
500 g	*boiled tripe*	I lb
2	*onions, peeled and chopped*	2
I tbsp	*salt*	I tbsp
IO–I2	*peppercorns*	IO–I2
	or	
½ tsp	*freshly ground pepper*	½ tsp
I tsp	*tabasco sauce*	I tsp
I tbsp	*fresh parsley, chopped*	I tbsp
500 g	*potatoes, peeled and diced*	I lb
2 tbsps	*flour*	2 tbsps
I20 ml	*water*	scant ¼ pint
I tsp	*marjoram, chopped*	I tsp
	——Dumplings——	
IOO g	*plain flour*	4 oz
½ tsp	*salt*	½ tsp
	freshly ground pepper	
I tsp	*baking powder*	I tsp
I tbsp	*butter, melted*	I tbsp
I	*egg*	I
3 tbsps	*milk*	3 tbsps

Put the veal shin or knuckle in a large pan with the water, parsley, bay leaf and thyme and bring to the boil. Skim off any scum that forms. Simmer for about 2 hours, then remove the veal shin from the broth, strip off the meat and cut it into cubes. Strain and reserve the broth.

Cut the boiled tripe into ½ cm (¼ inch) squares. Put the strained broth in a large pan with the onions, salt, peppercorns and tabasco and add the tripe and veal pieces. Simmer for 1½ hours.

Add the parsley and potatoes and cook for a further 30 minutes. Meanwhile prepare the dumplings. Sift the flour, salt, pepper and baking powder together and add the melted butter. Beat together the egg and milk and stir into the flour until well combined.

Mix the 2 tablespoons of flour with the water and remove the soup from the heat. Gradually stir in the flour mix, return to the heat, and cook, stirring constantly, until thickened.

Drop the dumpling batter into the thickened soup by teaspoons, add the marjoram, cover and cook for a further 15 minutes. Serve hot.

NOTE: This soup improves with re-heating.

——PEANUT SOUP——
Serves 5–6

25 g	*butter*	1 oz
4–5	*spring onions, finely sliced*	4–5
2	*stalks celery, finely diced*	2
2 tbsps	*flour*	2 tbsps
175 g	*peanut butter*	6 oz
1¼ litres	*light stock (e.g. chicken)*	2 pints
½ tsp	*Worcestershire sauce*	½ tsp
½ tsp	*salt*	½ tsp
	pepper or cayenne to taste	
250 g	*peanuts in their shells*	8 oz

Heat the butter in a saucepan and sauté the spring onions and celery for about 5 minutes. Add the flour and cook for a further 1–2 minutes. Add the peanut butter and cook until it forms a smooth paste. Remove from the heat and gradually stir in the stock. Add the Worcestershire sauce, salt and pepper or cayenne. Bring to the boil, stirring constantly, then cover the pan and simmer for 10 minutes.

Meanwhile shell the peanuts and put them in a small baking pan or tray under a hot grill to lightly brown, turning frequently. When ready to serve, pour the soup into warmed bowls and sprinkle over handfuls of the freshly roasted peanuts.

——BLACK BEAN SOUP——
Serves 8

This soup has diverse origins – some claim it comes from the Caribbean, as it is a special favourite of the Cubans. Certainly it is commonly found in the southern states of America, but it is also claimed by those of Jewish origin and can be found in areas with large numbers of middle European immigrants. The Spanish influence can be seen in the addition of ham hocks.

NOTE: A little diced bacon, sautéed with the onions, may be added for flavour in place of the ham bone.

500 g	dried black beans	1 lb
2 litres	water	3½ pints
40 g	butter	1½ oz
2	onions, peeled and chopped	2
2	cloves garlic, peeled and crushed	2
3	sticks celery, chopped	3
1	bouquet garni (parsley, thyme and bay leaf)	1
1–1¼ kg	beef bones	2–3 lb
1	ham bone (optional)	1
1½ litres	chicken stock	2½ pints
6	peppercorns	6
1 tsp	salt	1 tsp
1 litre	water	1¾ pints
2 tbsps	lemon juice	2 tbsps
120 ml	Madeira or brandy	scant ¼ pint

——To garnish——

1	lemon, very thinly sliced	1
2	hard-boiled eggs	2
2 tbsps	parsley, finely chopped	2 tbsps

Put the beans in a large bowl, cover with water and leave to soak overnight.

Next day, strain the beans and discard the water. Melt the butter in a large stockpot and sauté the onions, garlic and celery until softened but not browned. Add the *bouquet garni*, beef bones, ham bone, chicken stock, peppercorns, salt, beans and water. Bring to the boil, then reduce the heat, skim the top and simmer, partially covered, for 4 hours or until the beans mash easily against the side of the pot.

Discard the beef and ham bones and the *bouquet garni*. Purée the soup through a food mill or coarse strainer. Add the lemon juice and Madeira or brandy, and if the soup is too thick add extra hot stock or water. Check the seasoning, and serve garnished with lemon slices and sprinkled with chopped hard-boiled egg and parsley.

——SENATE BEAN SOUP——
Serves 6–8

The story goes that this soup became famous in 1904 when 'Uncle Joe' Cannon, speaker of the US House of Representatives, bellowed: 'From now on, hot or cold, rain, snow or shine, I want it on the menu every day.' It is still a popular item on the politicians' menu.

500 g	*dried white navy (pea) beans*	*1 lb*
2–3 litres	*cold water*	*3½–5 pints*
1	*large, meaty ham bone*	*1*
3 litres	*hot water*	*5 pints*
175 g	*cooked and mashed potato*	*6 oz*
2	*onions, peeled and finely chopped*	*2*
4	*sticks celery, finely chopped*	*4*
2–3	*cloves garlic, peeled and crushed*	*2–3*
3 tbsps	*parsley, finely chopped*	*3 tbsps*
1 tsp	*salt*	*1 tsp*

½ tsp	*freshly ground black pepper*	*½ tsp*
2–3	*rashers of bacon, cooked till crisp*	*2–3*

Rinse the dried beans well in a colander, put in a large bowl, and cover with plenty of cold water. Leave to soak overnight.

Next day, drain the beans and rinse again. Put in a large pot with the ham bone, and add the hot water. Cover and simmer gently for 2½ hours. Add the mashed potato, onion, celery, garlic, parsley, salt and pepper. Simmer for a further 1 hour or until the beans are tender.

Remove the ham bone, dice the meat and return the meat to the soup. Check the seasoning, adding more salt if necessary. Serve hot with crisp, crumbled or finely chopped bacon on top.

——HOT AND SOUR SOUP——
Serves 4–6

Most of the recipes in this book are long-established, traditional dishes, unlike this soup which is a newcomer to American cuisine. As regional Chinese restaurants specializing in the different cooking styles of provinces (for example, Szechwan, Hunan and Yunnan) become more popular, recipes like this one are beginning to creep into the American repertoire. The 'hot' part is provided by black pepper and the 'sour' by vinegar.

12	*trees' ears, cloud ears or wood's ears (a dried fungus – dried black mushrooms might be a suitable substitute)*	*12*
10	*dried lily buds or flowers or golden needles*	*10*
1 tbsp	*oil*	*1 tbsp*
250 g	*lean pork, thinly sliced into strips*	*8 oz*
50 g	*bamboo shoots, shredded*	*2 oz*
1 litre	*chicken stock*	*1¾ pints*

¼ tsp	salt	¼ tsp
3 tbsps	white rice wine vinegar or white wine vinegar	3 tbsps
1 tbsp	soy sauce	1 tbsp
2 tbsps	cornflour	2 tbsps
3 tbsps	cold water	3 tbsps
1	bean curd, cut into small cubes (about 32)	1
1 tsp	hot oil (oil with chili)	1 tsp
½–1 tsp	black pepper, ground	½–1 tsp
2	eggs, lightly beaten	2

——To serve——

2 tbsps	spring onions, finely chopped	2 tbsps
	fresh coriander (Chinese parsley), finely chopped (optional)	

a wok (Chinese all-purpose pan) or large saucepan

Soak the trees' ears and dried lily buds in a small bowl of boiling water for 10–15 minutes. Drain and thinly slice the trees' ears, removing any hard centres. Cut the lily buds in half, removing any hard ends.

Heat the oil in the wok or saucepan and stir-fry the pork for about 3 minutes. Add the bamboo shoots, stock, salt, vinegar and soy sauce and bring to the boil. Dissolve the cornflour in the cold water, then add a little of the hot soup to the mixture before adding it to the soup. Stir until the soup has thickened and is opaque. Add the bean curd cubes and cook until heated through. Add the hot oil and the pepper and remove from the heat. Cool for a couple of minutes.

Add a little of the hot soup to the lightly beaten eggs, then pour the egg mixture into the soup and stir until thick and creamy. Serve garnished with chopped spring onions and fresh coriander.

——LYNETTE'S CHICKEN POT PIE——
Serves 4–6

My Pennsylvania Dutch friend, Lynette Chattanow, prepared this speciality of her people for me on a couple of occasions. Pot pie (or 'bot boi' as the locals call it) is actually a noodle soup, and is typical of the simple, hearty food for which these people are renowned. Some modern interpretations prepare 'pot pie' more like a chicken pie covered in squares of pastry and baked, but Lynette's recipe below is the old traditional method.

In Pa. Dutch country you can buy bags of ready-made square noodles called 'pot pie'.

1½ kg	whole chicken or chicken pieces	3–3½ lb
1	onion, peeled and sliced	1
2	stalks celery, sliced (optional)	2
2	carrots, peeled and sliced, (optional)	2
	salt	
	peppercorns	
	large pinch saffron	

——The 'pot pie'——

250 g	plain flour	8 oz
½ tsp	salt	½ tsp
4	egg yolks	4
4–6 tbsps	hot water	4–6 tbsps

Put the chicken or chicken pieces into a large pot with the onion, celery and carrots, salt and peppercorns. Cover with water, bring to the boil, then cook long and slowly for 1½–2 hours.

Remove the chicken, take out the bones and discard them. Cut the flesh into bite-sized pieces and return to the pan with the saffron. Simmer very gently.

Meanwhile, prepare the 'pot pie'. Sift the flour and salt, make a well in the centre and add the egg yolks and hot water as needed to make a firm dough. Knead lightly (Lynette preferred rough-textured noodles, so little kneading was required). Roll out the dough on a lightly floured surface, but not too thinly. Cut into 5 cm (2 inch) squares (a pizza cutter makes this an easy job). Drop the noodle squares into the boiling chicken broth and cook for at least 20 minutes. The longer the noodles cook the thicker the broth will become.

NOTE: Pa. Dutch people serve pot pie with a selection of their 'seven sweets and seven sours' – the latter being dishes like red beet eggs (page 144), watermelon rind (page 281) and pepper slaw (page 141).

FISH AND SHELLFISH

America has thousands of miles of seashore, stretching from the cold waters of Alaska to the warm Gulf waters of the south. In addition it has thousands of rivers and fresh-water lakes – for example the Mississippi, the greatest of all American rivers, with its off-shoots and inlets, and the Great Lakes which America shares with Canada in the north-east. So fish and shellfish in and around these areas are an important part of the local cuisines.

Certain areas are especially renowned for different fish or shellfish – the state of Maine is famous for its lobster, Maryland for its crabs, Louisiana for its shrimps, soft-shelled crabs, pompano, frogs' legs and the tiny fresh-water crawfish, Washington and Oregon for salmon, New England states for their quahogs or hard-shelled clams, Florida for conch (pronounced 'conk'), California for abalone, the geoduck (pronounced 'gooeyduck') clams and the large Dungeness crabs, and Alaska for its Alaskan King crabs with their giant-size claws.

Most of the fish or shellfish used in the following recipes are available in ordinary fishmongers' shops and in many supermarkets. Unusual items such as quahogs (hard-shelled clams) and pompano can be found only at fish markets like Billingsgate in London, but substitutes have been suggested.

CIOPPINO

Serves 8–10

The Italian name of this spicy fish stew belies its origin. It was in fact invented in San Francisco, some say by a Genoese sailor called Giuseppe Buzzaro; others claim it was the creation of fishermen at the colourful Fisherman's Wharf, calling out to their friends to 'chip-in-o' or contribute some of their day's catch to the steaming pots of stew. Traditionally it is served with sourdough bread, and any number and variety of fish or shellfish can be added to the stew.

1 1/4 kg	firm-fleshed fish, e.g. sea bass, whiting, mackerel, halibut, mullet	3 lb
2	crabs, cooked	2
	or	
1	lobster	1
12	mussels or oysters or clams, or a mixture of each	12
120 ml	olive or cooking oil	6 tbsps
2	onions, peeled and chopped	2
2–3	cloves garlic, peeled and crushed	2–3
1	green pepper, de-seeded and chopped	1
800 g	tinned tomatoes, chopped	26 oz
500–600 ml	red wine	3/4–1 pint
150 g	tin tomato paste	5 oz
1 litre	fish stock (i.e. from mussels, crab and fish trimmings)	1 3/4 pints
2	bay leaves	2
1 tsp	basil	1 tsp
1 tsp	oregano	1 tsp
2 tsps	salt	2 tsps
	freshly ground pepper	
500 g	prawns, cooked	1 lb
5–6 tbsps	fresh parsley, chopped	5–6 tbsps
1	lemon, sliced	1

Clean the fish, reserving the heads, bones and all trimmings for the stock. Cut the flesh into large serving pieces. Remove the top shell from the crabs and discard the gills and intestines. Break the crabs in half, reserving the shell and any of the yellow fat for making stock.

Steam the well-cleaned mussels (or oysters or clams) in a little water until the shells just open. Strain the broth through triple layers of cheesecloth or muslin and reserve.

To make the stock, combine the fish trimmings, crab shell and fat and reserved broth, add 1 litre (1¾ pints) of water, and simmer, covered, for 30 minutes. Strain through triple layers of cheesecloth or muslin, and if necessary make up to 1 litre (1¾ pints) with extra water.

Heat the oil in a large pan and sauté the onion, garlic and green pepper until softened – about 5 minutes. Add the stock and all the remaining ingredients except the prawns, parsley and lemon. In a large saucepan or casserole, arrange the fish and prawns in layers. Pour over the sauce, cover and cook over a low heat for 20 minutes. Add the crab halves and the mussels and cook for a further 5 minutes. The cioppino is ready when the fish flakes easily with a fork. Check the seasoning, and serve in bowls with parsley sprinkled over the stew and slices of lemon twisted on to the sides of the bowls. Have plenty of napkins and spare bowls at hand as the shellfish will need shelling. Serve with sourdough bread (page 182) or sourdough French bread (page 183).

POMPANO EN PAPILLOTE – FISH IN PAPER
——PARCELS——
Serves 4–6

Louisiana is the leading pompano fishing area in the world, so it is small wonder that this particular recipe should be so popular in New Orleans, where it was created at Antoine's. The pompano, which is unknown in European waters, is a slim-bodied, fatty-fleshed fish with a forked tail and can weigh up to 5 kg (10 lb).

It is unlikely, however, that many of you will have access to the pompano, even though imported ones are available at London's Billingsgate fish market. Other fish may be successfully substituted, for example mackerel, mullet, or shad (a type of herring). Lean fish such as sole, flounder, whiting, turbot, striped bass, etc. may also be used.

240 ml	*dry white wine*	*scant* ¹/₂ *pint*
240 ml	*stock or water*	*scant* ¹/₂ *pint*
4 large or 8 small	*pompano fillets (or other recommended substitute)*	4 large or 8 small
50 g	*butter*	2 oz
2 tbsps	*flour*	2 tbsps
4	*spring onions with 5 cm (2 inch) green tops, chopped*	4
1 tbsp	*fresh parsley, chopped*	1 tbsp
	pinch cayenne	
	pinch thyme	
	salt	
	freshly ground pepper	
100 g	*cooked and peeled prawns, sliced into quarters*	4 oz
100 g	*crabmeat*	4 oz

baking trays; parchment or brown paper

Preheat the oven to 200°C, 400°F, gas mark 6.

Combine the white wine with the stock or water and heat in a flat pan or large skillet to almost boiling point. Lower the heat and gently poach the fish fillets in the liquid until they are half-done – about 4–5 minutes, or less if smaller fillets are being used. Drain the fillets from the pan and set aside. Reserve the poaching liquid.

Melt the butter in the pan, add the flour and blend well. Add the spring onions and parsley and cook until the onions are soft and transparent – about 5 minutes. Add the poaching liquid gradually and cook, stirring constantly, until the sauce is thickened. Add the cayenne, thyme, salt, pepper, prawns and crabmeat, stirring very gently to avoid breaking up the crabmeat. Cook over a low heat for 5 minutes.

Meanwhile cut out eight 26 × 30 cm (11 × 14 inch) heart-shaped pieces of parchment. (Any brown paper or even white paper may be used instead. Aluminium foil will suffice if absolutely necessary.) Butter the parchment or paper well, then fold the hearts in half down the middle. Put each fish fillet on one side of the heart next to the centre fold. Divide the seafood sauce equally over all the fillets. Fold the other side of the paper over and bring the edges together. Roll up the edges of the paper and crimp slightly to form a well-sealed package.

Place the parcels on buttered baking trays and bake for 15 minutes in the preheated oven until the packages are puffed and lightly browned. Serve the fish in their bags.

——POACHED SALMON AND EGG SAUCE——
Serves 3–4

This recipe is traditionally served in New England to celebrate Independence Day on 4 July.

500 g	*salmon steaks*	*1 lb*
3 tbsps	*white wine*	*3 tbsps*
240 ml	*water*	*scant ½ pint*
1	*small carrot, peeled and halved*	*1*
1	*slice onion*	*1*
½	*stalk celery, sliced*	*½*
1 tsp	*fresh parsley, chopped*	*1 tsp*
½	*bay leaf*	*½*
¼ tsp	*salt*	*¼ tsp*
	a few peppercorns	
	thin slice lemon	

——The sauce——

25 g	*butter*	*1 oz*
3 tbsps	*flour*	*3 tbsps*
180 ml	*milk*	*generous ¼ pint*
120 ml	*reserved fish stock (from above)*	*scant ¼ pint*
1	*egg, hard-boiled, shelled*	*1*
3 tbsps	*cream*	*3 tbsps*
¼ tsp	*salt*	*¼ tsp*
	freshly ground pepper	

——To serve——

*boiled or steamed young
peas*

Put the salmon steaks, wine, water, carrot, onion, celery, parsley, bay leaf, salt, peppercorns and slice of lemon in a saucepan, and bring to the boil. Cover the pan and simmer gently for about 7–10 minutes until the salmon is tender. (Whole pieces of salmon will take longer.) Remove the fish to a warm serving dish and strain the stock. Boil rapidly until reduced to 120 ml (scant ¼ pint), and reserve for the sauce.

Heat the butter in a medium saucepan, add the flour and cook for 2 minutes. Remove from the heat and gradually stir in the milk and the reserved fish stock. Return the pan to the heat and, stirring constantly, bring to the boil until thickened.

Chop the hard-boiled egg and add to the sauce with the cream, salt and pepper. Heat through, but do not boil. Pour the sauce over the salmon steaks and serve with young peas, the traditional accompaniment.

——FILLETS OF SOLE MARGUÉRY——
Serves 4

Although this recipe was named after the famous Parisian eating place, the Restaurant Marguéry, where it was created, its subsequent arrival and success in America warrants its inclusion in this book. One of America's most famous and most prodigious eaters of the late nineteenth and early twentieth centuries – the colourful 'Diamond' Jim Brady – was responsible for arranging the stealing of the Marguéry recipe from Paris. The beautiful Marguéry sauce can be enjoyed with many different fish.

——The fish stock——

¾–1 kg	*fish trimmings, bones and heads*	1½–2 lb
1	*onion, peeled and chopped*	1
2	*cloves garlic, peeled*	2
1	*lemon, sliced*	1

4–5	stalks fresh parsley, chopped	4–5
240 ml	dry white wine	scant 1/2 pint
1	bay leaf	1
1/4 tsp	saffron powder	1/4 tsp
1/4 tsp	dried basil	1/4 tsp
	or	
1/2 tsp	fresh basil	1/2 tsp
1/4 tsp	dried thyme	1/4 tsp
	or	
1/2 tsp	fresh thyme	1/2 tsp
10	peppercorns	10
1 1/2–2 tsps	salt	1 1/2–2 tsps
1 1/2 litres	water	2 1/2 pints

——The Marguéry sauce——

75 g	butter	3 oz
75 g	mushrooms, sliced	3 oz
3 tbsps	flour	3 tbsps
120 ml	milk	scant 1/4 pint
240 ml	fish stock (see above)	scant 1/2 pint
12	oysters, shelled	12
100 g	prawns, peeled	4 oz
120 ml	cream	scant 1/4 pint

——The fish——

4 large or 8 small	fillets of sole or plaice or whiting	4 large or 8 small
480 ml	fish stock (see above)	generous 3/4 pint
2	whole cloves	2
1	bay leaf	1
6	peppercorns	6
2	lemon slices	2

——To garnish——
fresh parsley and lemon slices

a poaching pan, large skillet or heavy frying pan

Put all the fish stock ingredients into a large pan, bring to the boil, and simmer for 30–40 minutes. Strain well through cheesecloth or muslin, and reserve the stock.

To make the sauce, heat 25 g (1 oz) of the butter in a skillet and sauté the sliced mushrooms until wilted. Remove the mushrooms and their juice from the pan. Add the remaining 50 g (2 oz) of butter, and when melted add the flour. Cook for several minutes, remove from the heat and gradually stir in the milk and fish stock. Return to the heat and, stirring constantly, cook until thickened. Return the mushrooms to the pan with their juice and add the oysters and prawns. Do not add the cream until just before coating the fish with the sauce.

Put the fish fillets in a poaching pan, skillet or frying pan and completely cover with the fish stock. Add the remaining ingredients and bring to the boil. Lower the heat and simmer very gently until the fish flakes when tested with a fork. This should take about 10 minutes, but will vary with the size and thickness of the fillets. Take care not to overcook the fish or the fillets will break up.

To serve, gently lift the fillets from the pan, drain briefly and lay in a warmed serving dish. Add the cream to the hot Marguéry sauce, heat through and pour over the fillets. Garnish with fresh parsley and slices of lemon.

NOTE: Freeze the remaining fish stock for later use, or use in other fish recipes, for example, cioppino (page 52).

——BAKED SHAD OR HERRING——
Serves 3–4

The shad is prized in America, both for its tasty fillets and its roe. In early colonial days, the rivers were so thick with shad that people could virtually scoop them out of the waters by the bucket. However, river pollution has taken its toll on the now less plentiful shad.

Fillets of this fish may be prepared like other fish, by grilling or frying in butter, but longer, slower cooking helps to dissolve the multitude of small bones which characterize this large herring-like fish. A similar variety of shad can be found in European waters.

500 g	shad fillet (or other herring fish)	1 lb
15 g	butter	large knob
2 tbsps	onion, peeled and chopped	2 tbsps
2 tbsps	green pepper, chopped	2 tbsps
2 tbsps	celery, chopped	2 tbsps
75 g	fresh breadcrumbs	3 oz
1	egg, lightly beaten	1
1 tbsp	fresh parsley, finely chopped	1 tbsp
	salt and pepper to taste	
	extra butter	
120 ml	fish (or other light) stock, or wine or cider	scant ¼ pint

a 1¼ litre (2 pint) ovenproof dish

Preheat the oven to 160°C, 325°F, gas mark 3.

Get your fishmonger to remove as many of the bones from the fillet as possible. This should leave the fillet split down the centre and across to each side, thus giving plenty of room in the centre of the fish for the stuffing.

Heat the butter in a pan and sauté the onion, green pepper and celery for about 5 minutes to soften. Put in a small bowl with the breadcrumbs, egg, parsley, salt and pepper, and mix well. Stuff the cavity of the fillet with the mixture and lay back the top portion of the fish.

Cut a large piece of aluminium foil in which to wrap the fish. Butter the inside of the foil and sprinkle with salt and pepper. Lay in the fillet and pour over the stock, wine or cider.

Fold over the sides and ends of the foil to make a parcel. Place the parcel in the ovenproof dish and bake in the preheated oven for 1 hour.

——BROILED SCROD – GRILLED COD——
Serves 4

Scrod is the American name for young codfish, and scrod fillets and steaks are common in fish shops along the coastlines.

1 kg	scrod or cod	2 lb
1/2 tsp	salt	1/2 tsp
1/4 tsp	freshly ground pepper	1/4 tsp
100 g	butter, melted	4 oz
75 g	fresh breadcrumbs	3 oz
1/2	green pepper, de-seeded and chopped	1/2
1/2	onion, peeled and chopped	1/2
1 tbsp	made mustard	1 tbsp
1 tsp	Worcestershire sauce few drops tabasco	1 tsp
3 tbsps	lemon juice	3 tbsps
2 tbsps	sherry	2 tbsps
3 tbsps	grated parmesan cheese	3 tbsps

Cut the fish into four serving pieces and season with salt and pepper. Place the fish on the grill tray, brush with 25 g (1 oz) of melted butter, and grill for 5 minutes.

Meanwhile combine the rest of the butter with the breadcrumbs, green pepper, onion, mustard, Worcestershire sauce, tabasco, lemon juice and sherry. Turn the fish pieces, top with the butter/crumb/vegetable mixture, and sprinkle with parmesan cheese. Grill for a further 7 minutes or until the fish flakes easily and the top is lightly browned.

——CODFISH CAKES OR BALLS——
Makes 12 cakes or 24–30 balls

This traditional New England recipe makes use of salt cod, still available even with the domination of freezer and canned foods. Fresh cod may be substituted, in which case there is no need to soak the fish overnight; the potatoes should be salted and the fishcake mixture seasoned to taste.

350–400 g	salt cod (bacalao)	12–14 oz
3/4 kg	potatoes	1 1/2 lb
15 g	butter or margarine	large knob
1	egg, lightly beaten	1

*pinch ground mace or
ginger (optional)
freshly ground pepper
dried breadcrumbs or
flour to coat
oil for deep-frying*

Soak the salt cod overnight in a large bowl of cold water. The following day, drain the cod and put it in a saucepan with fresh water. Bring to the boil, then cover the pan and simmer for 10–15 minutes until the fish flakes easily. Strain the fish from the water, remove the bones and skin, and flake the flesh.

Meanwhile, peel the potatoes and cut into even sizes. Cook in a pan of unsalted water for 15–20 minutes until tender. Drain and mash with the butter or margarine. (This should yield about 250 g (8 oz) of mashed potatoes.

Mix together the flaked fish, mashed potatoes, egg, mace or ginger, and pepper. Form the mixture into cakes or balls, roll in the breadcrumbs or flour, and deep-fry in hot fat until browned all over. Drain on kitchen paper and serve hot.

——MARYLAND CRABCAKES——
Makes 6–8

Maryland is famous for its delicious crab creations, of which crabcakes and crab soup are two good examples. Marylanders celebrate the bounty of their seashores with glorious crab feasts where crabcakes are the traditional fare.

500 g	crabmeat	1 lb
50 g	fresh breadcrumbs (i.e. 2–3 slices of bread)	2 oz
1 tsp	dry mustard	1 tsp
3 tbsps	mayonnaise	3 tbsps
1	egg, lightly beaten	1
1 tsp	Worcestershire sauce	1 tsp
	dash of cayenne	
1/2 tsp	salt	1/2 tsp
	flour or dry breadcrumbs	
25–50 g	butter	1–2 oz

a skillet or heavy frying pan

Flake the crabmeat into a medium bowl. Add the breadcrumbs, mustard, mayonnaise, lightly beaten egg, Worcestershire sauce, cayenne and salt. If the mixture is too soft, chill first; if it is too stiff, add extra mayonnaise or fresh cream.

Shape the mixture into 6 or 8 fat crabcakes. Lightly toss in sifted flour or roll in dry breadcrumbs.

Heat the butter in the skillet or frying pan and sauté the crabcakes for 4–5 minutes on each side until lightly browned. Serve hot.

NOTE: If desired you can add a little finely chopped onion or parsley to the mixture before cooking.

——LOBSTER À L'AMÉRICAINE——
Serves 4

This is a delightful dish and by far the nicest way I know of cooking lobster. It ought to be made with a live lobster in preference to the pre-cooked shellfish so frequently on sale in Australia and Britain, if you wish to re-create the genuine dish. Lobster à l'Américaine has long been the subject of controversy – French cooks claiming that the use of oil and tomatoes makes it a classic Provençal dish. The authoritative *Larousse Gastronomique* says that this dispute was finally settled when it was discovered that the recipe was indeed invented by a French chef, Pierre Fraisse, in his restaurant in France (previously Fraisse had been a chef in America, particularly in Chicago). He named his lobster creation in honour of the tourists who first sampled it. (K.C.)

2 × 1 kg or	*live lobsters*	2 × 2 lb or
4 × 500 g		4 × 1 lb
1 tsp	*salt*	1 tsp
½ tsp	*freshly ground pepper*	½ tsp
6 tbsps	*olive or other oil (e.g. corn)*	6 tbsps
75 g	*butter*	3 oz
1–2	*cloves garlic, peeled and crushed*	1–2

1	onion, peeled and finely chopped	1
4	spring onions, finely chopped	4
1	bouquet garni (bay leaf, parsley, thyme)	1
8–10	large tomatoes, peeled and chopped	8–10
480 ml	dry white wine	generous 3/4 pint
1/4 tsp	cayenne	1/4 tsp
120 ml	brandy	scant 1/4 pint
120 ml	dry sherry or fish stock	scant 1/4 pint
5 tbsps	fresh parsley, finely chopped	5 tbsps

a skillet or large frying pan

Kill the lobsters by plunging them head first into a large pan of boiling water. Cut them in half lengthwise (i.e. from the head to the end of the tail). Carefully remove and discard the head and intestines. The tail and meat in the upper part of the body should be in one piece, with the shell still on the tail. Reserve all claws and legs of edible size.

Rub salt and pepper into the lobster halves. Heat the oil and 50 g (2 oz) of the butter in the skillet or pan, and cook the lobsters over a high heat until the shells turn red. Remove from the pan. Cook the legs and claws the same way.

Add the remaining 25 g (1 oz) of butter to the skillet, and sauté the garlic, onion and spring onions until softened and beginning to brown. Return the lobster halves to the pan with the *bouquet garni*, tomatoes, dry white wine and cayenne. Cover the pan and cook for a further 5 minutes over high heat.

Remove the lobster halves, claws, etc. and keep warm. Add the brandy and the sherry or fish stock to the sauce in the pan and bring to the boil. Boil the sauce until it is reduced by one third. Check the seasoning. Arrange the lobster halves and claws on a large warm dish and pour over the sauce. Sprinkle with parsley.

——LOBSTER NEWBURG——
Serves 4 as an appetizer or 2 as a main meal

It is said that a sea captain by the name of Ben Wenberg invented this dish in the kitchens of his favourite New York City restaurant, the classy Delmonico's, whose owner, Charles Delmonico, added 'Lobster à la Wenberg' to his menu. However, Delmonico and Wenberg fell out and the dish was withdrawn. Later Delmonico re-introduced it, but changed the name to Newberg. The mis-spelling continued as it became Lobster Newburg. The recipe may be adapted to other shellfish, for example Shrimp Newburg.

360 ml	*double cream*	*generous ¹/₂ pint*
3	*egg yolks, well beaten*	*3*
¹/₄ tsp	*salt*	*¹/₄ tsp*
	pinch freshly ground pepper	
	pinch cayenne	
	pinch nutmeg	
1 kg	*whole lobster, to yield about 3 cups cooked and diced meat*	*2 lb*
1 tbsp	*sherry or brandy*	*1 tbsp*
1 tbsp	*butter*	*1 tbsp*

——To serve——

cooked rice

Heat the cream in the top of a double boiler until hot. Remove from the heat and whisk in the egg yolks, seasonings and spices. Return to a low heat, and being careful not to allow the water to boil, cook, stirring continuously, until the mixture coats the back of the spoon. Add the lobster and continue to cook until the lobster is warmed through – about 5 minutes. Finally, just before serving, add the sherry or brandy and butter and stir for 1 minute. Serve hot on a bed of rice.

——BAKED STUFFED CLAMS——
Serves 4

16	clams or other molluscs,	*16*
	e.g. mussels	
1 litre	boiling water	*1³/4 pints*
25 g	fresh brown breadcrumbs	*1 oz*
25 g	cheese, grated	*1 oz*
3	slices bacon	*3*
50 g	mushrooms, sliced	*2 oz*
¹/2	lemon, juice only	*¹/2*
	salt and freshly ground pepper	

a large baking tray

Preheat the oven to 200°C, 400°F, gas mark 6.

Scrub the shellfish well and put several at a time in a large saucepan with the boiling water to cover. Boil until the shells open – about 5–10 minutes (see note on page 28). Drain the opened shellfish from the water and remove the flesh, reserving the shells. Mince the flesh with some of the strained juice into a small bowl. Add the breadcrumbs and the grated cheese.

Fry the bacon slices until crisp. Remove from the pan and leave to cool. Slice the mushrooms and sauté in the bacon fat for a few minutes until wilted. Add to the bowl with the lemon juice and seasonings.

Spoon the mixture back into the shells. Dice or crumble the bacon and sprinkle over the tops. Put the shells on a baking tray and bake on the shelf above the centre of the preheated oven for 15 minutes. Serve hot as an hors-d'œuvre or as a fish course for a dinner party.

——CLAMS OR OYSTERS CASINO——
Serves 4–6

4–6	slices bacon	*4–6*
2	spring onions, finely	*2*
	chopped	
¹/2	green pepper, de-seeded	*¹/2*
	and finely chopped	

1	*stalk celery, finely*	*1*
	chopped	
2–3	*stalks fresh parsley, finely*	*2–3*
	chopped	
1 tbsp	*lemon juice*	*1 tbsp*
	a few drops	
	Worcestershire sauce	
	salt and freshly ground	
	pepper to taste	
	rock salt	
24	*clams or oysters on the*	*24*
	half shell	

a skillet or frying pan; a large ovenproof dish

Preheat the oven to 200°C, 400°F, gas mark 6.

Fry the bacon in the skillet or pan until crisp. Drain from the pan and chop finely. Pour off any excess bacon fat. Sauté the spring onions, green pepper and celery in the remaining fat until softened – about 5 minutes. Stir in the parsley, lemon juice, Worcestershire sauce and salt and pepper to taste.

Spread the rock salt thickly over the base of the ovenproof dish. Spread a little of the vegetable mixture over each clam or oyster half, and put the shells side by side on the rock salt. Bake in the preheated oven for about 10 minutes until lightly browned. Alternatively, put under a hot grill until the clams or oysters are heated through. Serve as an hors-d'œuvre or a fish course.

——NEW ENGLAND CLAMBAKE——

This is one of those 'party' recipes where it is impossible to specify exact ingredients: it's a case of adding what you like and as much as you need for the party. For a clambake is very much a social occasion in America. It was originally an Indian method of cooking, and was soon adopted by the early settlers; in time, it became a popular electioneering event and even a big tourist attraction in New England.

It is prepared by digging out a pit in the sand of the beaches, lining the base with rocks or stones, and then setting a large wood fire above. By the time the fire has reduced almost to ashes, the stones beneath are extremely hot. These are then covered with wet, fresh seaweed which is layered between all the items to be cooked at the bake – clams in their shells, lobsters, any other fish wrapped in paper, sausages, potatoes in their jackets, husks of fresh corn. Even whole chickens are sometimes added.

It might be more accurate to call it a 'clamsteam' rather than a 'clambake', as the essential method of cooking is by the steam from the wet seaweed. I have even seen a clambake re-created in a large oil drum, and author Howard Mitcham* finds that a 'galvanized garbage can' works much better than the old method of a hole filled with stones, which he believes wastes the most delicious part of the clams – their juice. (See Mitcham's advice on the use of garbage cans in a 'shrimp boil', on page 71.)

Other sea-coast states in America have their own versions of the clambake. In Maryland it is called a crab feast (or fest); large quantities of crabs are steamed, or made into Maryland crabcakes, and then consumed with plenty of beer to wash them down. Further up the coast in New Jersey, the popular festivity there is known as the shad bake. The shad, a kind of herring, comes up river to spawn from late winter to late spring and is one of America's favourite fish. Customarily, the shad is nailed to a plank of wood and baked over a barbecue pit – another cooking method adopted from the Indians. In Maine, the abundance of lobsters gives rise to many enjoyable lobster bakes.

———OYSTERS ROCKEFELLER———
Serves 2 as a main course or 4 as an appetizer

Oysters Rockefeller was created around 1900 by Mr Jules Alciatore, owner of Antoine's, one of New Orleans' most famous restaurants. He is also credited with the invention of another classic New Orleans speciality – pompano en papillote (page 54).

This recipe gained its name from the superb flavour of its sauce, which was reckoned to be as rich as Rockefeller himself! Today there are as many different versions of oysters Rockefeller as there

---

* Howard Mitcham, *Provincetown Seafood Cookbook*, Addison-Wesley, Reading, Massachusetts, 1975.

are restaurants in the French Quarter of New Orleans. While attending a medical conference there I spent two very memorable days enjoying a gastronomic tour around the city, where I sampled oysters Rockefeller, among other things, and knew immediately that this was one recipe worthy of its reputation. (K.C.)

24	*oysters on the shell*	24
100 g	*butter*	*4 oz*
500 g	*spinach, fresh*	*1 lb*
2–3	*spring onions, finely chopped*	*2–3*
5–6 tbsps	*parsley, finely chopped*	*5–6 tbsps*
4–5 tbsps	*fresh breadcrumbs*	*4–5 tbsps*
1/4 tsp	*tabasco*	*1/4 tsp*
1 tbsp	*Worcestershire sauce*	*1 tbsp*
2	*anchovy fillets, finely chopped*	*2*
	or	
1 tsp	*anchovy paste*	*1 tsp*
2 tbsps	*Pernod, or ouzo or other aniseed-flavoured liqueur*	*2 tbsps*
	rock salt	
6 tsps	*parmesan cheese*	*6 tsps*

a large ovenproof dish

Preheat the oven to 200°C, 400°F, gas mark 6.

Wash the oysters thoroughly and open the shells carefully to retain all their juices. Wash the oyster flesh to remove any sand or shell particles. Strain the oyster juice through cheesecloth and reserve.

Melt the butter in a skillet or heavy frying pan and cook the washed, stemmed spinach and the chopped spring onions for 5 minutes until tender. Add the parsley, breadcrumbs, tabasco, Worcestershire sauce, anchovies or paste and Pernod. Cook for 2–3 minutes, then purée the sauce in a blender or finely chop the spinach.

Wash the deep half of each oyster shell, place an oyster in each half, and arrange the shells in an ovenproof dish containing a thick layer of rock salt – 1–2 cm (1/2–3/4 inch). (The rock salt helps to support the shells in place and also retains heat to keep the shells hot.)

Place the dish under a hot grill and cook for 2–3 minutes until the edges of the oysters start to curl. Remove from the grill, add a teaspoon of oyster juice to each shell, and cover the oysters with the spinach sauce. Sprinkle the tops with parmesan cheese – about ¼ teaspoon per shell.

Bake the shells in the preheated oven for 5–10 minutes until hot, then place under the grill to lightly brown the tops. Serve in the pan of rock salt.

NOTE: Other popular additions to the spinach sauce are chopped green pepper, celery, lettuce or watercress and anise.

——OYSTER STEW——
Serves 2–3

The amazing Oyster Bar in New York's Grand Central Station has always been known for its oyster stew, a simple but delicious recipe.

12	*oysters in their shells*	*12*
25 g	*butter*	*1 oz*
240 ml	*milk*	*scant ½ pint*
240 ml	*double cream*	*scant ½ pint*
½ tsp	*celery salt*	*½ tsp*
	salt and pepper	

a skillet or large frying pan

Shell the oysters, reserving the oyster liquor. Strain the liquor. Heat the butter in the skillet or pan and gently sauté the oysters until their edges curl.

Meanwhile scald the milk and cream in a saucepan and add to the oysters with the reserved oyster liquor, celery salt and extra salt and pepper to taste. Heat through, without boiling, and serve immediately with crackers.

NOTE: Americans serve 'oyster crackers' with this stew – these are tiny octagonal crackers specially invented to complement oysters. The people of Maine like to adapt their prize catch – the lobster – to make a similar stew.

——A LOUISIANA SHRIMP BOIL——

Down in Louisiana, the shrimp (or prawns as we know them), crabs and crawfish (crayfish, crawdads or mudbugs as they are also called) are so plentiful in the Gulf waters and bayous that little excuse is needed for a shrimp boil, crab boil, or crawfish boil party. In Louisiana you can buy special mixtures of shrimp and crab boil spices and herbs which are an essential part of the cooking. Our crab boil spice jar contained bay leaves, mustard seed, coriander, allspice and dried red pepper, among other things.

We were particularly enchanted by Howard Mitcham's amusing description of how he and his friends organize a shrimp boil party – by cooking 400 lb of shrimp in a pillowcase lowered into a 30-gallon galvanized garbage can (dustbin)!

However, before cooking can begin, it is important to ensure that you have the *right* kind of garbage can and that it is properly prepared. As Mr Mitcham told us in a letter, some people have been made ill by not following these procedures carefully. First, always make sure that the can has been *welded* together and *not soldered* together, as solder is lead and therefore poisonous. Second, the can (a new one, of course) should be scrubbed out thoroughly with a generous amount of bicarbonate of soda and hot water to 'neutralize any of the residues of the acids that were used in the galvanizing process'. Once the can is prepared, this is how Mr Mitcham goes about feeding the hungry hordes:

'Fill your 30-gallon pot one third full of water and add 6 large onions, coarsely chopped; a whole bunch of celery with leaves, coarsely chopped; 2 whole heads of garlic, coarsely chopped; 3 lemons, sliced, 1 lb of salt and ½ lb of cayenne; 5 3-ounce packages of "shrimp boil" spices; and ½ a bottle of Worcestershire sauce; and a quart of white wine. Boil all this stuff to make a good strong liquor. Put 25 lb of shrimp in a pillowcase and lower them into the pot of boiling liquor. Make sure they're loosely packed so that the hot water can circulate all around them. By trial and error we found that the ideal cooking time for 25 lb is approximately 25 minutes. Of course the time is much less for smaller batches. Use the same cooking liquor over and over for each new batch; it gets richer and richer all the time. Allow 2 lb of shrimp for each guest.

Serve with chili sauce made with onion, parsley, lemon, poppy seeds and tabasco.'*

That extract is sufficient proof of what voracious shrimp-eaters they are in the Gulf states!

——SHRIMP REMOULADE——
Serves 3–4

A popular New Orleans speciality.

1 tbsp	shrimp (prawn) boil spice (i.e. a mixture of crushed bay leaf, coriander, red pepper flakes, peppercorns, allspice, mustard seed – see page 71)	*1 tbsp*
500 g	fresh prawns, uncooked	*1 lb*

——For the sauce——

1 tsp	dry mustard	*1 tsp*
1 tbsp	vinegar	*1 tbsp*
2 tsps	paprika	*2 tsps*
	large pinch cayenne	
1/4 tsp	salt	*1/4 tsp*
1	clove garlic, peeled and crushed	*1*
1/2	stick celery, finely diced	*1/2*
1	large spring onion, finely sliced	*1*
3 tbsps	oil (e.g. peanut, olive)	*3 tbsps*

——To serve——

shredded lettuce
fresh parsley

Put the spices in a medium pan half filled with water and bring to the boil. Boil for 5 minutes before adding the prawns. Cook for

* Howard Mitcham, *Creole Gumbo and All That Jazz*, Addison-Wesley, Reading, Massachusetts, 1978.

2-3 minutes until the shells turn pink, then strain from the pan. Remove the shells, heads and legs and reserve the flesh.

To make the sauce, put the sauce ingredients into a bowl and mix together well. Alternatively, blend all the ingredients in an electric blender, leaving the sauce slightly chunky. To serve, lay the prawns on a little shredded lettuce and either pour over the remoulade sauce or serve it separately. Sprinkle with chopped fresh parsley.

——BROILED SCALLOP KEBABS——
Serves 2-4

There are two kinds of scallops in America – sea scallops, which are larger, and the tiny bay scallops for which New York's Long Island is famous. The American sea scallop differs only slightly from those found in the English Channel, off the French Atlantic coast, and in Australia. The coral is normally removed before sale, as is its distinctive fluted shell, which is sold separately in cookware shops.

Scallops are also served breaded and fried or sautéed in butter and herbs. Broiling or grilling is, however, a very common American way of cooking fish.

250 g	scallops without their shells	8 oz
6	slices of bacon	6
100 g	mushrooms (16 medium size)	4 oz
25 g	butter, melted	1 oz
	salt and freshly ground pepper	
	paprika	

4 kebab sticks or skewers

If you are using the larger sea scallops cut these into bite-sized pieces.

Grill the bacon slices, but do not allow them to become crisp. The bacon should be soft enough to roll up. Cut each slice in half and fold up each piece into a small roll.

Wipe the mushrooms and remove the stems (which can be used later to flavour soups, stews, or stocks). Thread the prepared ingredients on to the kebab sticks, alternating the bacon rolls and whole mushrooms between the scallops. Brush the kebabs with melted butter and sprinkle with salt, pepper and a little paprika. Cook under a hot grill, turning once, until lightly browned – about 5–7 minutes. Serve hot as an hors-d'œuvre or a fish course.

——FROGS' LEGS IN WINE——
Serves 3–4

Frogs' legs are revered as a great delicacy in Southern Louisiana, where the swampy inlets or creeks (known as bayous) around the Mississippi delta provide ideal hunting grounds for the frog hunters. Prime frog-hunting time is at night, often in special airboats to skim over the uncertain terrain of the swamps and always with 'frogging lights' – a sort of miner's head-lamp with which to find the quarry in the dark.

The meat of frogs' legs tends to be dry, and so must be cooked with care to ensure that the natural juices do not evaporate.

12 medium or 6–8 large	*pairs frogs' legs*	*12 medium or 6–8 large*
360 ml	*white wine*	*generous ½ pint*
	salt	
	freshly ground pepper	
	cayenne	
100 g	*butter*	*4 oz*
2 tbsps	*flour*	*2 tbsps*
1	*small green pepper, de-seeded and chopped*	*1*
3	*spring onions, sliced*	*3*
100 g	*fresh mushrooms, sliced*	*4 oz*
2 tbsps	*fresh parsley, chopped*	*2 tbsps*
1	*lemon, juice only*	*1*
3 tbsps	*cream*	*3 tbsps*

a skillet or heavy frying pan

Divide the paired frogs' legs into single legs, like chicken drumsticks. Parboil them for 3 minutes and leave to cool. Put 240 ml (scant ½ pint) of the white wine with an equal quantity of water in a bowl, season with salt and pepper and add the frogs' legs. Marinate the legs for at least 1 hour.

Drain the frogs' legs from the marinade and pat dry with kitchen paper. Rub them with salt, black pepper and a little cayenne. Heat the butter in a skillet or pan and sauté the legs for 3–4 minutes until golden brown on both sides. Drain from the butter and keep warm.

Add the flour to the butter and cook for 1 minute. Add the green pepper, the sliced spring onions and mushrooms and the parsley. Stir in the remaining 120 ml (scant ¼ pint) of white wine and cook until the vegetables are soft – about 10 minutes. Add the lemon juice and cream, and season with salt and pepper and cayenne to taste, remembering that to achieve an authentic 'Cajun' dish the sauce should be spicy hot. If you do not like spicy food, you may omit the cayenne.

Finally, return the frogs' legs to the sauce and heat through. Serve as an hors-d'œuvre for an impressive start to a dinner party.

MEAT AND POULTRY

Beef, in the form of steak, rib roast or ground (minced) beef for hamburgers, is the meat most commonly associated with American cooking. The American fondness for steak is now legendary – an obsession which led to the famous cowboy era of the cattle trails during the second half of the 1800s. As good historians Waverley Root and Richard de Rochemont put it: 'The pursuit of beef was about to open up an indigenous American life style so romantic, to outsiders at least, that it has been supporting the moving picture industry ever since.'* (A similar claim has been made for the role of popcorn in helping to keep cinemas profitable.)

Root and de Rochemont also discuss the next link in the chain – the development of a certain style of cowboy cooking which gave rise to such dishes as chuck wagon stew, buckaroo (which means 'cowboy') beans and 'son-of-a-bitch stew' (presumably this was not the most popular of dishes, judging by its name and by the fact that its ingredients included all the parts of the cattle normally disdained by Americans, for example, tongue, liver, heart, sweetbreads and marrow gut).

However, it was steak that remains the cowboys' and all of America's favourite repast. It became synonymous with the American idea of the good life, though recently inflation, declining beef production and rising prices have taken their toll on the American dream. Steak, and in particular 'prime' graded steak, is becoming a luxury food.

Another part of the cattle that is popular if expensive in America

* Waverley Root and Richard de Rochemont, *Eating in America – A History*, William Morrow and Co. Inc., New York, 1976.

is calves' liver, which is by far the most tender and tasty of all livers. It is still commonly served in the old British manner – sautéed, and served with sautéed onion rings and gravy.

Chicken and chicken livers are comparatively cheap in America and, as a result, cookbooks abound with ideas of ways to cook both. Turkey, a native species of America, is also readily available both fresh and smoked, and poultry is often successfully combined with seafood to create such interesting and tasty dishes as jambalaya, gumbo filé, and turkey with oyster stuffing.

Pork is also fairly inexpensive, as is the preserved salt pork used in chowders and baked beans. Smoked hams are popular, especially the famous Smithfield hams of Virginia, which are produced from pigs fattened on peanuts.

——SURF AND TURF——
Serves 1

Americans love to combine meat and seafood, giving rise to such aptly named dishes as 'surf and turf'. In our recipe below the beef steak is served with an oyster 'blanket', although we have also been served with steak and lobster claws or prawns. Other examples of this meat and seafood combination can be found in oyster stuffing for turkeys (page 114), gumbo filé (page 38) and jambalaya (page 106), to name a few.

175–250 g	*steak, e.g. Porterhouse,* *sirloin*	*6–8 oz*
6–8	*oysters, shelled*	*6–8*
	pinch salt	
	pinch freshly ground *black pepper*	
1 tbsp	*butter*	*1 tbsp*
1 tbsp	*fresh parsley, chopped*	*1 tbsp*

Choose a nice thick steak about 5 cm (2–2½ inches) thick. Grill to taste (i.e. rare, medium, well done) until nearly ready. Spread the oysters over the steak, add the salt and pepper, and dot with the butter. Put the steak under the grill for just a few minutes more until the oysters become plump. Sprinkle with parsley and serve at once.

——STEAK TERIYAKI——
Serves 3–4

This Japanese speciality has quickly won its way into the hearts of American cooks and lovers of good food. It is an easily prepared and delicious dinner.

½ tsp	*ground ginger*	*½ tsp*
1	*clove garlic, peeled and crushed*	*1*
3 tbsps	*soy sauce*	*3 tbsps*
3 tbsps	*oil (e.g. peanut, cooking)*	*3 tbsps*
2 tbsps	*saké (rice wine) or sherry or port*	*2 tbsps*
500 g	*sirloin steak*	*1 lb*

——To serve——
cooked rice

a skillet or heavy frying pan

Mix together the ginger, garlic, soy sauce, oil, and saké (or substitute) in a wide bowl or dish. Add the whole piece of steak and marinate the meat for several hours, turning the steak periodically.

To cook, drain the steak from the marinade, put in a salted, fat-less skillet or pan, and brown the steak on both sides over a high heat. Cook the steak to taste (i.e. rare, medium, well done). Remove to a warm serving dish and keep warm.

Add the marinade to the pan juices, stir and bring to the boil. Serve the teriyaki sauce over the steak, with boiled rice to accompany.

NOTE: If you are using chopsticks to eat the steak, thinly slice the beef first before pouring over the sauce.

——SHAKER FLANK STEAK——
Serves 3–4

Flank steak is found below the ribs of a beef carcass. Skirt of beef is a similar cut which could be substituted.

The Shakers were a strict religious sect, originating in

Manchester, England, who established settlements in New England and Ohio. Their distinctive recipes survive to this day because they wrote them down and, to feed hundreds daily, had to measure ingredients carefully.

1 kg	flank steak	*2 lb*
25 g	butter	*1 oz*
1	medium onion, peeled and sliced	*1*
1	stalk celery, sliced	*1*
1	carrot, peeled and cut into strips	*1*
1/2	green pepper, de-seeded and thinly sliced	*1/2*
1 tbsp	fresh parsley, chopped	*1 tbsp*
1/2	lemon, juice only	*1/2*
120 ml	stock or water	*scant 1/4 pint*
3 tbsps	tomato ketchup	*3 tbsps*

skillet or heavy frying pan

Score the surface of the flank steak with a sharp knife. Heat the butter in the skillet or frying pan and fry the meat until lightly browned on both sides. Remove from the pan and keep warm.

Add the sliced onion and celery, carrot strips and pepper slices to the pan and sauté until softened – about 5 minutes. Add the parsley, lemon juice, stock or water and tomato ketchup, and stir to combine. Finally, return the flank steak to the pan, cover, and simmer gently for 1½ hours. To serve, slice the meat and pour over the vegetables and their juices.

——YANKEE POT ROAST——
Serves 6–8

1 1/4 kg	beef roast, e.g. rump, sirloin, top end, etc.	*3 lb*
2 tbsps	bacon fat	*2 tbsps*
2	cloves garlic, peeled and crushed	*2*
360 ml	water	*generous 1/2 pint*

120 ml	red wine	scant ¼ pint
1 tsp	salt	1 tsp
¼ tsp	pepper	¼ tsp
1	bay leaf	1
100 g	whole cranberries	4 oz
4	medium carrots, peeled and thickly sliced	4
6	medium potatoes, peeled and halved	6
4	onions, peeled and left whole	4
1 tbsp	flour	1 tbsp

a heavy saucepan or Dutch oven

First brown the roast – heat the bacon fat in the saucepan or Dutch oven and brown the roast on all sides. Add the crushed garlic and cook for 2–3 minutes. Add the water, wine, salt, pepper and bay leaf. Cover the pan and cook slowly until the meat is tender – about 1½–2 hours.

Thirty minutes before the end of the cooking time, add the cranberries, carrots, potatoes and onions. When cooked, remove the meat and vegetables from the pan on to a warm serving dish. Blend the flour with a little water and add to the pan. Cook, stirring constantly, until the gravy has thickened. Serve the pot roast cut into slices, with the vegetables and gravy to accompany.

———SAUERBRATEN———
Serves 6

Wherever people of German origin have settled in the USA – in cities like Philadelphia, Baltimore, Cincinnati and Milwaukee – this marinated pot roast with its distinctive sweet and sour flavour has remained a firm favourite. Preparations must start several days in advance of cooking.

2 kg	beef joint, e.g. topside, rump or rolled beef	4 lb

———For the marinade———

480 ml	red wine vinegar	generous ¾ pint

240 ml	white wine	scant 1/2 pint
2	onions, peeled and chopped	2
2	carrots, peeled and sliced	2
2	sticks celery, diced	2
10	peppercorns	10
4	whole cloves	4
2	bay leaves	2
3	whole allspice, crushed	3
1 1/2 tsps	salt	1 1/2 tsps

——For the sauce——

80 g	butter	3 oz
4 tbsps	oil	4 tbsps
3 tbsps	flour	3 tbsps
100 g	gingersnaps, crushed	4 oz

Put the beef in a deep bowl. Combine the vinegar, wine, onions, carrots, celery, peppercorns, cloves, bay leaves, allspice and salt in a large saucepan. Bring to the boil then pour over the beef. Turn the meat several times in the marinade, then cover and refrigerate for 2–3 days, turning several times each day.

Remove the beef from the marinade and dry with paper towels. Heat 40 g (1 1/2 oz) of the butter with the oil in a deep pan and brown the beef on all sides. Pour off some of the excess fat, then add the marinade. Simmer for approximately 3 hours until the meat is tender.

Remove the meat from the pan and keep hot. Strain the liquid in the pan and skim off as much fat as possible. In a saucepan, melt the remaining 40 g (1 1/2 oz) butter, add the flour and cook for a couple of minutes. Gradually add the strained liquid and, stirring constantly, cook until thickened. Add the crushed gingersnaps to the gravy and simmer for a few minutes more. Check the seasoning before serving the sauce over the sliced pot roast. Traditionally, potato pancakes (latkes) (page 194) accompany sauerbraten.

NOTE: Some German cooks achieve the sweet and sour flavour by adding sugar and sour cream to their gravy instead of gingersnaps.

——KENTUCKY BURGOO——
Serves 10–12

This meal-in-one stew is Kentucky's most famous dish and is traditionally served at large outdoor gatherings such as political and church meetings and the equally famous Kentucky Derby Day races. Original recipes made good use of the abundant wildlife such as squirrels, rabbits and game birds, and listed enormous quantities of ingredients. Later chicken, beef, pork and salt pork came to replace those original ingredients, but the quantities still ran into thousands of pounds of meat and tons of potatoes and vegetables. Our recipe below is of more manageable proportions, but it is still an ideal party dish.

500 g	beef, cubed (e.g. chuck, stewing steak)	1 lb
1	beef bone, cracked	1
1–1½ kg	chicken, cut into pieces	2–3 lb
500 g	pork, cubed	1 lb
2 tsps	salt	2 tsps
½ tsp	black pepper	½ tsp
¼ tsp	cayenne	¼ tsp
2½ litres	water	4 pints
3	medium onions, peeled and diced	3
2	medium potatoes, peeled and diced	2
4	sticks celery, diced	4
4	carrots, scraped and sliced	4
1	green pepper, de-seeded and diced	1
250 g	tinned butter beans, drained	8 oz
350 g	sweetcorn	12 oz
350 g	medium tomatoes, skinned and diced	12 oz
250 g	okra, sliced	8 oz
2	cloves garlic, peeled and crushed	2

2	*bay leaves*	2
1 tsp	*dried thyme*	*1 tsp*
	or	
2 tsps	*fresh thyme*	*2 tsps*
3–4	*sprigs fresh parsley, chopped*	*3–4*

a preserving pan or very large pot

Put the cubed beef, cracked beef bone, chicken pieces, cubed pork, salt, pepper, cayenne and water in the pan or pot, bring to the boil, then simmer for 2 hours.

Add the onions, potatoes, celery, carrots, green pepper and butter beans to the pan and simmer covered for a further hour, then remove the cover and simmer for 1 hour more.

Add the sweetcorn, diced tomatoes, okra, garlic, bay leaves and thyme, and simmer gently for one more hour. Before serving, remove the beef and chicken bones and stir in the parsley.

The burgoo is best served in large soup bowls with crusty home-made bread to accompany, for example Anadama (page 179) or sourdough French (page 183).

BOILED NEW ENGLAND DINNER
—(CORNED BEEF)—
Serves 6

Corned beef to those of us of British origin immediately brings to mind tinned corned beef from South America. So it came as something of a surprise to discover that Americans (and Australians, for that matter) have preserved the habit of salting beef to cure it and that the traditional New England boiled dinner of the settlers' time is still as popular as ever. Also, the traditional dish served to celebrate St Patrick's Day in America is corned beef and cabbage (very similar to the recipe given below), a reminder of the bacon and cabbage dish usually served in Ireland.

The mustard sauce is not traditional but is our addition to the dinner.

1¼ kg	*corned beef brisket*	*3 lb*
	water to cover	
500–700 g	*potatoes*	*1–1½ lb*

250 g	*carrots*	*8 oz*
250 g	*swede, turnip, or parsnip*	*8 oz*
½	*large cabbage*	*½*
	salt and pepper to taste	

————For the mustard sauce————

150 ml	*corned beef stock*	*¼ pint*
2 tbsps	*red wine vinegar*	*2 tbsps*
2 tbsps	*sugar*	*2 tbsps*
1 tsp	*dry mustard*	*1 tsp*
25 g	*butter or margarine*	*1 oz*
1	*large egg*	*1*

Put the corned beef in a large heavy saucepan, cover with water and bring to the boil. Cover the pan and simmer gently for 2½ hours.

Meanwhile peel the potatoes and cut into even sizes. Peel the carrots and swede (or turnip or parsnip) and cut into strips or large dice. Add all the vegetables to the corned beef, season, cover and cook for a further 15 minutes.

Remove the hard centre core from the cabbage and cut into wedges. Add to the pan and cook for a further 15 minutes.

While the beef and vegetables are still cooking, strain off 150 ml (¼ pint) of the corned beef stock for the sauce. Put the stock, wine vinegar, sugar, mustard and butter or margarine into a small pan and bring to the boil.

Lightly beat the egg in a small bowl and add a few tablespoons of the hot sauce to it. Pour the egg mixture into the sauce and heat gently to thicken, but do not boil the sauce or the egg will curdle.

To serve, place the corned beef on a warmed carving tray and surround with the vegetables (or serve the vegetables separately in a warmed serving dish). Pour the mustard sauce into a gravy boat and serve over the sliced beef.

NOTE: Left-over corned beef and its vegetables may be used the following morning to make corned beef hash or red flannel hash (page 161) for a traditional American 'brunch'.

———TEX-MEX CHILI CON CARNE———
Serves 3–4

Chili con carne is as hot an issue in America and Mexico as its spicy flavour, for this is another dish whose origin and ingredients cause furious arguments on all sides. The problems centre around the following questions:

Is it a Mexican dish or did it originate in Texas?

Should cubed steak or minced beef be used?

Should real chilis or chili powder be used?

Should tomatoes be added? And what about onions?

Should beans be added to the stew, or served separately, or not served at all?

Mexicans themselves hotly deny parentage of chili con carne, while Texans are delighted to accept full responsibility for the dish which is one of the state's most famous specialities. But that doesn't stop people asserting that the dish is a Mexican invention.

From my point of view, I prefer cubed beef to minced, chili with tomatoes *and* onions, and with beans added to the stew. From a purely practical point of view, chili powder* is far more readily available throughout the world than the fresh red Mexican *ancho*** chilis that are part of a perfectionist's chili.

100 g	*dried red kidney beans*	*4 oz*
	or	
500 g	*tinned red kidney beans, drained*	*1 lb*
500 g	*stewing beef*	*1 lb*
1–2 tbsps	*fat or oil*	*1–2 tbsps*
1	*medium onion, peeled and chopped*	*1*
1–2	*cloves garlic, peeled and finely chopped or crushed*	*1–2*
1–2 tbsps	*chili powder*	*1–2 tbsps*

* Chili powder was first created in the early 1900s in Texas by a German who extracted pulp from the pods and mixed it with other spices (e.g. cumin, oregano).

** The *ancho* chili is the most frequently used of Mexico's more than twenty different chilis. Chilis, the main seasoning of the Inca and Aztec Indians, were unknown in Europe until Columbus discovered them along with the Americas.

$^1/_2$ tsp	ground cumin	$^1/_2$ tsp
$^1/_2$ tsp	dried oregano	$^1/_2$ tsp
	or	
1 tsp	fresh oregano, finely chopped	1 tsp
$^1/_2$–1 tsp	salt	$^1/_2$–1 tsp
120 ml	stock or water	scant $^1/_4$ pint
500 g	tinned tomatoes, puréed or finely chopped	1 lb

————To serve————
tortillas (optional)

Soak the dried kidney beans in water overnight. Drain and boil in fresh water for 1$^1/_2$ hours until tender. Drain again.

Meanwhile trim any excess fat from the beef and cut the meat into cubes. Heat the fat or oil in a medium pan, add the onion and garlic, and sauté for 3–4 minutes. Add the cubed beef and brown, turning frequently. Add the chili powder (2 tablespoons for those who like it hot) and the cumin, and sauté for a further 2 minutes.

Add the oregano, salt, stock and tomatoes, then cover the pan and simmer gently for 1–1$^1/_4$ hours. Finally, add the drained beans and cook for a further 30 minutes. Serve with tortillas – or popadums, the nearest substitute we can think of for the ground corn tortillas.

NOTE: If dried chilis are available, use three red chilis instead of the chili powder for each 500 g (1 lb) of meat. Cut the chilis in half, remove the stems and seeds, and soak in hot water for 1 hour. Mince or purée the chilis with the stock or water used in the recipe.

NORWEGIAN MEATBALLS WITH
————GJETOST SAUCE————
Serves 6–8

There are many similar Scandinavian meatball recipes which have been adopted into the American cuisine. Gjetost cheese is a Norwegian full fat whey cheese, made with cow's and goat's milk and then smoked. The brand we used was 'Ski Queen', which we found in New York, London and Perth, Western Australia (the latter with some difficulty). Order this cheese from a merchant who deals in speciality food imports or cheeses. A substitute for this cheese could be found in other smoked cheeses (e.g. Austrian), although these won't have the slightly sweet taste of gjetost.

3/4 kg	*lean minced beef*	*1 1/2 lb*
250 g	*minced pork or veal*	*8 oz*
1 1/2 tsps	*salt*	*1 1/2 tsps*
1/2 tsp	*pepper*	*1/2 tsp*
2	*eggs, beaten*	*2*
240 ml	*milk*	*scant 1/2 pint*
2 tbsps	*capers, finely chopped*	*2 tbsps*
50 g	*fine dried breadcrumbs*	*2 oz*
	oil for frying	

————For the sauce————

25 g	*butter*	*1 oz*
2 tbsps	*flour*	*2 tbsps*
120 ml	*milk*	*scant 1/4 pint*
120 ml	*cream*	*scant 1/4 pint*
120 ml	*chicken stock or broth*	*scant 1/4 pint*
250 g	*gjetost cheese, grated*	*8 oz*
150 ml	*sour cream*	*1/4 pint*
2 tbsps	*parsley or dill, chopped*	*2 tbsps*

a skillet or large frying pan

To make the meatballs, mix together the beef, pork or veal, salt, pepper, eggs, milk, capers and breadcrumbs and shape into small balls about 1 1/2 cm (3/4 inch) in diameter. This mixture will make about 150 meatballs.

Heat the skillet or pan, filling it to a depth of about 1 cm (1/2 inch) with the oil. Cook the meatballs over a moderate heat, turning several times. Do not overcook – the outside should be brown and the inside just no longer pink. Remove the meatballs and drain on absorbent paper.

To make the sauce, melt the butter in a separate pan, add the flour and cook for several minutes. Remove from the heat and

gradually blend in the milk, cream and chicken broth. Bring to the
boil, stirring constantly, and cook until thickened. Gradually mix
in the cheese and continue to cook over a low heat until it has
melted. Remove from the heat, add the sour cream, stir to blend,
then finally add the meatballs and heat through.

Serve sprinkled with chopped parsley or dill.

——MEAT LOAF——
Makes a 500 g (1 lb) loaf

This recipe may also be made adding 175 g (6 oz) of fresh
breadcrumbs to the mixture.

500 g	*beef (e.g. sirloin, rump or braising)*	*1 lb*
100 g	*bacon*	*4 oz*
1	*medium onion, peeled*	*1*
1–2	*cloves garlic, peeled*	*1–2*
3 tbsps	*tomato ketchup*	*3 tbsps*
1 tsp	*salt*	*1 tsp*
1 tsp	*Worcestershire sauce*	*1 tsp*
2 tbsps	*red wine*	*2 tbsps*
1	*egg*	*1*

a 500 g (1 lb) loaf tin

Preheat the oven to 180°C, 350°F, gas mark 4.

Mince together the beef, bacon, onion and garlic. (Alternatively, ask your butcher to mince together the beef and bacon;
peel and finely chop the onion and garlic before adding to the
minced meats.)

Add the ketchup, salt, Worcestershire sauce, red wine and egg
to the meat and mix well together. Press the mixture into the loaf
tin, smoothing over the surface. Bake in the preheated oven for
about 1¼ hours until the loaf is fully cooked. Strain the surrounding fat from the pan before inverting the meatloaf on to a warm
serving plate. Gently scrape away any white fat from the surface of
the loaf. Serve hot or cold.

NOTE: Americans like to eat meat loaf hot with spaghetti and a

tomato sauce. Hot meat loaf is also a favoured filling for heroes
(page 213).

——CHOP SUEY——
Serves 4

Like chow mein (page 111), chop suey is a genuine American/
Chinese dish. Some say it was invented by the Chinese cooks
whose job it was to feed the Chinese labour force imported into
America for the building of the trans-American railroad. Other
stories tell of the dish (whose name means 'miscellaneous odds
and ends') first being served in an American–Chinese restaurant
to some gullible customers, who, nonetheless, thoroughly enjoyed
it.

350–400 g	*cooked meat (e.g. chicken, beef, pork)*	*12–14 oz*
3 tbsps	*soy sauce*	*3 tbsps*
1 tbsp	*sherry or red wine*	*1 tbsp*
1 tbsp	*cornflour*	*1 tbsp*
1	*medium onion, peeled*	*1*
1	*clove garlic, peeled*	*1*
1–2 tbsps	*oil*	*1–2 tbsps*
2	*sticks celery, sliced*	*2*
1/2	*green or red pepper, de-seeded and sliced*	*1/2*
100 g	*mushrooms, sliced*	*4 oz*
50 g	*water chestnuts, sliced*	*2 oz*
50 g	*bamboo shoots, sliced*	*2 oz*
250 g	*beansprouts*	*8 oz*
1/2 tsp	*salt*	*1/2 tsp*
1/4 tsp	*monosodium glutamate (MSG) (optional)*	*1/4 tsp*
3 tbsps	*chicken, beef or pork stock*	*3 tbsps*

a wok (Chinese all-purpose pan), skillet or large frying pan

Chop the cooked meat into bite-sized pieces. Mix 2 tablespoons
of the soy sauce with the sherry or wine and the cornflour. Add
the meat and stir to coat. Leave to marinate for 1 hour.

Slice the onion and the garlic. Heat the oil in the wok, skillet or pan and sauté the onion and garlic to soften – about 2–3 minutes. Add the celery and green or red pepper and sauté for a further 2–3 minutes. Add the mushrooms and sauté for 2 more minutes. Add the marinated meat and fry briskly to brown lightly. Add the water chestnuts, bamboo shoots, beansprouts, salt, MSG, stock and the remaining 1 tablespoon of soy sauce to the pan. Stir until the sauce has thickened and serve hot with fried rice (page 157) or plain boiled rice.

——PIROSHKI OR PIROZHKI——
Makes 20–24

Piroshki (or 'little pies' as their Russian name signifies) are good for buffet parties or as 'finger food'. They are often served as accompaniments to Jewish soups, and can be filled with many different mixtures from potato to cream cheese or fish – the piroshki below have a meat filling. They may also be called 'pirogen' or 'pirojok', and can be made with a yeast dough instead of pastry, and deep fried instead of baked.

250 g	plain flour	8 oz
	pinch salt	
100 g	butter or fat	4 oz
1	egg yolk	1
2–3 tbsps	iced water	2–3 tbsps
15 g	butter	large knob
1	medium onion, peeled and finely chopped	1
1	clove garlic, peeled and finely chopped or crushed	1
100 g	mushrooms, thinly sliced	4 oz
350 g	minced beef	12 oz
1/2 tsp	salt	1/2 tsp
	freshly ground pepper	
2–3	stalks fresh parsley, finely chopped	2–3
1 tsp	Worcestershire sauce	1 tsp

| 3 tbsps | stock | 3 tbsps |
| 1 | egg yolk, to glaze | 1 |

baking trays or sheets; an 8–10 cm (3–4 inch) round cutter

To make the pastry, sift the flour and salt and rub in the butter or fat to resemble fine breadcrumbs. Lightly beat the egg yolk with the iced water and add to the flour to make a dough. Cover and leave in a cool place to rest for 15 minutes.

Meanwhile heat the butter in a medium pan, add the onion and garlic and sauté for 2–3 minutes. Add the sliced mushrooms and sauté for a further minute.

Add the minced beef and cook, stirring frequently, until browned. Finally, add the salt, pepper, parsley, Worcestershire sauce and stock, cover the pan and simmer for 15 minutes.

Preheat the oven to 200°C, 400°F, gas mark 6.

Roll out the pastry fairly thinly and cut into 8–10 cm (3–4 inch) circles. Mix the egg yolk with a little cold water and lightly brush around the edges of the circles of pastry. Put a spoonful of meat mixture on to the centre of each circle and fold over into a half-moon shape, sealing the edges by pinching together the pastry (or by using a fork). Prick the top of the pies twice with a fork to let steam escape, and brush the pastry with the remaining egg glaze. Put the piroshki on baking trays or sheets and bake in the preheated oven for 12–14 minutes until golden brown. Serve hot.

NOTE: Larger patties, similar to Cornish pasties, can be made in exactly the same way, except that the pastry circles are cut 13–15 cm (5–6 inches) in diameter. These are called 'piroghi'.

——BOSTON IRISH STEW——
Serves 4–6

This famous stew was traditionally served to exhausted runners after they crossed the finishing line of one of the world's best known, oldest, and most fiercely contested races – the Boston Marathon. In 1980, however, this long appreciated custom was dropped on the advice of nutritionists – a decision that was greeted with a clamour of protest from disappointed contestants who now have to make do with yoghurt and vitamin drinks instead.

1¼ kg	stewing, neck or breast of lamb	3 lb
3	carrots	3
2	onions	2
2–3	leeks (optional)	2–3
4	medium potatoes	4
2	parsnips	2
600 ml	lamb or chicken stock	1 pint
½ tsp	salt	½ tsp
	pepper	
1	bay leaf	1
¼ tsp	dried thyme	¼ tsp
2 tsps	cornflour	2 tsps
3 tbsps	water	3 tbsps

Trim any excess fat from the lamb. Peel and dice the carrots and onions. Wash, trim and slice the leeks, if desired, including some of the green part. Peel and halve the potatoes. Peel the parsnips and cut into large dice or strips. Put the lamb and prepared vegetables into a large pot with the stock, salt, pepper, bay leaf and thyme. Bring to the boil, cover the pan and simmer for 2 hours until the meat is tender.

Skim off the fat from the top of the stock. Slake the cornflour with the water. Remove the pan from the heat and stir in the dissolved cornflour. Return to the heat, and bring to the boil, stirring, until thickened. Test for seasoning and serve hot as a complete meal.

——BARBECUED SPARE RIBS——
Serves 2–3

These pork spare ribs show a Chinese influence in the addition of soy sauce, wine (or sherry) and garlic. See page 209 for American barbecue sauce for beef ribs and chicken.

500 g	pork spare ribs	1 lb
5 tbsps	soy sauce	5 tbsps
3 tbsps	water	3 tbsps
2 tbsps	red wine or sherry	2 tbsps

2 tbps	tomato ketchup	2 tbsps
1 tsp	sugar	1 tsp
1	clove garlic, peeled and crushed	1
small piece	root ginger, finely chopped (optional)	small piece

Cut the ribs into separate portions if necessary and remove any excess fat. Mix together the soy sauce, water, wine or sherry, ketchup, sugar and crushed garlic in a wide bowl or casserole dish, and add the ginger if desired. Marinate the spare ribs in the sauce for at least 1 hour, turning occasionally.

When ready to cook, remove the ribs from the marinade (reserving the liquid) and cook under a hot grill for about 10 minutes on each side, turning once, until the ribs are cooked and darkly brown.

Alternatively, the ribs may be baked in the oven, preheated to 190°C, 375°F, gas mark 5. Thread the ribs on to a long skewer and place the skewer on an oven rack. Put a large pan or tray beneath the hanging ribs to catch any drippings, and bake for 40–45 minutes until cooked and crisp.

Heat the reserved marinade in a small pan and serve hot as a sauce for the ribs.

——INDIAN STEW——
Serves 4

100 g	salt pork or bacon, diced	4 oz
1 kg	pork spare ribs	2 lb
2	medium onions, peeled and diced	2
1	clove garlic, peeled and crushed	1
1	green pepper, de-seeded and diced	1
2 tbsps	plain flour	2 tbsps

3	ears fresh corn, stripped of kernels	3
	or	
350 g	tinned or frozen corn kernels	12 oz
3–4	fresh tomatoes, skinned and chopped	3–4
120 ml	stock or water	scant 1/4 pint
4	sweet potatoes or yams, peeled and quartered	4

Fry the salt pork or bacon in a large heavy saucepan until crisp, then drain from the pan and set aside. Trim any excess fat from the spare ribs. Brown them in the fat remaining in the saucepan, then drain and keep hot.

Add the onion and garlic to the pan and sauté until lightly browned – about 5 minutes. Add the green pepper and the flour and cook a few minutes more. Add the corn kernels, tomatoes and stock or water, and stir until thickened. Return the spare ribs to the pan and put the sweet potatoes on top. Cover the pan and simmer for 50 minutes until the meat is tender. Five minutes before the end of cooking time, return the salt pork or bacon to the pan to warm through. Serve hot as a complete meal.

——SWEET AND SOUR PORK——
Serves 4–5

3/4 kg	lean, boneless pork, cut into cubes	1 1/2 lb
3 tbsps	cornflour	3 tbsps
	fat or oil for deep-frying	
1	medium onion, peeled and sliced	1
2	cloves garlic, peeled and crushed	2
1/2 tsp	salt	1/2 tsp
1	medium green pepper, de-seeded and cut into strips	1

1	*large carrot, peeled and cut into sticks*	*1*
2 tbsps	*soy sauce*	*2 tbsps*
2 tbsps	*sugar*	*2 tbsps*
3 tbsps	*white rice wine vinegar* *(or white wine or ordinary white vinegar)*	*3 tbsps*
240 ml	*pork or other light stock*	*scant 1/2 pint*
1 tbsp	*cornflour*	*1 tbsp*
2 tbsps	*pineapple juice or syrup*	*2 tbsps*
175 g	*pineapple chunks*	*6 oz*

a wok (Chinese all-purpose pan), skillet or large frying pan

Spread the pork cubes on a large plate or tray and sift over the cornflour, turning several times to coat the pieces all over. Heat the fat or oil in the wok, skillet or frying pan and deep-fry the pork pieces until crisp and lightly browned. Drain from the pan and place on absorbent paper in a warm serving dish. Keep warm.

Remove all but two tablespoons of the oil from the pan, add the sliced onion and crushed garlic with the salt, and sauté until 'pungent' – about 2–3 minutes. Add the pepper strips and carrot sticks and continue to fry until the vegetables are beginning to soften but are still crisp and crunchy – about 4–5 minutes.

Meanwhile mix the soy sauce, sugar, vinegar and stock together in a small bowl. Add to the pan and bring to the boil. Mix the cornflour with the pineapple juice and add to the pan. Stir constantly until thickened. Finally add the pineapple chunks, heat through, and fold in the crispy pork. Turn the mixture on to a hot serving plate and serve with Chinese fried rice (page 157) or plain boiled rice.

——SCHNITZ UND KNEPPE——
Serves 4–6

This well-known Pennsylvania Dutch recipe makes use of the dried and cured foods which were so necessary in the pre-refrigeration era. Yet despite the introduction of modern preserving methods the old ways have survived easily, thanks to the old-fashioned values of many of these people, and this stew/soup has remained as popular as ever.

Schnitz (dried 'cut' apples) und Kneppe (dumplings) may be made with fresh cooking apples – 500 g (1 lb) – however, the dish will not be as authentic. Customarily, the dumplings were made from a yeast-leavened bread dough, though the more modern baking powder dumplings are usually substituted.

250 g	*dried apple rings*	*8 oz*
1¼–1¾ kg	*ham joint*	*3–4 lb*
25 g	*flour*	*1 oz*
25 g	*brown sugar*	*1 oz*

———For the dumplings———

175 g	*flour*	*6 oz*
2 tsps	*baking powder*	*2 tsps*
1 tsp	*salt*	*1 tsp*
	freshly ground pepper	
2 tsps	*parsley, finely chopped*	*2 tsps*
15 g	*butter or margarine, melted*	*large knob*
1	*egg, lightly beaten*	*1*
5–6 tbsps	*milk*	*5–6 tbsps*
	extra parsley to decorate	

Soak the dried apples in water for 2–4 hours. Put the ham in a large saucepan (or a Dutch oven as many Americans use), cover with water and cook slowly for 3 hours. Remove the meat and strain 360 ml (generous ½ pint) of stock for use later. Remove the rind from the ham and cut the flesh into bite-sized pieces. Return the meat to the pot with the soaked apples and their water. Simmer for 30 minutes.

Meanwhile, to make the gravy, brown the flour in a heavy-based saucepan over a low heat, stirring constantly. When brown, remove from the heat, and add the sugar and the reserved ham liquid. Stir until smooth, return to the heat and bring to the boil, stirring continuously. When thick, add to the ham and apple mixture.

To make the dumplings, sift together the flour, baking powder, salt and pepper. Stir in the parsley, melted butter or margarine and egg. Add sufficient milk to make a stiff but moist dough.

About 20 minutes before serving, drop the dumpling batter by teaspoonfuls into the simmering mixture. Cover the pan tightly and cook for 15 minutes. Do not uncover the pan at all, or the dumplings will collapse. Serve in large bowls, sprinkled with extra parsley.

HAM OR GAMMON STEAKS WITH ——RED-EYE GRAVY——
Serves 4

The idea of virtually pouring a cup of hot coffee over a ham steak may seem hard to swallow – but the surprising thing about this recipe is how good it tastes and how unobtrusive the coffee flavour is. Opinions vary, in fact, about whether you should add coffee or just plain water to the pan after cooking the ham, so you may do either and still produce a traditional American dish. You may also make red-eye gravy from the pan juices of a whole baked ham.

4	ham or gammon steaks	*4*
25–50 g	butter	*1–2 oz*
1/2 tsp	instant coffee granules (optional)	*1/2 tsp*
120 ml	hot water	scant *1/4 pint*

a skillet or heavy frying pan

Remove any rind from the ham or gammon steaks. Heat the butter in the skillet or frying pan and gently fry the steaks till lightly browned on each side – about 10 minutes in all. Remove from the pan and keep the steaks warm on a heated plate or dish.

Dissolve the coffee in the hot water, add to the pan in which the steaks were cooked, and stir to include all the ham juices and browned pieces from the bottom of the pan. Serve the red-eye gravy in a warmed sauceboat.

——HOT SAUSAGES AND PEPPERS——
Serves 3–4

500 g	hot Italian pork sausages (see note overleaf)	*1 lb*
	oil for frying	
1 large	stalk of celery, diced	*1 large*

3	spring onions, chopped	3
1	green pepper, de-seeded and cut into strips	1
120 ml	stock	scant ¼ pint
2 tbsps	tomato purée	2 tbsps
	salt and freshly ground pepper	
½ tsp	paprika	½ tsp
	home-made egg noodles (page 153)	

a skillet or heavy frying pan

If desired, cut the sausages into 8 cm (3 inch) lengths.

Heat the oil in a skillet or heavy frying pan and fry the sausages with the celery, spring onions and green pepper strips for 5 minutes. Mix together the stock and tomato purée, and add to the pan with the salt and pepper to taste. Add the paprika, cover the pan, and simmer for about 30 minutes.

Boil the egg noodles in salted water as detailed on page 154. Drain, toss in a little butter, and pile into a warm serving dish. Spoon the hot sausages and peppers with the tomato sauce over the noodles.

NOTE: If spicy hot sausages are not available, add some chili powder, according to taste, when sautéing the vegetables. Plain sausages may also be used.

——HAWAIIAN RUMAKI——
Makes 26–28

This recipe shows the oriental influence in Hawaii, where the Japanese and Chinese are the two major immigrant groups in this island state.

350 g	chicken livers	12 oz
250 g	canned water chestnuts	8 oz
13–14	slices lean bacon (streaky)	13–14
120 ml	soy sauce	scant ¼ pint
2 tbsps	saké or dry white wine	2 tbsps

1 tbsp	honey	1 tbsp
1/4 tsp	ground ginger	1/4 tsp
1	clove of garlic, crushed	1

toothpicks

Cut the chicken livers in half. Drain the water chestnuts from their liquid and cut each into 2–3 slices. Cut the bacon slices in half across the middle. Lay each bacon half-slice flat, place one half chicken liver at one end of each slice, top with a piece of water chestnut, and roll up the bacon into a mini-roll. Secure each one with a toothpick.

Place the soy sauce, saké or wine, honey, ginger and crushed garlic in a large bowl and mix to blend well. Add all the bacon rolls to the bowl and leave to marinate for at least 1 hour.

Heat the grill (or a barbecue for outdoor cooking) and cook the rumaki, turning once, until they are deeply browned all over and the chicken liver inside is tender – about 5 minutes each side. Serve hot as an hors-d'œuvre or as part of a buffet.

——JEWISH CHOPPED CHICKEN LIVERS——
Makes about 500 g (1 lb)

1	large onion, peeled and chopped	1
1	clove of garlic, peeled and chopped (optional)	1
1	stalk of celery, chopped (optional)	1
2 tbsps	chicken fat, other fat or oil	2 tbsps
500 g	chicken livers	1 lb
2	eggs, hard-boiled	2
1 tsp	salt	1 tsp
	freshly ground pepper	
1/2 tsp	garlic salt	1/2 tsp

a skillet or large frying pan

Formerly this pâté-like mixture was made by finely chopping all the ingredients and mixing them together. However, if you have a mincer everything may be minced together. If not, finely chop the onion, garlic and celery.

Heat the chicken fat (or other fat or oil) in a skillet or frying pan and sauté the chopped vegetables until softened – about 5 minutes. Add the chicken livers and sauté for a further 6–7 minutes, turning occasionally.

Shell the eggs and, if not using a mincer, chop finely. Remove the pan from the heat and leave the contents to cool slightly, before finely chopping the chicken livers. Mix well with the other ingredients.

If using a mincer, put the livers and vegetables and the hard-boiled eggs through the machine.

Season the mixture well with salt, pepper and garlic salt. Serve like pâté with crackers, slices of toast, or thinly sliced rye or brown bread.

——SOUTHERN FRIED CHICKEN——
Serves 4–8

This is surely the most famous American chicken recipe, gaining in popularity as fast food chains like 'Kentucky Fried Chicken' continue to spread abroad. Home-cooked, it has certainly become one of our family favourites. There are literally dozens of different ways to prepare southern fried chicken, from simply dipping in plain or seasoned flour and deep-frying, to coating in batter, breadcrumbs or cracker crumbs before deep-frying.

8	pieces of chicken (or a 1¼ kg/3 lb chicken, jointed)	8
120 ml	buttermilk (or milk and 1 tsp lemon juice)	scant ¼ pint
8 tbsps	flour	8 tbsps
1 tsp	salt	1 tsp
	freshly ground pepper	
1 tsp	dried marjoram	1 tsp
1 tsp	dried parsley	1 tsp
	fat for deep-frying	

——————For the cream gravy——————

2 tbsps	bacon drippings or other fat	2 tbsps
2 tbsps	flour	2 tbsps
240 ml	chicken stock	scant ½ pint
2–3 tbsps	double cream	2–3 tbsps
	salt and pepper	

a deep-fat frying pan

Remove the skin from the chicken pieces if desired. Place the chicken in a large bowl with the buttermilk (or the milk and lemon juice mixture) and marinate for at least 1 hour.

Sift the flour and salt into a small bowl, and stir in the pepper, marjoram and parsley.

Heat the fat in the frying pan. Shake the chicken pieces gently to remove any excess buttermilk, and dip the pieces into the herbed flour, to coat all over. Deep-fry the pieces fairly slowly so that they can cook right through – taking about 15–20 minutes in all and turning once to brown both sides. Drain on kitchen paper and serve with cream gravy.

To make the gravy, heat the bacon drippings or other fat in a medium pan, add the flour and cook for one minute. Remove from the heat and gradually stir in the chicken stock. Return to the heat and cook, stirring constantly, until thickened. Cook for 2 minutes, then remove from the heat and stir in the cream, salt and pepper to taste. Re-heat if necessary, but do not boil.

——————CHICKEN MARYLAND——————
Serves 4

Chicken Maryland is one dish which *has* crossed the Atlantic and become popular in countries like Britain. However, somewhere in the transition process it adopted extra ingredients like batter-coated bananas and pineapples rings (nowhere in our library of American cookbooks could we find mention of these additions), and lost the traditional cream gravy which prevents this dish from being too dry.

1 1/4 kg	chicken thighs or drumsticks (i.e. 8 pieces)	2 1/2 lb

——For the batter——

100 g	plain flour	4 oz
1 tsp	baking powder	1 tsp
1/2 tsp	salt	1/2 tsp
	freshly ground pepper	
1	egg	1
120 ml	milk	scant 1/4 pint
	fat for deep-frying	

——For the corn fritters——

2	fresh ears of corn	2
	or	
250 g	frozen or tinned corn kernels	8 oz
	left-over batter from above	

—— To serve——

8	slices of bacon	8
	cream gravy (see southern fried chicken page 100)	

a deep-fat frying pan or large skillet

Remove the skin from the chicken pieces if desired. Sift the flour, baking powder, salt and pepper into a medium bowl. Beat the egg and milk together and gradually mix into the flour to make a smooth, thickish batter.

Heat the fat in the deep-fat frying pan or skillet until hot but not smoking.

Meanwhile, dip each chicken piece into the batter to coat thoroughly, allowing any excess batter to drip off before deep-frying the chicken in the hot fat. (Reserve the left-over batter for the corn fritters.) Fry the chicken gently for about 10 minutes on each side, turning once, until the batter is lightly browned all over.

Drain from the pan and lay on absorbent kitchen paper in a warm serving dish. Keep warm while the rest of the pieces are cooking.

Meanwhile, parboil the corn-on-the-cob ears for 5 minutes in boiling but not salted water. Drain and leave to cool. When cool enough to handle, run a sharp knife down the cobs to remove the kernels. Add the kernels to the remaining batter (thin with a little extra milk if necessary).

When all the chicken is cooked, strain the hot fat to remove any batter sediment, then return some of the fat to the pan and fry spoonfuls of corn batter until golden brown, turning once. Drain on absorbent paper and keep warm.

Meanwhile, grill the bacon slices and prepare the cream gravy as on page 101.

To serve, lay the chicken pieces in the centre of a large hot serving dish or plate, and surround with the corn fritters and grilled bacon. Pour the cream gravy over the chicken pieces (or serve separately in a gravy boat). Serve with baked potatoes, chips (French fries or *pommes frites*) or a green salad.

——SPICY BARBECUED CHICKEN——
Serves 6–8

Barbecued chicken and barbecued ribs are two of the all-time favourites in America, especially in the South and especially for outdoor barbecues (see page 208).

1 ½ kg	*whole chicken or chicken pieces*	*3 lb*
1 quantity	*spicy barbecue sauce (see page 209)*	*1 quantity*

Skin the chicken or chicken pieces if desired, or leave the skin on. Brush with the barbecue sauce and marinate if possible for a few hours.

To cook, preheat the oven to 190°C, 375°F, gas mark 5, and bake the chicken, basting frequently with the pan juices and extra barbecue sauce. Whole chickens will take about 45 minutes to 1 hour and chicken pieces 20–30 minutes.

Alternatively, grill the pieces under a hot grill for 30–40 minutes, turning the pieces occasionally to baste. Serve with any hot barbecue sauce that is left over.

NOTE: *Barbecued beef ribs* may be grilled in the same way. An easier barbecued recipe can be made by sprinkling the chicken or ribs with barbecue spice powder or seasoning or brushing with ready prepared barbecue sauce.

ROAST CORNISH HEN OR POUSSIN WITH ——TAHITIAN STUFFING——
Serves 2–4

The Cornish hen is a miniature chicken or 'poussin' weighing from ½–1 kg (1–2 lb). This stuffing is not a traditional recipe, but one of our own favourites which makes use of the abundant supply of dried fruits and nuts readily available in America, and which complements the Cornish hens beautifully.

2	*Cornish hens or poussins*	2
50 g	*fresh breadcrumbs (e.g. sourdough bread, page 182)*	*2 oz*
75 g	*dried tropical fruit and nut mixture (or 'Tahitian Combo'), e.g. raisins, dried pineapple and papaya, roasted nuts (peanuts, cashews, chopped walnuts and almonds), soybeans, chopped dates, grated or desiccated coconut*	*3 oz*
15 g	*butter*	*large knob*
120 ml	*chicken or turkey stock*	*6 tbsps*
2 tbsps	*sherry or tequila*	*2 tbsps*
2	*Cornish hens' livers*	2
	salt and freshly ground pepper	
	butter	
	oil or fat for roasting	

a roasting pan

Preheat the oven to 200°C, 400°F, gas mark 6.

Remove the giblets from the Cornish hens, reserve the livers, and cook the remainder with water to make stock for gravy.

Put the breadcrumbs in a medium bowl. Make up the dried fruit and nut mixture according to availability of the suggested ingredients. Dice the fruit and chop the larger nuts coarsely. Leave smaller nuts (e.g. peanuts) whole.

Put the prepared mixture into a small saucepan with the butter, stock, the sherry or tequila and the hens' livers. Cover the pan and stew gently for 7–8 minutes. Remove and chop the livers and add them, the fruit and nut mixture and the stock to the breadcrumbs. Season to taste with salt and pepper, mix well, then divide between the two hens, stuffing the cavities and trussing by sewing or with small skewers. Rub the skin of the hens with butter.

Heat the oil in the roasting pan in the preheated oven, add the stuffed hens, and roast for 15 minutes before reducing the heat to 180°C, 350°F, gas mark 4. Continue roasting for a further 30–40 minutes, basting occasionally. Serve with giblet gravy.

——COUNTRY CAPTAIN——
Serves 4–6

This recipe shows an obvious Indian/Pakistani influence. Perhaps it got its name from a far-travelled trader and sea captain.

1–1¼ kg	chicken	2½–3 lb
4 tbsps	flour	4 tbsps
2 tsps	salt	2 tsps
	freshly ground pepper	
50 g	butter or margarine	2 oz
1	medium onion, peeled and chopped	1
1–2	cloves garlic, peeled and crushed	1–2
½	red pepper	½
½	green pepper	½
1 dsp	curry powder	1 dsp
500 g	tinned tomatoes, finely chopped	1 lb

½ tsp	*dried thyme*	½ tsp
	or	
1 tsp	*fresh thyme, finely*	1 tsp
	chopped	
50 g	*currants or sultanas*	2 oz
240 ml	*chicken stock*	scant ½ pint

———To serve———
toasted almonds, grated
or desiccated coconut,
mango or fruit chutney
cooked rice

Cut the chicken into 8–10 serving pieces. Put the flour, 1 teaspoon of the salt and some pepper in a small bowl and toss each piece of chicken in the mixture to coat, shaking off any excess flour.

Heat the butter or margarine in a large heavy saucepan and fry the chicken pieces to brown on all sides. Drain the pieces from the pan and keep them warm. Sauté the chopped onion and crushed garlic in the fat until softened – about 5 minutes.

Meanwhile, remove the seeds from the peppers and cut the flesh into short strips. Add to the pan with the curry powder and fry for a few minutes longer. Add the chopped tomatoes, thyme, currants or sultanas, chicken stock and the remaining 1 teaspoon of salt. Stir until blended, then return the chicken pieces to the pan, cover, and simmer gently for about 45 minutes until the chicken is tender and the sauce thickened.

Serve the country captain with small bowls of toasted almonds, coconut and chutney, and with cooked rice.

———CHICKEN JAMBALAYA———
Serves 8–10

With so many cultural influences at work in the Louisiana area, it is often difficult to tell the exact origin of a dish. Jambalaya is strongly reminiscent of Spanish paella and is well suited to the shrimp-rich waters of the Gulf and the important rice industry of the South. The name probably derives from the Spanish word *jamón* or the similar French word *jambon*, meaning 'ham'. When it comes to making a good jambalaya, almost anything goes into the pot as far as Creoles are concerned. You may adapt this recipe to make pork or seafood jambalaya.

2–2¼ kg	uncooked chicken plus giblets	4–5 lb
300 ml	water	½ pint
I	large onion	I
I–2	cloves garlic	I–2
4–5	spring onions	4–5
I	medium green pepper	I
2–3	stalks celery	2–3
50 g	butter or oil	2 oz
250 g	smoked sausages, e.g. Spanish chorizo or German frankfurters	8 oz
100 g	ham	4 oz
500 g	tinned tomatoes	1 lb
I	bay leaf	I
½ tsp	dried thyme	½ tsp
½ tsp	ground cumin	½ tsp
3	whole cloves	3
3–4	allspice berries, crushed or	3–4
¼ tsp	ground allspice berries	¼ tsp
¼ tsp	cayenne	¼ tsp
300–350 g	uncooked long-grain rice	10–12 oz
175 g	peeled and cooked prawns	6 oz
	salt to taste	

a large heavy saucepan

Put the chicken and giblets in a heavy saucepan with the water, bring to the boil, then cover and simmer gently for 1–1½ hours until the chicken is tender. Strain the stock from the pan and reserve. Leave the chicken to cool slightly, then remove the flesh from the bones and cut into strips. Dice the chicken liver if desired. Discard the rest of the giblets, bones and skin. Clean any scum from the pan. When cold, skim the fat off the surface of the chicken stock.

Meanwhile, peel and chop the onion and crush the cloves of garlic. Trim the spring onions, including the green parts, and slice them. Halve the pepper, remove the seeds and white pith and cut the flesh into strips. Trim the celery and cut into slices.

Heat the butter or oil in the saucepan, add all the vegetables, and sauté, stirring frequently, for 3-4 minutes. Cut the smoked sausage into slices and add to the pan. Fry for a further 5 minutes. Dice the ham and add to the pan with the roughly chopped tomatoes and their juices, the bay leaf, thyme, cumin, cloves, allspice and cayenne. Add 300 ml (½ pint) of the reserved chicken stock and return the sliced chicken and diced liver (optional) to the pan.

Rinse the rice under cold water and add to the pan. Bring the contents to the boil, then cover the pan and cook for about 20 minutes, until the rice is tender and the stock has been absorbed. If the jambalaya looks too moist, remove the lid towards the end of the cooking time to allow the remaining liquid to evaporate. Five minutes before the end of the cooking time, stir in the peeled prawns. Before serving, season to taste with salt and add extra cayenne if a spicy flavour is to your liking.

This recipe makes a good party dish.

——CHICKEN TETRAZZINI——
Serves 10-12

This pasta dish is believed to have been invented in San Francisco in honour of the famous Italian soprano, Luisa Tetrazzini, who sang at the Opera House in San Francisco in the early 1900s.

2–2¼ kg	*uncooked chicken plus giblets*	*4–5 lb*
600 ml	*water*	*1 pint*
250 g	*uncooked spaghetti*	*8 oz*
50 g	*butter or margarine*	*2 oz*
250 g	*mushrooms, sliced*	*8 oz*
50 g	*plain flour*	*2 oz*
240 ml	*single cream*	*scant ½ pint*
3 tbsps	*sherry, vermouth or marsala*	*3 tbsps*

large pinch grated nutmeg
salt and freshly ground
pepper to taste

25 g   *parmesan cheese, grated*   *1 oz*

paprika

a 4 litre (7–8 pint) ovenproof casserole, greased

Put the chicken and its giblets into a large saucepan, add the water and bring to the boil. Cover the pan and simmer gently for 1–1½ hours until tender. Strain off the stock and reserve. Discard the giblets. Leave the chicken to cool slightly before removing the flesh from the bones. Discard the bones and skin and cut the chicken into bite-sized pieces. Skim the fat from the surface of the cooled stock.

Preheat the oven to 190°C, 375°F, gas mark 5.

Cook the spaghetti in boiling salted water for 8–10 minutes. Drain well.

Heat the butter or margarine in a medium pan, add the sliced mushrooms and sauté for 3–4 minutes, turning occasionally. Strain the mushrooms from the pan and keep warm.

Add the flour to the pan and fry for 2 minutes, then remove from the heat. Gradually stir in 600 ml (1 pint) of the reserved stock, then return the pan to the heat and, stirring constantly, bring to the boil to thicken. Cook for 2 minutes, then remove from the heat and stir in the single cream, sherry, vermouth or marsala, nutmeg, salt and pepper to taste.

Put the drained spaghetti and sautéed mushrooms in the base of the casserole dish, hollowing out the centre. Pour over some of the cream sauce. Stir the chicken pieces into the remaining sauce and pile the mixture into the centre of the casserole. Sprinkle the top with grated parmesan cheese and a little paprika, and bake the dish in the preheated oven for 30–35 minutes until the top is lightly browned.

NOTE: 25–50 g/1–2 oz toasted flaked or slivered almonds make a tasty addition to the chicken mixture before it is baked.

——BRUNSWICK STEW——
Serves 6–8

This is another recipe that can trace its origins back to the Indians, who used to throw anything and everything edible into their stew pots. Squirrel was one of the favourite ingredients in the early years of settlements in the United States, and in some areas squirrel can still be bought as a meat. However, in time, it was replaced by chicken.

Three places lay claim to lending their name to this hearty stew – Brunswick County in Virginia, Brunswick County in North Carolina, and Brunswick in Georgia. But the balance of opinion seems to favour Virginia's claim.

2–2¼ kg	*chicken with giblets*	4–5 lb
	salt and pepper	
50 g	*butter*	2 oz
2	*medium onions, peeled and chopped*	2
2	*large cloves garlic, peeled and crushed*	2
3–4	*stalks celery, finely sliced*	3–4
1	*large green pepper, de-seeded and sliced*	1
2	*dried chili or hot peppers*	2
	or	
4–6	*small pickled or canned hot peppers*	4–6
500 g	*tinned tomatoes, drained and roughly chopped*	1 lb
2	*bay leaves*	2
3–4	*sprigs parsley, chopped*	3–4
240 ml	*chicken stock (made with the giblets)*	scant ½ pint
1 tbsp	*Worcestershire sauce*	1 tbsp
1–1¼ kg	*medium potatoes*	2–3 lb
300 g	*fresh, frozen or tinned and drained butter beans*	10 oz
	or	

100 g	dried butter beans, soaked overnight and cooked until tender	4 oz
300 g	fresh, frozen or canned and drained sliced okra	10 oz
500 g	frozen, tinned and drained, or fresh sweetcorn kernels	1 lb

a very large flameproof casserole

Cut the chicken into 8 or 9 serving pieces and remove the skin if preferred. Put any left-over chicken bones or carcass and the giblets in a saucepan, cover with water, bring to the boil and simmer, covered, for at least 1 hour. Strain and reserve the stock. Discard the bones and giblets.

Sprinkle the chicken pieces with salt and pepper. Heat the butter in a large flameproof casserole and sauté the chicken on all sides to brown. Strain and keep the pieces warm.

Sauté the onions, garlic, celery and green pepper in the same butter until softened, about 5 minutes. If using dried chili peppers, add them to the casserole (if using bottled or canned peppers do not add these until the last addition of ingredients to the stew). Add the chicken pieces, tomatoes, bay leaves, parsley, reserved chicken stock and Worcestershire sauce. Bring the stew to the boil, then cover and cook for 15 minutes.

Meanwhile, peel the potatoes, cut them into 2 or 3 pieces, and add them to the casserole. If using fresh or frozen butter beans or dried, cooked ones, add them now. Cover and cook for a further 15 minutes.

Finally, if using bottled or tinned chili peppers and tinned and drained butter beans, add these to the casserole. Add the okra and corn, cover, and cook for a further 15 minutes until all the ingredients are tender. Serve hot as a complete meal.

——CHICKEN CHOW MEIN——
Serves 4–6

This recipe is a classic example of 'melting pot cookery' – it is an original American–Chinese dish, unheard of in China until its introduction there by American travellers. Concoctions like this one are believed to have been introduced to feed the large Chinese labour force imported into America to help build the Western Railroad in the 1860s. From chow mein came the American word 'chow' applied to any food.

American supermarkets carry ready-made Chinese fried noodles, but you can make your own easily by deep-frying thin noodles.

1–1¼ kg	chicken and giblets	2½–3 lb
250 g	thin noodles (see page 153)	8 oz
	oil for deep-frying	
3–4	stalks celery, diced	3–4
1	large onion, peeled and chopped	1
½	Chinese or Dutch white cabbage, sliced	½
½	green pepper, de-seeded and cut into strips (optional)	½
2 tbsps	peanut oil	2 tbsps
4–5 tbsps	soy sauce	4–5 tbsps
250 g	beansprouts, drained	8 oz
2–3 tbsps	cornflour	2–3 tbsps
2 tbsps	water	2 tbsps

a deep-fat frying pan; a wok (Chinese all-purpose pan) or skillet or heavy frying pan; a roasting pan

Begin preparations for this meal the day before or earlier in the day. Preheat the oven to 190°C, 375°F, gas mark 5. Remove the giblets from the chicken and roast the bird in the preheated oven in a roasting pan with a little bacon fat or lard. Roast for about 45 minutes, then leave to cool. When cold, strip the flesh from the chicken, cut into pieces and reserve. Put the bones and giblets in a large pan, cover with water, bring to the boil, then cover the pan and simmer for at least 1 hour. Strain the stock into a bowl – you will need about 240 ml (scant ½ pint).

About 1 hour before serving, bring a large pan of water to the boil, add the noodles and cook for 2 minutes. Drain from the pan and put the noodles into the top half of a steamer, cover the pan and steam the pasta for a further 5 minutes for home-made and 15 minutes for factory-made pasta.

Meanwhile, heat the oil in the deep-fat frying pan until hot but not smoking. Place forkfuls of noodles into the hot fat, and when browned underneath, turn over to brown the other side. Drain on absorbent kitchen paper, place in a warm serving bowl and keep hot. Continue until all the noodles are fried and crisp.

Prepare the vegetables. Heat the peanut oil in the wok, skillet or frying pan. Add the vegetables and sauté gently for about 5 minutes, stir-frying (regularly turning the vegetables). Add the soy sauce, chicken pieces, 240 ml (scant ½ pint) of reserved stock and the beansprouts. Heat through, stirring occasionally, for 2–3 minutes.

Dissolve the cornflour in the water, add to the pan and stir until thickened. Serve the chicken and vegetables over the crispy noodles, with extra soy sauce.

ARROZ CON POLLO
——(RICE WITH CHICKEN)——
Serves 4–6

This popular dish from Mexico and Puerto Rico has become a firm favourite wherever these people have settled in America, for example, New York City.

1¼ kg	chicken	3 lb
1 tsp	salt	1 tsp
	freshly ground pepper	
2 tbsps	olive or other oil	2 tbsps
2	medium onions, peeled and chopped	2
1–2	cloves garlic, peeled and crushed	1–2
500 g	tomatoes, skinned and chopped	1 lb
½	green pepper, de-seeded and sliced	½

¹/₂	*red pepper, de-seeded and sliced*	*¹/₂*
	small piece of saffron	
480 ml	*chicken stock*	*generous ³/₄ pint*
175 g	*long-grain rice*	*6 oz*
100 g	*tin or jar of pimientos*	*4 oz*

Cut the chicken into serving pieces and sprinkle each piece with salt and pepper. Heat the oil in a large heavy saucepan and fry the pieces until browned on all sides. Remove with a draining spoon and keep warm.

Add the chopped onion and garlic to the pan and sauté gently until softened and golden – about 5 minutes. Add the tomatoes and the green and red pepper strips and cook for a further 3 minutes. Add the saffron, chicken stock and chicken pieces to the pan, cover, and cook for 30 minutes. Add the rice and the chopped pimientos and cook for a further 15 minutes until the liquid has almost evaporated and the rice is cooked. Serve hot as a complete meal.

ROAST TURKEY WITH OYSTER
——STUFFING——

This quantity is for a 4–4¹/₂ kg (8–10 lb) bird. For larger birds up to 8 kg (20 lb), double the quantities. An alternative cornbread stuffing is given below.

4–4¹/₂ kg	*turkey*	*8–10 lb*
12	*fresh oysters to yield about 600 ml (1 pint) oysters and liquor*	*12*
1	*small onion*	*1*
1	*stick celery*	*1*
large knob	*butter*	*large knob*
1	*turkey liver*	*1*
50 g	*fresh breadcrumbs*	*2 oz*
1 heaped tbsp	*fresh parsley, finely chopped*	*1 heaped tbsp*
¹/₂ tsp	*salt*	*¹/₂ tsp*

	freshly ground pepper	
1	*egg, lightly beaten*	*1*
	fat for roasting	
6–8	*bacon slices (optional)*	*6–8*

a roasting pan

Preheat the oven to 220°C, 425°F, gas mark 7.

Remove the giblets and wipe the turkey inside and out. Reserve the liver for the stuffing, and use the rest of the giblets to make turkey gravy.

Prize open the oysters using an oyster knife, screwdriver or can opener, and, adding all their liquor, scoop out the flesh into a bowl.

Peel and chop the onion and dice the celery. Heat the butter in a small pan and sauté the onion and celery till softened – about 5 minutes. Add the turkey liver and cook for a further 4–5 minutes, turning once. Remove from the heat, chop the liver and add it and the vegetables to the oysters.

Add the breadcrumbs, parsley, salt, pepper and egg to the bowl and mix together until well blended. Stuff the breast cavity of the turkey with the mixture and truss or sew up the opening. (In America this is not always easy, owing to the awkward habit butchers have of removing the surrounding skin, cutting it back to the breast flesh.)

Meanwhile, heat the fat in the roasting pan, add the turkey with slices of bacon over its breast, if desired, and cover the bird during the first half of the cooking time with a large piece of aluminium foil. Remove the foil during the second half of the cooking time to brown the turkey skin. Roast in the preheated oven for 20 minutes, then reduce the temperature to 180°C, 350°F, gas mark 4, and cook for a further 2¾–3¼ hours.

Serve with candied yams (page 131), maple-glazed onions (page 133), cranberry mould (page 283), roast potatoes and giblet gravy.

——CORNBREAD STUFFING——

Quantities given are for a 2¼ kg (5 lb) chicken. For a 5 kg (10–12 lb) turkey, double the quantities.

175 g	*bacon, diced*	*6 oz*
1	*small onion, peeled and chopped*	*1*
1	*stalk celery, finely sliced*	*1*
½	*green pepper, de-seeded and thinly sliced*	*½*
⅓	*loaf cornbread (see page 185), crumbled*	*⅓*
3 tbsps	*chicken or turkey stock*	*3 tbsps*
1	*egg, lightly beaten*	*1*
1 tsp	*dried sage*	*1 tsp*
	or	
2 tsps	*2 tsps fresh sage, chopped*	*2 tsps*
½ tsp	*dried marjoram*	*½ tsp*
	or	
1 tsp	*fresh marjoram, chopped*	*1 tsp*
	salt and freshly ground pepper	

a skillet or frying pan

Fry the bacon in the skillet or frying pan until crisp. Drain from the pan and put in a medium bowl. Sauté the chopped onion, sliced celery and green pepper in the bacon fat until softened – about 5 minutes. Add to the bowl with the crumbled cornbread, chicken or turkey stock, lightly beaten egg, sage and marjoram. Season to taste with salt and pepper. Mix well together, then stuff the cavity of the bird with the mixture. Truss and roast the bird as normal.

——ROAST STUFFED DUCKLING——
Serves 2–4

International ways of cooking duck, like the French favourites *à l'orange* or *à la cerise* (cherries), and the variety of ways the Chinese serve it, have become popular in the USA. This recipe, though, is a combination of two American ideas for cooking duck, with a nut stuffing and an apricot glaze and sauce.

1 × 2–2¼ kg	*duckling and giblets*	*1 × 4–5 lb*
	salt	

———For the stuffing———

1	*duck liver*	*1*
25 g	*butter or margarine*	*1 oz*
1	*medium onion, peeled and chopped*	*1*
1	*stick celery, sliced*	*1*
100 g	*fresh brown breadcrumbs*	*4 oz*
25 g	*pecans or walnuts, chopped*	*1 oz*
1	*egg, lightly beaten*	*1*
¼ tsp	*salt*	*¼ tsp*
	freshly ground pepper	
1 tbsp	*fresh parsley, chopped*	*1 tbsp*
	or	
1 tsp	*dried parsley*	*1 tsp*

———For the apricot glaze and sauce———

5 tbsps	*apricot jam*	*5 tbsps*
300 ml	*duck stock (from giblets)*	*½ pint*
½	*lemon, little grated rind and the juice*	*½*
1 tbsp	*cornflour*	*1 tbsp*
	salt and pepper	

a roasting pan; a wire rack

Wipe the duck dry with kitchen paper and rub the skin with salt. Put the giblets in a medium pan, cover with water and bring to the boil. Cover the pan and simmer for about 45 minutes, then strain and reserve the stock. Chop the duck liver and place in a bowl.

Preheat the oven to 200°C, 400°F, gas mark 6.

Heat the butter or margarine in a small pan or frying pan and sauté the chopped onion and sliced celery until softened – about 5 minutes. Add to the duck liver with the breadcrumbs, chopped nuts, egg, salt, pepper and parsley. Mix together to make a fairly dry stuffing, press into the duck cavity and truss.

Put the stuffed duck on a wire rack over a roasting pan and roast in the preheated oven for 10 minutes before reducing the temperature to 180°C, 350°F, gas mark 4. Cook for 1 hour longer, basting the duck occasionally with the pan juices.

To prepare the apricot glaze, mix the apricot jam with 2 tablespoons of the reserved duck stock, a little grated lemon rind and the juice of the half lemon. Fifteen minutes before the end of the cooking time, brush the surface of the duck several times with the glaze, reserving the remainder for the sauce. Return to the oven.

Put the apricot glaze in a small pan. Dissolve the cornflour in a few tablespoons of the duck stock and add to the pan with the remaining stock. Cook, stirring constantly, until the sauce has thickened and become opaque. Season with salt and pepper to taste.

As there is comparatively little eating on a duck, a 2–2¼ kg/4–5 lb bird will feed two people very well. Cut the carcass in two down the breast bone and serve with the sauce. If intended for a family of four, cut the carcass into quarters, or carve the meat as usual.

VEGETABLES

The most traditional vegetables in America are corn, beans and squash – the Indian triad of vital crops on which the tribes' survival depended.

CORN

The word 'corn' means different things to different nationalities, sometimes describing wheat, oats, or rye. But to an American, corn is ears of maize with its golden and white kernels. So vital was it to the survival of both tribes and settlers that it provided many different uses. Fresh corn stalks were a source of sweetening like sugar, and the dried stalks and leaves can be used as animal feed. Corn husks can be used for mattress fillings and for making the Mexican dish 'tamales', where the husks are used as wrappers for the minced meat and cornmeal filling. Corn cobs boiled with water and sugar make corn cob syrup and corn cob jelly; dried cobs are good fire fuel.

From field corn is also produced corn oil and corn cereals, and from the very finely ground white cornmeal comes cornflour. Fermented corn supplies America with its favourite whisky – bourbon. Only 10 per cent of the US corn crop is sweetcorn for eating.

Ground, dried corn provides such southern dishes as cornbread, spoonbread, hush puppies and cornmeal mush. Southerners are also partial to 'hominy' – corn soaked in ashes, wood lye and water until the hulls can be easily removed; and to ground, dried hominy known as 'grits', traditionally eaten with milk and butter at breakfast.

Yet another kind of field corn is popcorn, of which several varieties have been specifically developed because of their superior 'popping qualities'.

BEANS

American Indians are believed to have cultivated beans thousands of years ago, eventually producing beans of many different sizes and shapes, and all kinds of colours. These days the most commonly available beans in America are pink (pinto), red kidney, black, black-eyed peas, white lima and the small white 'pea or navy' beans.

SQUASH (including gourds and pumpkins)

There is some confusion as to what exactly is meant by squashes, gourds and pumpkins. Those vegetables which Americans call 'winter squashes' we in Europe call vegetable marrows. Summer or green squashes or zucchini as they are known in America are courgettes to most Europeans.

American pumpkins are the large orange vegetables which provide so much fun at Hallowe'en. They are usually served in America in sweet dessert pies rather than as a savoury vegetable. Australian pumpkins, by contrast, have grey skins.

——To prepare sweetcorn for cooking——

Ideally the freshest, sweetest corn of all is that rushed straight from the field to the kitchen pot, before the sweetness of the cob is lost. Once picked, the sugar in the corn quickly turns to starch, though refrigeration immediately after picking will slow this process a little. Removing the husks also accelerates the sugar conversion.

However, few of us in this day and age of urban living can enjoy the luxury of freshly picked corn. What we can do, though, is ensure that the corn we do have is not overcooked. As with all vegetables, the younger and fresher the corn, the quicker it will cook. When corn is ready for eating the cob should have a dried silk (the tassel of thick hair that grows around the top of the cob). Blackened silks are a sign that the corn has passed its peak, and over-mature corn is tough and chewy instead of crisp and sweet.

Pull back some of the green husk surrounding the cob and prick a kernel with your fingernail. If it is ripe the kernel will leak some corn 'milk'.

To prepare the cobs for cooking (other than baking or barbecuing, see below), pull back and remove the husks and all of the silk.

——BOILED CORN-ON-THE-COB——

Bring a pan of water to the boil – but *do not* add salt as this toughens the corn. Some Americans like to add a little sugar to the water – from one teaspoon to one tablespoon, depending on the amount of corn to be cooked. Others like to boil their corn in a mixture of half milk and half water.

If the corn is young and fresh, add the prepared cobs to the boiling liquid, cover the pan, and immediately remove from the heat. Leave the corn in the hot liquid for 5 minutes, then drain. Serve with salt, pepper and butter.

Alternatively, add the cobs to the boiling liquid, cover the pan and cook for from 3 to 7 minutes depending on the size and age of the corn. Drain well and serve as above.

——STEAMED CORN-ON-THE-COB——

Bring a little water to the boil in a pan or the bottom part of a steamer, lay the prepared cobs in the steamer, cover the pan and steam for 5–9 minutes. Serve as above.

NOTE: Many Americans run a corn cutter down the cobs before eating them to ensure that only the digestible kernels are eaten and not the indigestible hulls. To remove kernels from the cobs, run a sharp knife, a corn cutter or the pointed tip of a vegetable peeler down the lines of kernels, pushing to one side until the line gradually pops out.

——BAKED CORN-ON-THE-COB——

Select plump, ripe ears of fresh corn with their husks completely enveloping the corn.

Preheat the oven to 180°C, 350°F, gas mark 4.

Carefully pull down the leaves of the husk to expose the dried silk (the hair-like tassel at the end of the cob). Remove the silk as completely as possible, then carefully replace the husk leaves over the corn. Tie the top of the husk with cotton thread to prevent exposure of the corn kernels during baking.

Bake in the preheated oven for 15 minutes. The husk will be brown and crisp and should be removed before serving the corn with butter and a light sprinkling of salt and pepper if desired.

Corn cooked in this manner is deliciously crisp and loses none of its flavour or vitamins.

NOTE: For *Barbecued Corn-on-the-Cob*, place the prepared cobs on the barbecue grill and turn occasionally during the cooking time.

——SUCCOTASH——
Serves 4

Modern-day succotash is now served only as a vegetable dish, although in the early days of the colonization of New England it was often a meal in its own right, cooked with whole chickens, salt pork and corned beef. Succotash was definitely an Indian dish passed on to the settlers, who quickly adopted it as part of their staple diet. The name derives from the Indian word *misickquatash*, used by the Narragansett tribe of latter-day Rhode Island. Originally the corn and the beans (two of the Indians' three most important crops) were cooked in bear grease, which reputedly added a sweet touch to the dish. Succotash is traditionally served in Plymouth, Massachusetts, on Forefathers' Day (21 December).

175 g	*dried butter beans*	*6 oz*
	or	
350 g	*cooked, fresh, tinned or frozen butter or broad beans*	*12 oz*
350 g	*sweetcorn kernels (i.e. 3 fresh ears corn) or frozen or tinned corn*	*12 oz*
25 g	*butter*	*1 oz*

1/2 tsp	salt	1/2 tsp
	freshly ground pepper	
2 tbsps	stock or water	2 tbsps
5 tbsps	cream	5 tbsps

Soak the dried beans overnight if using. The following day drain the beans, add fresh water, and cook covered until tender – about 30–40 minutes. Drain again.

Scrape the corn kernels from the cobs (see page 121). Melt the butter in a medium pan, add the beans, corn, salt and pepper, stock or water. Cover the pan and simmer gently, stirring occasionally, for about 10 minutes. Remove from the heat and stir in the cream. Heat gently to warm through, but do not boil. Serve hot.

——CORN OYSTERS——
Makes about 8

This recipe probably got its name because some eaters mistook these deep-fried vegetables for oysters.

2	ears fresh corn	2
	or	
250 g	tinned or frozen corn	8 oz
	kernels	
1	egg, separated	1
2 tbsps	flour	2 tbsps
1/4 tsp	salt	1/4 tsp
	freshly ground pepper	
	oil for deep-frying	

a skillet or deep frying pan

If using fresh corn, remove the husks and silk. Either grate the corn from the cobs or strip the kernels and grind them through a mincer or mouli vegetable mill. (You may leave the kernels whole, but you will not create the same oyster effect.) Drain tinned corn or de-frost frozen kernels.

Put the corn into a medium bowl with the egg yolk and sift in the flour, salt and pepper. Mix together.

Heat the oil in a skillet or pan. Meanwhile, beat the egg white until stiff and gently fold into the corn mixture. Drop spoonfuls of the corn into the hot fat and fry until golden brown all over, turning once. Drain on absorbent paper. Serve as a vegetable accompaniment (for example with chicken) or as a light lunch.

NOTE: This recipe may be adapted to use up left-over cooked corn on the cob. Scrape off the kernels, mince them, and proceed with the recipe.

——CORN PUDDING——
Serves 3–4

500 g	*tinned or frozen sweetcorn kernels*	1 lb
	or	
300–350 g	*sweetcorn kernels off the cob (i.e. 3–4 large cobs)*	10–12 oz
2 tbsps	*flour*	2 tbsps
240 ml	*milk*	scant 1/2 pint
25 g	*butter or margarine*	1 oz
2	*large eggs, lightly beaten*	2
1/2 tsp	*salt*	1/2 tsp
	cayenne to taste	

a 1 1/4–1 3/4 litre (2–3 pint) ovenproof dish, greased

Preheat the oven to 180°C, 350°F, gas mark 4.

Drain the corn from the liquid in the can or prepare the cooked cobs and strip off the kernels (see page 121). Put the corn in a medium bowl and sift over the flour. Stir to combine.

Heat the milk and butter in a small saucepan and slowly pour over the beaten eggs, stirring constantly. Stir in the salt and cayenne to taste. Finally, stir the milk/egg mixture into the corn and flour, and when well combined, pour the pudding into the greased baking dish. Bake in the preheated oven for about 1 hour until set.

NOTE: There are many different versions of this classic dish. To make the pudding creamier, substitute some single cream for part of the milk. To give the pudding a tasty topping, sprinkle over 25–50 g (1–2 oz) of grated cheese before baking.

You may also add any of the following extras to the corn: 1/2 a diced green pepper; 100 g (4 oz) of chopped ham or 4 slices of grilled and diced bacon; 1–2 chopped spring onions; 1–2 skinned and chopped tomatoes.

——BAKED BEANS——
Serves 6–8

This is one of New England's best known dishes, the traditional Saturday night dinner, and the reason why Boston is known as 'bean town'. In the olden days, the Puritans of New England began to celebrate the Sabbath from Saturday night onwards, so food had to be prepared ahead as no work was allowed on the Sabbath. Often the beans were cooked in large earthenware bean pots at the local baker's ovens. The pots were collected by the baker on Saturday morning and returned that night in time for dinner. Usually large quantities were baked, leaving plenty for the following morning's breakfast, some for cold baked bean sandwiches for lunch, and even some for freezing. One American friend's old family cookbook describes how a cloth bag filled with baked beans was hung by a strap outside to freeze and chunks of beans were hacked off as needed.

The beans usually used in this dish are the small round pea or navy beans, though a more interesting 'bean pot' can be made using many other varieties of dried beans, for example, pink (pinto), small red kidney or baby lima (butter) beans. The sweetening was originally maple syrup or sugar, later treacle (molasses), and least traditionally, brown sugar.

Baked beans are usually served with steamed Boston brown bread (see page 177).

500 g	*dried pea (navy) beans or other dried beans*	*1 lb*
250 g	*salt pork or a slab of bacon*	*8 oz*
1	*onion, peeled*	*1*
3 tbsps	*treacle*	*3 tbsps*
1 tsp	*dry mustard*	*1 tsp*
1/2–1 tsp	*salt*	*1/2–1 tsp*
	freshly ground pepper (optional)	

a 4 litre (7 pint) ovenproof casserole

Soak the beans overnight in a large bowl filled with cold water. The following day, drain the beans and put them in a large pot with fresh water to cover. Bring to the boil, then cover the pan and simmer very gently for about 45–50 minutes until the beans are cooked. Drain, reserving the bean water.

Preheat the oven to 130°C, 250°F, gas mark ½.

Slash the rind of the salt pork and put it in the casserole with the whole onion. Cover with the beans, exposing only the pork rind. Mix about 300 ml (½ pint) of the reserved bean water with the treacle, mustard and salt and pour over the beans. Add a further 300 ml (½ pint) of bean water and the pepper, if desired.

Gently shake the pot to blend the liquids, cover the casserole and bake in the preheated oven for about 6 hours. Check the liquid content, especially during the last half of cooking time when the beans may begin to dry up, adding extra bean water as necessary. (*Note*: some New Englanders top up the liquid with beer.)

Before serving, remove and discard the onion. Remove some of the excess fat from the salt pork or bacon and dice or slice the meat and return to the beans. Check the seasoning before serving with frankfurters or sausages and steamed brown bread.

——BUCKAROO OR COWPOKE BEANS——
Serves 6–8

This western version of New England baked beans is a spicier dish, stewed in a pot. Originally the cowboys (or buckaroos as they are also known) stewed their beans over an open camp fire. Beans are still a traditional part of outdoor barbecues and camping meals.

500 g	dried beans	1 lb
250 g	salt pork or slab bacon	8 oz
1	onion, peeled	1
1–2	cloves garlic, peeled	1–2
1–2 tbsps	brown sugar	1–2 tbsps
1 tsp	dry mustard	1 tsp
2–3 tsps	chili powder (optional)	2–3 tsps

½ tsp	ground cumin	½ tsp
1	bay leaf	1
500 g	tinned tomatoes, finely chopped	1 lb
	or	
5–6	fresh tomatoes, skinned and chopped	5–6
½–1 tsp	salt	½–1 tsp

a 4 litre (7 pint) saucepan or pot

Soak the dried beans and cook as directed in the previous recipe.

Slash the rind of the salt pork and put it in the pan or pot with the whole onion and the cloves of garlic. Cover with the beans. Mix about 300 ml (½ pint) of the reserved bean water with the sugar, mustard, chili powder (if desired) and cumin. Pour over the beans. Add the bay leaf and the tomatoes with their juice. If necessary add extra bean water to ensure that the beans are fully covered. Stir in the salt.

Cover the pot and simmer very gently for 5–6 hours, checking during the latter part of cooking that the pot doesn't run dry. Top up with more bean water if necessary.

FRIJOLES REFRITOS – MEXICAN RE-FRIED ——BEANS——
Serves 4

Rumour has it that Mexicans serve their staple pinto beans with almost every dish at every meal, but I thought these stories were exaggerated – until I visited Mexico. It is also surprising to discover that left-over beans are even more popular served 're-fried' than they are as ordinary boiled beans. As far as a Mexican is concerned, the beans get better and better the more they are re-fried, so don't throw out your left-over left-overs! However, re-fried beans are rather bland in flavour – probably to offset the highly spiced foods they usually accompany. The American addition of onion and garlic makes this a more interesting version.

300–350 g	cooked pinto (pink) beans	10–12 oz
1–2 tbsps	bacon fat	1–2 tbsps

3 tbsps	onion, peeled and finely chopped (optional)	3 tbsps
1	clove garlic, peeled and crushed (optional)	1
1–2 tbsps	meat stock	1–2 tbsps

Mash the cooked beans. Heat the fat in a pan and sauté the onion and garlic for 3–4 minutes. Add the mashed beans and meat stock and cook, stirring occasionally, until hot and the mixture is dry. Serve with Mexican specialities, for example huevos rancheros (page 164).

NOTE: ½ a teaspoon of chili powder may be added to the pan while sautéing the onion and garlic. Grated parmesan or other cheese may be sprinkled over the beans on serving.

BAKED STUFFED SQUASH OR
——MARROW——
Serves 3–4

1	medium squash or vegetable marrow	1
4	slices bacon	4
1	small onion, peeled and chopped	1
1	medium tomato, chopped	1
	salt	
	Worcestershire sauce	
	pinch of nutmeg	
	oil	

a greased ovenproof dish

Preheat the oven to 190°C, 375°F, gas mark 5.

Halve the squash or marrow and scoop out the seeds from the centre.

Dice the bacon slices and fry until crisp. Drain from the pan, then pour off any excess bacon fat and sauté the chopped onion in the remaining fat until softened – about 5 minutes. Add the chopped tomato and sauté for a further 2–3 minutes. Stir in salt to taste, a few shakes of Worcestershire sauce and a pinch of nutmeg. Stir in half the diced bacon and divide the stuffing between the two squash halves. Sprinkle the remaining bacon over the top of the stuffing. Lightly brush the exposed surface of the squash or marrow with oil, place the halves on a baking dish, and bake in the preheated oven for about 50 minutes until the vegetables are tender. Serve as a vegetable accompaniment.

——POTATO (SARATOGA) CHIPS——
Serves 3–4

Potato chips (or crisps as we know them in Britain) are very much an American invention and the biggest selling of all snack foods. But before they achieved this distinction, potato chips were first known as Saratoga chips. American food lore gives yet another fascinating, almost unbelievable, explanation of the origin of these chips. The chef concerned was reputedly an American Indian with the apt name of George Crum, who worked at Moon's Lake House in Saratoga Springs, a popular New York State spa. A guest at the Lake House kept sending back his helping of French fried potatoes, complaining that they were not thin enough. In a rage George Crum sliced up some potatoes wafer-thin, dropped them in hot fat – and inadvertently began a multi-million dollar industry!

The British call these freshly made chips 'game chips', as they are usually served with game such as pheasant and grouse.

500 g	*white potatoes*	*1 lb*
	fat or oil for deep-frying	
	salt	

a deep-fat frying pan

Peel the potatoes and either cut them with a sharp knife or grate them into paper-thin slices. Keep the potatoes in a bowl of cold water until ready to fry, then drain the slices thoroughly, patting them dry with kitchen paper or a clean tea cloth.

Heat the fat or oil in the deep-fat frying pan until hot but not smoking. Fry the chips in batches until lightly puffed and browned. Drain on absorbent paper. Sprinkle with salt and serve hot.

——HASHED BROWNS——
Serves 4

Served with fried eggs, hashed browns are still one of the most popular of all American breakfasts. They can also be served as a vegetable accompaniment to steaks, etc.

3	*medium/large potatoes*	*3*
2 tbsps	*bacon dripping or other fat*	*2 tbsps*
	salt and freshly ground pepper	

a skillet or heavy frying pan

Peel the potatoes and grate them coarsely into a large bowl of cold water. Heat the bacon dripping in the pan or skillet. Meanwhile, drain the grated potatoes from the bowl into a colander or large sieve and press gently to remove most of the excess water. Turn the potatoes into the pan, season well with salt and pepper, then press the potatoes into the pan with the back of a fish slice or spatula. Partially cover the pan with a lid, and fry for about 20 minutes until a dark brown crust forms on the base of the potatoes and the top is cooked. If desired the potatoes may be carefully turned over to brown the other side, too, though usually they are served just by inverting a warmed serving plate over the pan, then turning the frying pan upside down so that the hashed browns are served brown side up. Serve with fried eggs for breakfast or brunch, or as a vegetable accompaniment to the main meal.

——POTATOES HUNGARIAN-STYLE——
Serves 3

These fried paprika potatoes are often served with eggs for breakfast in restaurants and cafés in America.

350 g	*cooked potatoes*	*12 oz*
1	*small onion, peeled*	*1*
25 g	*butter or fat*	*1 oz*
1/2 tsp	*paprika*	*1/2 tsp*

1	*tomato, peeled and diced*	1
	salt and freshly ground	
	pepper	

a skillet or frying pan

Dice the potatoes and chop the onion. Heat the butter or fat in a skillet or pan and sauté the onion for 3–4 minutes. Add the paprika and cook for a further 1–2 minutes. Add the potatoes, diced tomato, salt and pepper to taste. Cover the pan and cook gently for 8–10 minutes, turning occasionally. Serve hot.

——CANDIED YAMS OR SWEET POTATOES——
Serves 3–4

This is *the* traditional accompaniment to the Thanksgiving turkey dinner, an annual celebration shared by all Americans no matter what their ethnic origins or religious beliefs. Yams are often believed to be merely a darker-fleshed variety of sweet potato, although they each belong to a different plant family. A popular modern adaptation of this dish features the addition of marsh-mallows!

500 g	*yams or sweet potatoes*	1 lb
25 g	*brown sugar*	1 oz
3 tbsps	*sherry*	3 tbsps
25–50 g	*butter*	1–2 oz

an ovenproof baking dish

Peel the yams or sweet potatoes and cut into even-sized pieces as you would ordinary potatoes. Cook, covered, in boiling salted water for 20–25 minutes until tender. Drain and leave to cool slightly.

Meanwhile, preheat the oven to 190°C, 375°F, gas mark 5.

Generously butter the base and sides of an ovenproof dish and slice the yams or sweet potatoes into the dish, overlapping their edges. Heat the sugar and the sherry in a small pan until the sugar has dissolved, then pour over the vegetables. Dot the top with butter and bake in the preheated oven for about 30 minutes until caramelized. Serve hot.

———FRIED YAMS———
Serves 3–4

500 g	*yams*	*1 lb*
	oil, fat or butter for frying	

a skillet or heavy frying pan

Scrub the yams and boil whole in their jackets for about 25–30 minutes. Cool slightly and then peel away the skins. Alternatively, peel the yams first, cut into evenly sized pieces, and boil for about 10 minutes until they are becoming tender but still firm. Drain well and cool slightly, then cut into slices.

Heat the oil, fat or butter in the skillet or frying pan and fry the yams briskly until browned on both sides. Drain on absorbent paper.

NOTE: The yams are particularly tasty when fried in the same pan that German smoked chops (or bacon chops) or ham steaks have been cooked in, giving a sweet and sour flavour.

———EGGPLANT (AUBERGINE) PARMIGIANA———
Serves 4–6

This popular recipe with its tasty tomato sauce and cheese combination can be adapted to veal cutlets to make veal parmigiana and to chicken pieces for chicken parmigiana.

500 g	*eggplant (aubergine) (1 large)*	*1 lb*
6 tbsps	*olive oil*	*6 tbsps*
1	*medium onion, peeled and chopped*	*1*
1–2	*cloves of garlic, peeled and crushed*	*1–2*
500 g	*tin of tomatoes, roughly chopped*	*1 lb*
1 tsp	*dried oregano or*	*1 tsp*
2 tsps	*fresh oregano*	*2 tsps*
1 tsp	*dried parsley or*	*1 tsp*

2 tsps	fresh parsley	2 tsps
	salt and pepper to taste	
3–4 tbsps	plain flour	3–4 tbsps
75 g	grated parmesan cheese	3 oz
150 g	mozzarella or Bel Paese cheese, grated	6 oz
50 g	breadcrumbs, fresh	2 oz

a 1¼–1¾ litre (2–3 pint) ovenproof dish or casserole

Wipe the eggplant, slice it into ½ cm (¼ inch) slices, sprinkle generously with salt and leave for at least 30 minutes to draw out some of the vegetable's excess moisture.

Meanwhile, prepare the tomato sauce. Heat 2 tablespoons of the olive oil in a heavy saucepan and sauté the chopped onion and crushed garlic for about 5 minutes until softened and golden. Add the chopped tomatoes and their juice, the oregano and parsley, and season to taste with salt and pepper. Cover the pan and stew gently for about 20 minutes.

Preheat the oven to 190°C, 375°F, gas mark 5.

Pat the eggplant slices dry with kitchen paper then sift over the flour, turning the slices once to coat both sides. Heat the remaining 4 tablespoons of olive oil in a skillet or heavy frying pan and sauté the coated eggplant slices on both sides until lightly browned.

Gently mix together the grated parmesan cheese, the mozzarella or Bel Paese, and the fresh breadcrumbs.

Layer the three main ingredients – fried eggplant slices, tomato sauce and cheese mixture – in the ovenproof casserole, beginning with eggplant and ending with a layer of cheese and crumbs. Bake the dish uncovered in the preheated oven for 20–25 minutes until the top is lightly browned. Serve hot as an hors-d'œuvre, as a light meal, as a vegetable accompaniment to plain grilled steaks or chops, or as a filling for heroes (page 213).

——MAPLE-GLAZED ONIONS——
Serves 3–4

| 25 g | butter or margarine | 1 oz |
| 2 tbsps | maple syrup | 2 tbsps |

| 250 g | · | *baby onions, cooked and drained* | 8 oz |

a skillet or heavy frying pan

Heat the butter or margarine in the skillet or pan. Add the maple syrup, stir to combine, then add the baby onions. Sauté briskly, tossing occasionally until the maple glaze has almost disappeared – about 8–10 minutes. Serve hot with a Thanksgiving turkey or baked ham.

NOTE: Frozen onions may be used.

——HARVARD BEETS——
Serves 4

This sweet and sour vegetable dish is a speciality of New England.

350 g	*baby beets, cooked*	12 oz
	or	
500 g	*tinned beets, drained*	1 lb
25 g	*sugar*	1 oz
1/2 tsp	*salt*	1/2 tsp
2 tsps	*cornflour*	2 tsps
3 tbsps	*cider vinegar*	3 tbsps
2 tbsps	*orange marmalade*	2 tbsps
1/2 tsp	*ground ginger*	1/2 tsp
25 g	*butter*	1 oz

To prepare the beets, cut off the stem and root and gently press off the skins. If tinned beets are used, drain thoroughly. Leave baby beets whole and cut larger ones into slices.

Mix together the sugar, salt, and cornflour in the top of a double boiler. Stir in the vinegar and cook over direct heat, stirring constantly, until smooth and bubbly. Add the beets, marmalade, ginger and butter. Place the double boiler over simmering water and cook for about 30 minutes. Serve as a vegetable accompaniment.

PENNSYLVANIA DUTCH FRIED
——TOMATOES——
Serves 4

Putting sugar on vegetables is an old Pennsylvania Dutch habit which takes some getting used to. These tomatoes are probably best served with meats that suit a sweet and sour combination, for example ham or pork.

4–5	*large firm tomatoes, thickly sliced*	4–5
2 tsps	*salt*	2 tsps
	freshly ground black pepper	
50 g	*flour*	2 oz
50–75 g	*butter*	2–3 oz
2 tbsps	*brown sugar, sifted*	2 tbsps
240 ml	*double cream*	scant ¹/₂ pint
1 tbsp	*fresh parsley, finely chopped*	1 tbsp

a large skillet or heavy frying pan

Sprinkle the tomatoes on both sides with salt and a little black pepper. Dip the slices in the flour to coat both sides thoroughly, gently shaking off any excess flour. In the skillet or frying pan, melt the butter over a moderate heat. Add the tomato slices and cook for 5 minutes until lightly browned. Sprinkle the tops with half the brown sugar then carefully turn the tomatoes over with a spatula or fish slice and sprinkle the other side with the rest of the sugar. Cook for 3–4 minutes and then remove and keep warm.

Pour the cream into the pan, raise the heat to high, and bring to the boil, stirring constantly. Boil briskly for 2–3 minutes or until the cream thickens. Check for seasoning then pour over the tomatoes. Sprinkle with the parsley and serve as a vegetable accompaniment.

——CREOLE TOMATOES——
Serves 2–3

3	*large tomatoes*	3
1 tbsp	*bacon fat*	1 tbsp

1	small onion, finely chopped	1
1/4	large green pepper, de-seeded and finely chopped	1/4
	salt	
	cayenne pepper	
2 tbsps	single cream	2 tbsps

a flameproof dish, buttered

Preheat the oven to 180°C, 350°F, gas mark 4.

To skin the tomatoes, put them in a bowl of boiling water for 30 seconds, then drain and remove the skins. Cut them in half and place side by side in the buttered dish.

Heat the bacon fat in a small pan and gently sauté the chopped onion and green pepper for about 5 minutes to soften them. Place a spoonful of onion mixture on top of each tomato half and sprinkle lightly with salt and cayenne (remember that only the smallest amount of cayenne is necessary to give a peppery bite to the dish).

Bake in the preheated oven for 20 minutes. Lift the tomatoes from the dish on to a warmed serving plate. Add the cream to the juices in the dish and put over a gentle heat to warm the cream through. Do not boil.

Pour the cream sauce over the tomatoes and serve as a vegetable accompaniment.

——BROCCOLI PURÉE——
Serves 4–6

Although it might at first seem a shame to purée this lovely vegetable, this is an interesting and different way to serve it.

500 g	broccoli	1 lb
1/4 tsp	salt	1/4 tsp
25 g	butter, melted	1 oz
1/4 tsp	freshly ground pepper	1/4 tsp
	pinch nutmeg	
2 tbsps	double cream	2 tbsps

| *1 tbsp* | *lemon juice* | *1 tbsp* |
| *1–2 tbsps* | *parmesan cheese, grated* | *1–2 tbsps* |

a 900 ml (1 ½ pint) ovenproof dish

Cut the broccoli into small pieces and cook in water with the salt until tender – about 10–12 minutes. Meanwhile, preheat the oven to 190°C, 375°F, gas mark 5.

Drain the broccoli well and purée in a blender or put through a mouli vegetable mill or a sieve. Add the butter, pepper, nutmeg, cream and lemon juice and blend well. Check for seasoning, then spoon into the ovenproof dish. Sprinkle the top with grated parmesan cheese and heat through in the preheated oven for 10 minutes.

SALADS AND DRESSINGS

Americans love salads, which they usually eat immediately before the main entrée or meat course. Most meals eaten out in restaurants automatically include a salad, and many eating establishments pride themselves on the selection they offer at their 'salad bars' – now in vogue in Britain – where diners can wander around helping themselves to their own choice of salads, pickles and dressings, often topped off with crumbled, grilled bacon and croûtons of fried bread cubes. The salad bar is a good idea – a great improvement on the very ordinary salads often served up, which comprise nothing more than a plate of lettuce leaves or other greens (e.g. spinach or endive), one slice of tomato and one or two of cucumber.

Another American salad invention which meets with less approval from this writer is the jellied salad. American cookbooks are full of recipes for amazing concoctions, sometimes made in different coloured layers and usually made with packets of 'jello' (or jelly as we know it). These salads are invariably too sweet for the European palate, which is not as attuned as the American palate to the very sweet and sour flavour combinations. The one jellied salad recipe we have chosen to use in this book is one of the originals which has become an all-time favourite – 'Perfection Salad'.

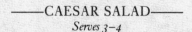

——CAESAR SALAD——
Serves 3–4

I first enjoyed this delicious and unusual salad after watching it being prepared at our table in a Las Vegas hotel. I was told that the salad originated in Tijuana, Mexico – a favourite shopping town for Americans making a day trip into Mexico, and less than four hours freeway drive from Los Angeles. I later learned that the story surrounding this popular salad's creation concerned a Tijuana restaurant called Caesar's. A group of Hollywood celebrities had stayed on late at Caesar's and were demanding something more to eat. The chef had only a few things left in the larder and the result was Caesar salad, one of our favourite recipes.

2	slices bread	2
	fat or oil for deep-frying	
1/2	head crisp lettuce, shredded	1/2
1–2	anchovy fillets	1–2
	large pinch dry mustard	
	few drops Worcestershire sauce	
1 tbsp	lemon juice	1 tbsp
1 tbsp	olive oil (garlic-flavoured if desired)	1 tbsp
1	raw egg	1
1 tbsp	grated parmesan cheese	1 tbsp
	salt and freshly ground pepper	

a deep-fat frying pan; a large salad bowl, preferably wooden

Cut the slices of bread into cubes. Heat the fat or oil in the frying pan and quickly fry the bread cubes until browned all over. Drain on absorbent kitchen paper and leave to get cold.

Shred the lettuce and keep to one side. Finely chop the anchovy fillets and add to the salad bowl with the mustard, Worcestershire sauce, lemon juice and olive oil. Mix well together. Crack the raw egg into the mixture and beat with a fork until well blended.

Stir in the parmesan cheese, salt and pepper to taste, then toss the lettuce into the dressing. Finally, fold in the cold croûtons of fried bread and serve immediately.

NOTE: Some versions of this recipe require that the egg be coddled for 1–2 minutes, i.e. placed in hot but not boiling water.

——WALDORF SALAD——
Serves 4

This now famous American salad was created by Oscar Tschirky, the *'maître d''* of the New York Waldorf Hotel.

2	*stalks celery, finely chopped*	*2*
I	*medium red-skinned apple, unpeeled, cored and diced*	*I*
50 g	*walnuts, chopped*	*2 oz*
180 ml	*mayonnaise (preferably home-made)*	*generous ¼ pint*
	freshly ground pepper	
	lettuce leaves	

a salad bowl

Mix together the celery, apple and walnuts and toss in the mayonnaise. Season with pepper. Line the salad bowl with leaves of lettuce and spoon the celery/apple mixture into the centre.

——CALIFORNIAN AVOCADO SALAD——
Serves 3–4

250 g	*fresh spinach*	*8 oz*
3–4	*cooked artichoke hearts (optional)*	*3–4*
50 g	*chick peas (garbanzos) (optional)*	*2 oz*
2	*tomatoes, quartered*	*2*
	or	
8	*baby cherry tomatoes, whole*	*8*
I	*large avocado*	*I*
	salt and freshly ground pepper	

——To serve——

grated parmesan cheese
French dressing

a salad bowl

Wash and shake dry the spinach. Remove any hard centre stems and shred the leaves if desired. Slice the artichoke hearts into four pieces and add to the bowl with the spinach, chick peas and tomatoes.

Peel the avocado, cut in half, remove the stone and slice the flesh into the bowl. Sprinkle with salt and pepper and toss lightly or the avocado pieces will break up. Sprinkle with a little grated parmesan cheese and serve immediately with French dressing. (Remember the avocado will soon begin to turn brown if left for any time.)

NOTE: If preferred, a mixture of spinach and lettuce may be used.

——COLESLAW——
Serves 4

The Dutch brought this now widespread salad with them to states like New York. The name was originally '*cool sla*', Dutch for cabbage salad. '*Cool*' soon became 'cold', and inevitably led in time to the creation of its opposite 'hot slaw' – cabbage cooked in vinegar, butter, salt and pepper and served hot. The Pennsylvania Dutch also love their 'pepper slaw' or 'pepper cabbage' – a coleslaw with chopped green peppers added.

250 g	*hard white cabbage, finely shredded*	*8 oz*

——For the dressing——

3 tbsps	*sour cream*	*3 tbsps*
2 tbsps	*double cream, whipped*	*2 tbsps*
2 tbsps	*cider vinegar*	*2 tbsps*
1 tsp	*sugar*	*1 tsp*
	salt and freshly ground pepper	

Put the shredded cabbage into a medium bowl. Beat together in a small bowl the sour cream, double cream, cider vinegar, sugar and seasonings until slightly thickened. Pour the dressing over the cabbage, toss to coat thoroughly, and chill before serving.

NOTE: Optional additions to the shredded cabbage are grated carrot, grated apple, chopped green pepper, and finely chopped spring onion. Other dressings, such as mayonnaise or boiled mustard dressing, may be substituted. Some people like to steam the cabbage lightly for 3–5 minutes. Cool before adding the dressing.

——GREEK SALAD——
Serves 4

½	clove garlic	½
½	head crisp lettuce, shredded	½
2–3	spring onions, finely sliced	2–3
½	small green pepper, de-seeded and thinly sliced	½
½	small cucumber, sliced	½

——For the dressing——

1	small lemon, juice only	1
4 tbsps	olive oil	4 tbsps
	salt and freshly ground black pepper to taste	
¼ tsp	dried oregano	¼ tsp
	or	
½ tsp	fresh oregano, chopped	½ tsp

——To garnish——

10–12	black olives	10–12
75–100 g	feta cheese, cut into small cubes	3–4 oz
2–3	medium tomatoes, cut into quarters or large dice	2–3

a large salad bowl, preferably wooden

Rub the garlic round the salad bowl. Add the lettuce, spring onions, green pepper and cucumber to the bowl, and mix together lightly.

Blend the dressing ingredients to form a thick, creamy-looking dressing (a good method is to put all the ingredients in a jar with a lid, seal, and shake until well combined). Toss the dressing into the salad and garnish with the black olives, feta cheese cubes and tomato pieces. Serve immediately.

——COLD POTATO SALAD——
Serves 3–4

500 g	potatoes	*1 lb*
1	spring onion, finely chopped	*1*
½	stalk celery, finely chopped	*½*
1 tbsp	fresh parsley, finely chopped	*1 tbsp*
1 tsp	cider or tarragon vinegar	*1 tsp*
1 dsp	oil	*1 dsp*
3 tbsps	double cream	*3 tbsps*
2 tbsps	mayonnaise	*2 tbsps*
¼ tsp	salt	*¼ tsp*
	freshly ground pepper	

——To serve——

lettuce leaves

Scrub the potatoes, but leave them in their skins. Put in a pan of cold salted water, bring to the boil, and cook for 15–20 minutes until tender. Drain and cool slightly before removing the skins.

When cold, dice the potatoes into a bowl. Add the spring onion, celery and parsley. Mix together the vinegar, oil, cream and mayonnaise, and add to the potatoes with the salt and pepper to taste. Toss to coat thoroughly. Serve chilled, on a bed of lettuce leaves.

NOTE: 1–2 tablespoons of finely chopped green pepper may be substituted for the celery.

——MACARONI SALAD——
Serves 4–5

This salad, which is a standard item in delicatessens in New York, is tastier than one would imagine.

75 g	uncooked macaroni	3 oz
2 tbsps	plain French dressing	2 tbsps
1 tsp	minced or grated onion	1 tsp
	large pinch salt	
	freshly ground pepper	
3 tbsps	mayonnaise	3 tbsps

Bring a pan of salted water to the boil. Add the macaroni and cook for 8–10 minutes until tender. Drain well. Stir in the French dressing and toss lightly. Leave to get cold.

When cold, stir in the onion, salt, pepper and mayonnaise and toss lightly. Serve chilled.

NOTE: Optional extras to give added flavour and colour contrast to the salad are grated carrot, finely chopped green or red pepper, finely chopped celery, and finely chopped fresh parsley. The salad tastes even better the following day when the onion is less dominant.

——RED BEET EGGS——
Makes 3–4

This traditional Pennsylvania Dutch salad (one of the 'seven sweets and seven sours') makes an unusual colour addition to the salad table.

3–4	hard-boiled eggs	3–4
500 g	jar, bottle or tin of baby	1 lb
	beetroots preserved in	
	vinegar	
	extra vinegar if necessary	

Shell the hard-boiled eggs and put them in a 1¼ litre (2 pint) jug. Add the baby beetroots and pour over the beetroot vinegar. Add extra vinegar if necessary to cover the beets.

Leave for several hours, possibly overnight. Turn the eggs occasionally to ensure that they colour evenly.

Serve the eggs whole or cut in half, with the beets in a separate dish.

——PERFECTION SALAD——
Serves 6–8

In 1905, Charles Knox of Knox's Gelatine ran a cookery contest. One of the judges was the legendary cookbook author Fannie Farmer. One of the winners was Perfection Salad, which, although it only gained third prize and a $100 sewing machine for the sender, Mrs John E. Cooke, went on to become an American classic.

Mrs Cooke, of New Castle, Pennsylvania, enclosed a letter to Charles Knox with her recipe in which she described it as 'one of the finest salads I have ever had . . . and can be served in so many different ways'. And she added: 'This salad is especially fine with fried oysters.'

This is the original recipe (with adaptations for modern measurements) as found for us in the Knox's Gelatine archives.

15 g	*powdered gelatine*	*2 tbsps*
120 ml	*cold water*	*scant ¼ pint*
120 ml	*vinegar*	*scant ¼ pint*
1	*lemon, juice only*	*1*
480 ml	*boiling water*	*generous ¾ pint*
100 g	*sugar*	*4 oz*
1 tsp	*salt*	*1 tsp*
250 g	*celery, cut into small pieces*	*8 oz*
100 g	*cabbage, finely shredded*	*4 oz*
2–3	*sweet red peppers (pimientos), finely cut*	*2–3*

a 1 litre (1½ pint) mould

'Soak the gelatine in cold water two minutes, add vinegar, lemon juice, boiling water, sugar and salt. Strain, and when beginning to set add remaining ingredients. Turn into a mould and chill. Serve on lettuce leaves with mayonnaise, or cut in dice and serve in cases made of red or green peppers.

'A delicious accompaniment to cold sliced chicken or veal.'

——THREE OR FOUR BEAN SALAD——
Serves about 6

100 g	*French (green) beans, topped and tailed and cut into 5 cm (2 inch) lengths*	*4 oz*
100 g	*yellow wax beans (optional), topped and tailed and cut into 5 cm (2 inch) lengths*	*4 oz*
100 g	*butter beans, cooked*	*4 oz*
100 g	*red kidney beans, cooked*	*4 oz*
6 tbsps	*French dressing (see page 151)*	*6 tbsps*
1	*small onion, peeled and finely chopped*	*1*
2 tbsps	*green pepper, finely chopped*	*2 tbsps*
	salt and pepper to taste	

Prepare all the beans, and boil or steam the French and wax beans for about 10 and 12 minutes respectively. Drain.

Mix together the three or four kinds of beans and toss in the French dressing. Add the onion, green pepper and seasonings to taste. Chill. Serve as part of a mixed buffet or salad dinner.

HORS-D'ŒUVRE, MAIN DISH AND VEGETABLE ACCOMPANIMENT SALADS

——CRAB LOUIS——
Serves 2–4

Some authorities say this dish was created in Seattle, Washington, others that it originated in San Francisco. Far from drowning the special crab flavour, the chili sauce complements the shellfish.

6 tbsps	mayonnaise	6 tbsps
3 tbsps	whipped cream	3 tbsps
3 tbsps	chili sauce	3 tbsps
2 tsps	grated onion	2 tsps
	dash cayenne (optional)	
	dash Worcestershire sauce	
	shredded lettuce	
250 g	fresh crabmeat	8 oz
2	hard-boiled eggs	2
8	ripe olives (optional)	8

Mix together the mayonnaise, whipped cream, chili sauce, grated onion, cayenne and Worcestershire sauce. Chill for at least 1 hour.

When ready to serve, shred the lettuce on to a serving dish. Pile the crabmeat into the centre and spoon over some of the prepared sauce. Serve the remaining dressing in a bowl. Peel the eggs and cut into quarters. Place around the edge of the dish, with an olive in between each piece. Serve as an hors-d'œuvre or as part of a cold buffet or main meal.

——CHEF'S SALAD——
Serves 3–4

This is a very popular American salad – in supermarkets you can even purchase packets of ready-made Chef's Salad which contain the meat and cheese ingredients sliced into strips for use in this recipe.

100 g	cooked chicken or turkey, cut into julienne strips	*4 oz*
100 g	cooked ham, cut into julienne strips	*4 oz*
100 g	Swiss cheese, cut into julienne strips	*4 oz*
1	small lettuce	*1*
2–3	tomatoes	*2–3*
2	hard-boiled eggs	*2*
	salt and freshly ground pepper	

Prepare the chicken or turkey, ham and cheese. (*Note*: Julienne strips are thin cuts about 5–7 cm (2–3 inches) in length.)

Wash the lettuce and shred into a salad bowl. If you wish to take care in the presentation of this salad, carefully lay rounds of each of the different strips around the entire surface of the lettuce, for example, the cheese strips around the outside, the chicken next and the centre covered neatly with ham strips. Alternatively, the three ingredients may be mixed together and scattered casually over the surface of the lettuce.

Quarter the tomatoes, shell and quarter the hard-boiled eggs, and place the tomato and egg quarters alternately around the edge of the salad. Sprinkle with salt and pepper and a few herbs, if desired. Serve as a luncheon or light supper dish with a favourite salad dressing, for example Thousand Islands (page 150), Green Goddess (page 151), or French (page 151).

——HOT CHICKEN SALAD——
Serves 2–3

250 g	cooked chicken, chopped	*8 oz*
2	stalks celery, chopped	*2*
1	spring onion or a few chives, finely chopped	*1*
50 g	slivered almonds, toasted	*2 oz*
1 tbsp	lemon juice	*1 tbsp*
6 tbsps	mayonnaise	*6 tbsps*
1/2 tsp	salt	*1/2 tsp*

| 25 g | *freshly ground pepper*
fresh breadcrumbs
(optional) | *1 oz* |

a 600 ml (1 pint) ovenproof dish, buttered

Preheat the oven to 190°C, 375°F, gas mark 5.

Mix together the chicken, celery, spring onion, almonds, lemon juice, mayonnaise, salt and pepper and put into the buttered ovenproof dish.

If desired, sprinkle over the fresh breadcrumbs, then bake the salad in the preheated oven for 15–20 minutes until the top is lightly browned. Serve hot.

NOTE: This salad is equally delicious served cold.

——HOT POTATO SALAD——
Serves 4

This is a dish which originated in Germany and is now popular in America. The recipe given below is the basic version, to which extra ingredients may be added according to fancy. You may also vary the dressing by using sour cream or mayonnaise in place of the oil.

1 kg	*potatoes*	*2 lb*
175 g	*bacon*	*6 oz*
50 g	*onion, peeled and finely chopped*	*2 oz*
4 tbsps	*oil (e.g. olive, peanut)*	*4 tbsps*
2 tbsps	*wine or cider vinegar*	*2 tbsps*
	salt and freshly ground pepper	
2 tbsps	*fresh parsley*	*2 tbsps*

a skillet or heavy frying pan

If the potatoes are new, scrub the skins and boil without peeling first. Otherwise peel the potatoes, cut into even sizes, and boil for 15–20 minutes until tender but still firm. Drain well and leave to cool slightly. Peel off the skins if necessary; dice the potatoes and keep warm in a serving bowl.

Meanwhile heat the skillet or frying pan and fry the bacon until crisp. Drain from the pan and reserve the bacon fat. Use 1 tablespoon of bacon fat to sauté the onion until tender – about 5 minutes. Add a further 2 tablespoons of bacon fat to the pan with the oil and the vinegar. Heat through and season to taste with salt and pepper.

Dice or crumble the bacon into the potatoes. Finely chop the parsley and add to the bowl. Pour over the hot dressing and toss lightly to distribute evenly. Serve immediately.

This salad is delicious with German smoked chops (or bacon chops) or ham or gammon steaks.

NOTE: Other favourite additions are finely chopped celery and dill pickles (page 277). Spring onions or chopped chives may be substituted for the onion.

SALAD DRESSINGS

——THOUSAND ISLANDS DRESSING——
Makes about 360 ml (generous ½ pint)

This well-known salad dressing must be named after the beautiful Thousand Islands scattered along a section of the St Lawrence River as it moves towards Lake Ontario. The islands are sandwiched between Ontario in Canada and New York State, USA.

240 ml	mayonnaise	scant ½ pint
5 tbsps	tomato ketchup	5 tbsps
1–2 tsps	chili sauce or tomato chutney	1–2 tsps
6	stuffed olives, finely chopped	6
2 tbsps	gherkins or dill pickles (see page 277), finely chopped	2 tbsps
1 tbsp	chives or spring onions, finely chopped	1 tbsp

1 tsp	fresh parsley, finely chopped	1 tsp
½ tsp	dried tarragon	½ tsp
	salt and pepper to taste	

In a small bowl, mix together all the above ingredients, seasoning to taste with salt and pepper. Chill and serve with salad dishes.

——GREEN GODDESS DRESSING——
Makes 240 ml (scant ½ pint)

This delicious dressing was created in the early 1920s at the Palace Hotel in San Francisco, in honour of British actor George Arliss's performance in *The Green Goddess*. It is equally good with green salads and as a cold dressing for fish.

180 ml	mayonnaise	generous ¼ pint
3	anchovy fillets, finely chopped	3
1 dsp	tarragon vinegar	1 dsp
1 tsp	chives or spring onions, finely chopped	1 tsp
1 tbsp	fresh parsley, finely chopped	1 tbsp
1 tsp	fresh tarragon, finely chopped	1 tsp
	or	
½ tsp	dried tarragon	½ tsp
	salt and pepper to taste	

Mix together the mayonnaise, anchovy fillets, vinegar, chives or spring onions, parsley, and tarragon. Season to taste with salt and pepper and blend well. Chill.

——FRENCH DRESSING, AMERICAN-STYLE——
Makes 240 ml (scant ½ pint)

| 3 tbsps | vinegar (e.g. white wine, tarragon or white) | 3 tbsps |

120 ml	*oil (e.g. olive, peanut)*	*scant 1/4 pint*
2 tsps	*lemon juice (optional)*	*2 tsps*
1 tbsp	*sugar*	*1 tbsp*
1/2 tsp	*onion salt*	*1/2 tsp*
1/4 tsp	*salt*	*1/4 tsp*
	freshly ground pepper	
	pinch cayenne	
1 tsp	*paprika*	*1 tsp*

Combine all the ingredients and blend in a liquidizer or shake well in a sealed bottle or jar until emulsified. Store in a cool place, and shake well before serving.

PASTA AND RICE

——HOME-MADE EGG NOODLES——
Makes about 500 g (1 lb)

Pasta fresca has become a popular feature in many of New York's gourmet or speciality shops – in some places you can watch through windows or over counters as the hand-made noodles are put through electric or hand-operated pasta machines. These machines, which roll the pasta dough to the required thickness and then cut it into noodles or spaghetti, are also available for purchase in the city cookware shops.

Once you have discovered fresh pasta as we did in New York, the factory-made product becomes a poor second. Aficionados prefer pasta fresca made with semolina flour, but plain white flour may be successfully substituted.

500 g	*semolina or plain flour*	*1 lb*
1 tsp	*salt*	*1 tsp*
2	*large eggs*	*2*
1 tbsp	*olive oil*	*1 tbsp*
2–3 tbsps	*water*	*2–3 tbsps*

Sift the flour and salt into a large bowl or on to a clean work surface. Make a well in the centre. Lightly beat together the eggs, olive oil and water and pour into the centre of the well. Gradually incorporate the flour into the liquid, stirring with the fingers or a fork until the mixture forms a ball of dough. Knead the dough until smooth (about 10 minutes) then cover and leave to rest for 20 minutes.

Roll out the dough on a lightly floured surface until it is the desired thickness for the noodles, keeping the dough in a long, rectangular shape. Trim the sides and leave on a clean tea cloth to dry for 1–2 hours, turning over occasionally. Cut the noodles about ½ cm (¼ inch) wide and dry for 1 hour before using.

To dry the noodles for storage, lay them out on a clean tea cloth and turn occasionally. When fully dried the noodles will be hard and breakable. Store in polythene bags in the refrigerator where they will keep for a week or so.

To cook pasta fresca, remember that home-made noodles always cook much quicker than packet pasta. These noodles require only 3–4 minutes cooking in boiling salted water. Drain before serving.

NOTE: This same dough will also make fresh lasagna (cut the dough into 5 cm (2 inch) wide lengths; cannelloni (roll the dough thinly and cut into 10–12 cm (4–5 inch) squares; and, if you have a pasta machine, spaghetti or spaghettini.

——SPAGHETTI WITH MEATBALLS——
Serves 4

500 g	minced beef	1 lb
	salt and pepper	
1 tbsp	olive or cooking oil	1 tbsp
1	medium onion, peeled and chopped	1
1–2	cloves garlic, peeled and finely chopped or crushed	1–2
500 g	tomatoes (e.g. Italian tinned), finely chopped	1 lb
2 tbsps	tomato purée or paste	2 tbsps
1 tsp	dried basil, oregano or mixed herbs	1 tsp
	or	
2 tsps	fresh herbs, chopped	2 tsps
1	bay leaf	1
	salt and freshly ground pepper to taste	

————To serve————

250 g	*uncooked spaghetti*	8 oz
	grated parmesan cheese	

Mix together the minced beef and seasonings to taste. Form into 16 round meatballs. Heat the oil in a medium pan, add the chopped onion and the garlic, and sauté for 4–5 minutes. Add the meatballs and brown on all sides, turning frequently.

Add the tomatoes, tomato purée or paste, herbs, bay leaf, salt and pepper. Cover the pan and simmer gently for 30 minutes. Meanwhile, bring a large pan of salted water to the boil. Cook the spaghetti for 10–12 minutes then drain. Lay the spaghetti around the outside of a large, warm serving dish, and spoon the meatballs and their sauce into the centre. Sprinkle with grated parmesan cheese.

NOTE: The meatball and tomato mixture is also a popular filling for a hot hero (page 213).

————FETTUCINE ALFREDO————
Serves 2–3

The classic Italian fettucine is made with butter, grated parmesan and black pepper. This is a richer, most delicious American version.

175 g	*fettucine noodles*	6 oz
	(see page 151)	
1	*egg yolk*	1
120 ml	*double cream*	scant ¼ pint
40 g	*grated parmesan cheese*	1½ oz
75 g	*butter, melted*	3 oz
	pinch grated nutmeg	
	freshly ground black	
	pepper	

Cook the fettucine noodles in a large saucepan of boiling salted water for 3–4 minutes for home-made noodles and 9–12 minutes for factory-made. The noodles should be cooked *al dente*, as the

Italians call it – not over-soft. Drain well and put in a warmed serving dish.

Meanwhile, beat the egg yolk lightly with the cream. Stir three-quarters of the parmesan into the melted butter and add the nutmeg and black pepper. Slowly stir the butter mixture into the egg and cream, then return the sauce to the pan and gently heat through without boiling.

Pour the sauce over the drained noodles, tossing lightly to disperse the sauce. Sprinkle the top with the remaining parmesan cheese and serve hot, either as an appetizer as the Italians like to serve their pasta, or as a light lunch or supper dish. It also makes a good accompaniment to grilled veal, pork or lamb chops.

——MACARONI CHEESE——
Serves 2–4

This is a good example of genuine American-Italian cooking. Whoever thought of mixing cooked macaroni with cheese sauce hit upon an all-time favourite combination!

100 g	*uncooked macaroni*	*4 oz*
25 g	*butter or margarine*	*1 oz*
3 tbsps	*flour*	*3 tbsps*
360 ml	*milk*	*generous ½ pint*
50 g	*grated Cheddar cheese*	*2 oz*
	salt and freshly ground	
	pepper	

an ovenproof casserole or serving dish

Heat a saucepan of salted water to boiling point, add the macaroni and cook, covered, for 10–12 minutes until tender. Drain well.

Meanwhile heat the butter or margarine in a medium pan. Add the flour and cook for 1 minute, then remove from the heat and gradually stir in the milk. Return to the heat and cook, stirring constantly, until the sauce has thickened. Cook for 2–3 minutes over a lower heat. Remove from the heat, stir in most of the grated cheese, and season to taste with salt and pepper. Add the drained macaroni and stir gently to combine well. Pour into the casserole or dish and sprinkle over the remaining cheese. Place under a hot grill for about 5 minutes to brown the top.

NOTE: A delicious extra taste can be added to this basic recipe by slicing fresh tomatoes over the macaroni cheese before sprinkling with the remaining grated cheese.

——CHINESE FRIED RICE——
Serves 5–6

250 g	uncooked rice	*8 oz*
3–4	slices bacon, diced	*3–4*
1	egg, lightly beaten	*1*
3–4	spring onions, chopped	*3–4*
	or	
1	small onion, peeled and finely chopped	*1*
25–50 g	cooked green peas (optional)	*1–2 oz*
	salt and pepper to taste	

a large skillet or heavy frying pan

Rinse the rice, drain, and put it in a large pan with a little salt. Cover with water, bring to the boil and simmer, uncovered, for 12 minutes until the rice is tender. Drain if necessary and rinse under running water. Drain again.

Meanwhile put the diced bacon in a large pan or skillet and fry until crisp. Drain from the pan and pour off any excess fat, leaving some in the pan. Pour the lightly beaten egg into the pan and fry, stirring occasionally to separate the egg into pieces. Remove from the pan and reserve.

Sauté the onions in the remaining bacon fat until softened – about 5 minutes. Return the rice, bacon, egg pieces and cooked peas to the pan and fry the mixture over a medium heat, turning frequently, for a further 6–7 minutes. Season to taste.

Serve in a warmed dish with Chinese food (chow mein, page 111; chop suey, page 89), or with barbecued ribs (page 92).

——WILD RICE AND MUSHROOMS——
Serves 4

Wild rice is not a true rice but the seed of an aquatic grass. America produces almost all the world's crop (it also grows in Asia), and of that, the bulk grows in Minnesota. American Indians used to harvest the rice almost exclusively, and such was its importance to them that tribal wars broke out over the wild rice areas.

In spite of mechanization, Indians still collect some of the rice in canoes. The scarcity of the crop keeps prices almost prohibitively high, although its unique taste makes it worth every cent. We decided to include this recipe, extravagant as it is cost-wise, in our book when Keryn managed to find wild rice on sale in remote Perth, Western Australia, and after seeing it served several times in London hotels.

100 g	*wild rice*	*4 oz*
450 ml	*boiling water*	*3/4 pint*
1 tsp	*salt*	*1 tsp*
75 g	*butter*	*3 oz*
4	*slices bacon, diced*	*4*
75 g	*fresh mushrooms, sliced*	*3 oz*

Cook the rice in the boiling salted water until tender – about 45 minutes. While the rice is cooking, melt the butter in a skillet, add the bacon, and cook until it is beginning to become crispy. Add the sliced mushrooms and continue cooking until the mushrooms are wilted. When the rice is cooked, drain and then toss with the bacon and mushrooms.

NOTE: Wild rice is particularly good with duck or other poultry dishes. It is often mixed with ordinary rice, which is one way to cut its prohibitive cost.

For other recipes using pasta and rice see the following:

Chicken pot pie (page 50)
Chicken Tetrazzini (page 108)
Chow mein (page 111)
Meat loaf (page 88)

Hot sausages and peppers (page 97)
Macaroni salad (page 144)
Arroz con pollo (page 113)
Chicken jambalaya (page 106)
Country captain (page 105)
Gumbo filé (page 38)

BREAKFAST AND BRUNCH

Eating breakfast or brunch in a restaurant or café is much more commonplace in America than in our homelands of Britain and Australia. Generally speaking, breakfast is one of the best value-for-money meals in the USA. A typical New York City breakfast of two eggs (any style) with fried or hashed brown potatoes, toast, butter and grape jelly (see page 284), plus coffee, sent into the office by delivery service, is almost as common to Americans as stopping to eat out before arriving at work.

Breakfast menus can range from enormous meals of steak or lamb chops, ham or gammon steaks, corned beef or red flannel hash (page 161), through the traditional British-style meal of sausage, bacon and eggs, to the European influence of rolls and coffee, Danish pastries (page 202), bagels (page 188) or toast.

The American taste for sweetness is amply demonstrated by the popularity of such breakfast choices as pancakes (page 172), waffles (page 171), French toast (page 173) and blintzes (page 174), which are usually served with maple or other flavoured syrups, and sometimes with whipped cream and fruit. Doughnuts (page 200) and American and English muffins (pages 169, 170) are also favourite breakfast foods.

In the old inns of New England you can still find a 'farmhands' special' on the breakfast menu – a substantial meal of steak, chops or hash with eggs, served with hot breads, rolls or muffins, followed by deep-dish apple pie with Cheddar cheese (page 252), and washed down with hot mulled cider and coffee! The popularity of coffee in America is usually attributed to the American tea embargo introduced after the notorious Boston Tea Party incident, when the British tried to impose a tea tax on the colonists.

In the southern states, hominy grits (dried, hulled corn), corn-meal mush (page 168) and hot biscuits (page 195) are popular for breakfast. In the south-west, Mexican specialities like eggs ranch-style (page 164) and re-fried beans (page 127) add spice to the morning meal.

Brunch is, of course, a uniquely American invention – a combination of breakfast and lunch which has become the traditional Sunday meal out for the whole family. The more substantial breakfast favourites like corned beef hash and eggs Benedict (page 163) are popular brunch dishes. Champagne brunches are a special way to start a lazy Sunday, and in New York you can find many places which offer live music – for example, 'Bach and Brunch' – to make the day even more relaxing.

———RED FLANNEL HASH———
Serves 2–3

This dish, part of a 'farmhand's breakfast' in New England, is a good way of using up left-overs from a boiled New England dinner (page 83). It makes a delicious brunch.

250–300 g	cooked or tinned corned beef	*8–10 oz*
2	medium cooked potatoes	*2*
1	small onion, peeled	*1*
15 g	butter or margarine	*large knob*
1	medium cooked beetroot	*1*
1 tsp	Worcestershire sauce	*1 tsp*
	salt and freshly ground pepper to taste	
2–3	poached eggs	*2–3*

a skillet or heavy frying pan

Dice or mince the corned beef. Dice the potatoes and onion. Heat the butter or margarine in the skillet or frying pan and sauté the onion until golden brown – about 5 minutes.

Meanwhile, dice the beetroot and add it with the beef and potatoes to the pan. Season with the Worcestershire sauce, salt and pepper. Cover the pan and fry briskly, turning the mixture over once.

Poach the eggs in lightly salted boiling water, drain, and serve on top of the hash on a warmed serving dish.

——SCRAPPLE——
Makes about 2¹/₄ kg (5 lbs)

This ingenious Pennsylvania Dutch speciality makes good use of the left-over parts of pigs for which there is less demand. Sometimes called 'ponhaws', it makes a delicious breakfast dish. We based our recipe on one used for generations by a Pennsylvania Dutch family, the Youndts, who make hundreds of pounds of scrapple for sale in the family butcher shop. Mrs Fern Youndt had this advice for us: 'Scrapple is very perishable and should be used within a week. To keep, I slice it slightly less than half an inch (1 cm) thick and wrap individually in freezer wrap and freeze. When I want to prepare it, I take as many slices from the freezer as I need and put the frozen scrapple into a hot pan that contains a tablespoon or more of oil. Brown and serve with syrup.'

1¹/₄ kg	*pork shoulder or neck*	*3 lb*
250 g	*pork liver*	*8 oz*
250 g	*pork skin*	*8 oz*
4	*pig trotters*	*4*
1 kg	*beef bones*	*2 lb*
4 litres	*water*	*7 pints*
300 g	*cornmeal*	*10 oz*
4 tsps	*salt*	*4 tsps*
480 ml	*cold water*	*generous ³/₄ pint*
2	*medium onions, peeled and finely chopped*	*2*
1 tbsp	*dried sage*	*1 tbsp*
1 tbsp	*dried marjoram*	*1 tbsp*
¹/₂ tsp	*ground thyme*	*¹/₂ tsp*
	dash ground cloves	
1 tsp	*ground pepper*	*1 tsp*

a preserving pan or very large saucepan; 2 × 1 kg (2 lb) and
1 × 500 g (1 lb) loaf tins

Chop the shoulder into small portions and put in the preserving
pan or large saucepan with the liver, skin, trotters, bones and
water. Bring to the boil, then cover the pan and simmer for 1½–2
hours until the meat falls away from the bones.

Strain the broth from the meat and bones, reserve and chill.
When cold skim off the layer of fat which will have solidified on the
surface. Remove the meat from the bones and discard the bones
and skin. Mince or finely chop all the meat.

Blend together the cornmeal, salt and cold water. Bring 1 litre
(1¾ pints) of the reserved broth to the boil and gradually stir
into the cornmeal. Return the mixture to the pan, and, stirring
constantly, bring to the boil. Cover the pan as the bubbling
cornmeal will spatter, and cook for about 10 minutes, stirring
frequently.

Stir in the minced or finely chopped meat, the finely chopped
onions, the sage, marjoram, thyme, cloves and pepper. Cover the
pan and simmer gently for 20 minutes, then remove the cover and
simmer for a further 10–20 minutes until thick. Pour the mixture
into the loaf tins and chill until set.

Cut the scrapple into slices and fry in a pan or skillet with a little
fat, oil or butter until it is crisp and browned, turning once. Serve
as a breakfast dish (for example with bacon and eggs) or – if you
can bear it – with syrup as the Pennsylvania Dutch enjoy it. (*Note*:
Syrup to an American is pancake syrup, not golden syrup. Most
supermarkets sell pancake syrup these days.)

——EGGS BENEDICT——
Serves 4–6

This is a common brunch dish to be found on most American
restaurant menus. It is a very tasty concoction providing the
Hollandaise sauce is not too overwhelming. The addition of
chicken stock to the sauce gives it a milder flavour.

4–6	*eggs*	*4–6*
2–3	*English muffins (page 169)*	*2–3*

4–6	*round slices ham (to match the diameter of the muffins)*	*4–6*

——For the hollandaise sauce——
Makes 120 ml (scant ¹/₄ pint)

2 tbsps	*lemon juice or wine vinegar*	*2 tbsps*
2	*egg yolks*	*2*
50 g	*butter*	*2 oz*
2–3 tbsps	*chicken stock*	*2–3 tbsps*
	salt and pepper to taste	

Poach the eggs in lightly salted water. Meanwhile, split the muffins into two rounds and toast under a hot grill to brown. Butter if desired.

Place each muffin on a warmed plate, lay on a slice of ham, then top with a drained poached egg. Keep the plates warm in the oven while preparing the hollandaise sauce.

Boil the lemon juice or vinegar in a small pan until reduced by half. Cool, then mix with the egg yolks in a small bowl over hot water. Whisk the mixture until the sauce begins to thicken, then gently whisk in small pieces of butter until well blended. Do not allow the sauce to boil. Stir in the chicken stock, add salt and pepper to taste, and when heated through, immediately pour over the eggs. Serve at once.

HUEVOS RANCHEROS – MEXICAN
——RANCH-STYLE EGGS——
Serves 4

These eggs are one of the most popular of Mexican breakfasts, as we soon discovered on visiting Mexico and the south-western states of America. No tourist could wish for a more filling meal on which to start a day's sight-seeing! It also makes a delicious brunch. Indian popadums are the nearest substitute I can think of for tortillas, though the latter are made from ground corn.

2 tbsps	bacon fat, lard or oil	2 tbsps
1	medium onion, peeled and finely chopped	1
1	clove garlic, peeled and crushed	1
1/2	green pepper, de-seeded and cut into strips	1/2
350 g	tomatoes, chopped	12 oz
1/2 tsp	salt	1/2 tsp
1–2 tsps	hot chili or tabasco sauce	1–2 tsps
	stock or tomato juice (if necessary)	
2–3 tbsps	oil for frying	2–3 tbsps
4	tortillas	4
8	eggs	8
120 ml	milk or single cream	scant 1/4 pint
	salt and pepper to taste	
	a knob of butter	
	frijoles refritos (re-fried beans – see page 127)	

a skillet or heavy frying pan

Heat the fat, lard or oil in a medium pan and sauté the onion and garlic for 2–3 minutes to soften. Add the pepper strips and sauté for a further 3–4 minutes. Add the tomatoes, salt and hot chili sauce or tabasco. If the mixture is not liquid enough, add a few tablespoons of stock or tomato juice. Cover the pan and simmer gently for 10–15 minutes.

Heat the oil in a skillet or frying pan. Fry the tortillas until lightly browned on both sides. Remove to a warm plate and keep hot.

Beat the eggs and milk or cream together. Add the salt and pepper. Heat the knob of butter in the skillet or pan and scramble the eggs, stirring occasionally until cooked but still soft.

Put one tortilla on each plate, spoon over the scrambled eggs, and cover the eggs with spoonfuls of the tomato sauce. Serve with re-fried beans and, for a more complete meal, with sautéed potatoes and grilled bacon.

NOTE: Fried or poached eggs may be substituted for scrambled eggs.

——WESTERN OMELETTE——
Serves 2–3

This dish is obviously the descendant of the Spanish omelette, as a result of Spanish influence on the cookery of the western and south-western states of America.

250–300 g	*potatoes*	*8–10 oz*
100 g	*bacon, diced*	*4 oz*
1	*small onion*	*1*
1/2	*small red or green pepper*	*1/2*
3	*large eggs*	*3*
120 ml	*milk*	*scant 1/4 pint*
	salt and freshly ground pepper to taste	

a skillet or heavy frying pan

Peel the potatoes, cut into even-sized pieces, and boil in salted water for 15–20 minutes until tender. Drain and leave to cool.

Put the diced bacon in the skillet or frying pan and fry until crisp. Drain from the pan and pour off any excess fat. Meanwhile, peel and dice the onion; remove the centre seeds from the pepper and cut the flesh into short strips. Sauté the onion and pepper in the remaining bacon fat.

Dice the potatoes and add to the pan. Sauté the vegetables until the potatoes are browning, turning once. Return the diced bacon to the pan.

Beat the eggs, milk, salt and pepper in a small bowl and pour the mixture over the vegetables in the pan. Cook until little bubbles start to appear on the surface, then put the pan under a hot grill to brown the surface of the omelette. Serve hot as a lunch or supper dish.

——HANGTOWN FRY——
Serves 3–4

This meal was supposed to have originated during the gold rush to the West in a Californian town called Hangtown (named after the hanging of five men from the same tree on the same day). Legend has it that after a gold miner struck it rich he arrived in town demanding the best meal money could buy – he was served with fried eggs, bacon and oysters, all expensive items in those days.

3	*rashers bacon, diced*	*3*
6	*eggs*	*6*
6 tbsps	*milk*	*6 tbsps*
1/4 tsp	*salt*	*1/4 tsp*
	pinch freshly ground black pepper	
50 g	*dried breadcrumbs*	*2 oz*
25 g	*flour*	*1 oz*
24	*oysters, shelled*	*24*
25 g	*butter*	*1 oz*
2 tsps	*parsley, chopped*	*2 tsps*
	lemon wedges	

a skillet or large frying pan

Fry the bacon in the skillet or pan until crisp. Drain, reserving the bacon drippings in the pan, and keep the bacon warm. In a bowl combine the eggs, 3 tablespoons of the milk, the salt and pepper, and beat slightly before setting aside. Combine the breadcrumbs and flour and first dip the shelled oysters in the remaining milk then roll in the crumb/flour mixture.

Add the butter to the bacon drippings in the pan and fry the oysters for 2–3 minutes until lightly browned, turning once. Return the bacon to the pan, then pour the egg mixture over all. Cook over a low heat until the bottom has cooked. Gently lift the edge of the omelette to allow the uncooked eggs to flow to the base of the pan. Do not overcook. Serve when the eggs are set, garnished with parsley and lemon wedges.

──CORNMEAL MUSH──
Serves 4–6

This American cereal, which may be eaten for breakfast or with meats, chili, etc., is very similar to Italian polenta and is especially popular in the southern states.

150 g	*cornmeal or polenta*	*5 oz*
2 tsps	*salt*	*2 tsps*
240 ml	*cold water*	*scant ¹/₂ pint*
480 ml	*boiling water*	*generous ³/₄ pint*

──To serve──

butter
milk

a double boiler

Mix together the cornmeal, salt and cold water. Gradually add the boiling water, stirring. Put the mixture in a large pan and cook, stirring constantly, over a fairly high heat until thickened. Either continue to simmer gently over a low heat for 40–45 minutes, stirring regularly, or transfer to a double boiler and cook, stirring occasionally, for about 30 minutes. Cover the pan in both cases, as the cornmeal mixture tends to spatter.

For a breakfast cereal, serve hot with butter and, if desired, a little milk.

──FRIED CORNMEAL MUSH──

Prepare the mush as above and pour the mixture into a loaf tin. Chill. Once set, cut into slices and fry in butter or fat until crisp and browned. Serve for breakfast with syrup, or with poultry or game.

NOTE: The slices may be dipped in beaten egg and coated with crumbs before frying.

———ENGLISH MUFFINS———
Makes about 20–24

If you haven't visited the United States of America you couldn't guess at the tremendous popularity of English muffins. As one famous brand name boasted in its television advertising, they are more popular for breakfast than toast.

scant 300 ml	lukewarm water	scant ½ pint
2 tbsps	sugar	2 tbsps
1 tbsp	dried yeast	1 tbsp
scant 300 ml	milk	scant ½ pint
1 tsp	salt	1 tsp
2 tbsps	oil	2 tbsps
¾ kg	white flour	1½ lb
	cornmeal or oatmeal	
	butter or margarine	

a skillet, heavy frying pan or griddle; 3 greased baking trays; an 8 cm (3 inch) plain round cutter

Measure the water into a jug, add 1 tablespoon of the sugar, and sprinkle over the yeast. Leave for 10–15 minutes in a warm place until frothy.

Heat the milk to scalding point and then leave to cool to lukewarm. Add the remaining 1 tablespoon of sugar, the salt and the oil. Meanwhile, sift 650 g (1¼ lb) of the flour and make a well in the centre. Mix together the yeast liquid and the milk, and mix into the flour to form a sticky dough.

Sift the remaining 100 g (4 oz) of flour on to the work surface and knead the dough until it is smooth and all the flour has been absorbed – about 10 minutes. Grease a large bowl, add the dough, turn once to grease the top and cover (for example, with greased polythene or cling-film). Leave in a warm place to prove for 1–2 hours, until double in size.

Punch the dough down and knead lightly. Grease the baking trays and sprinkle over a little cornmeal to coat the bases. Roll out the dough 2 cm (¾ inch) thick and cut into rounds with the cutter. Brush the tops of the muffins with a salt-water solution and sift over a little cornmeal. Put the muffins on the prepared baking trays, cover, and leave in a warm place for about 20 minutes.

Heat the skillet, frying pan or griddle and lightly grease the surface with butter or margarine. Over a fairly low heat, cook the muffins for about 7–8 minutes on each side, taking care that they do not burn before the inside is cooked through.

Periodically clean the skillet surface between batches of muffins. Alternatively, cook the muffins in the pan for only 2–3 minutes for each side to brown, and continue to cook in a warm oven (150°C, 300°F, Gas Mark 2) for about 20 minutes.

Serve hot with butter and grape jelly (page 284) or jam.

——AMERICAN MUFFINS——
Makes 10–12 large or 18 small

These muffins are more cake-like in texture than the older English muffins (see previous recipe). They are favourite snacks for breakfasts and even light lunches, and come in dozens of varieties – cornmeal, wholewheat, bran, apple sauce, cinnamon, blueberry, cheese, bacon, etc. This recipe is for the basic plain muffin.

250 g	*plain flour*	*8 oz*
2 tsps	*baking powder*	*2 tsps*
1/2 tsp	*salt*	*1/2 tsp*
50 g	*sugar*	*2 oz*
1	*egg, lightly beaten*	*1*
240 ml	*milk*	*scant 1/2 pint*
50 g	*butter or margarine, melted*	*2 oz*

a muffin tray or deep-cup bun tray, greased

Preheat the oven to 200°C, 400°F, gas mark 6.

Sift the flour, baking powder and salt into a bowl. Stir in the sugar. Lightly beat the egg with the milk. Pour the melted butter or margarine into the flour ingredients and add the egg and milk. Stir *only* to combine into a rough batter. *Do not overmix*, or it will spoil the final texture of the muffins.

Drop spoonfuls of batter into the greased tray to half fill the cups. Bake in the preheated oven for 20 minutes until risen and lightly browned. Serve warm with butter and jam, jelly or honey.

NOTE: For *Cornmeal, Wholewheat or Bran Muffins*, substitute 100 g (4 oz) of cornmeal, wholewheat or bran for half of the plain flour.

For *Cheese Muffins*, omit the sugar and add 25–50 g (1–2 oz) of finely grated cheese to the dry ingredients before adding the liquids.

For *Blueberry Muffins*, fold 100 g (4 oz) frozen, fresh, or tinned blueberries into the dry ingredients before adding the liquids.

For *Spiced Muffins*, sift ½ teaspoon of ground cinnamon or mixed spice with the flour.

——WAFFLES——
Makes 5–6

Like many other of their favourite dishes, Americans wholeheartedly adopted the waffle from Europe and made it their own. Thomas Jefferson, the third president of the USA, brought a waffle iron back to America with him after discovering waffles in Holland. However, unlike Europeans, Americans usually serve waffles at breakfast, although they may be served as a dessert with ice-cream as the Belgians do.

Unfortunately it is impossible to create the distinctive lattice pattern of the waffle without a waffle iron or electric waffle maker.

100 g	*flour*	*4 oz*
1 tsp	*baking powder*	*1 tsp*
¼ tsp	*salt*	*¼ tsp*
1 tbsp	*sugar*	*1 tbsp*
180 ml	*milk or buttermilk (or milk with 1 tsp lemon juice added)*	*generous ¼ pint*
1	*large egg*	*1*
3 tbsps	*butter, melted*	*3 tbsps*
	extra oil	

a waffle iron or electric waffle machine

Sift the flour, baking powder, salt and sugar into a bowl. In a large jug, measure the milk or buttermilk, add the egg and beat lightly. Beat in the melted butter and gradually stir the liquid into the flour until a smooth batter results.

Heat the waffle iron on both sides, or heat the machine according to the manufacturer's instructions. Brush the inside of the waffle iron with oil, and when hot, but not smoking, pour in a little of the waffle batter to fill the lower portion of the iron. Shut the iron and cook until brown and crisp, turning the hand iron once to brown the other side. Serve hot with butter and maple syrup, spice or orange syrup (page 176), or with cream or ice-cream.

NOTE: For lighter, crisper waffles, separate the egg and whisk the egg white till stiff. Fold gently into the batter before cooking.

——PANCAKES——
Makes 6 large or 12 small

The pancake can be found on almost every American breakfast menu under a wealth of different disguises. Each area in the United States has its own favourite name for the ubiquitous pancake – griddle cakes, hotcakes, flapjacks and flats are merely regional variations on the same theme. Pancakes can also be adapted to different flours (for example, cornmeal and buckwheat), to different liquids (for example, buttermilk, sour cream and sourdough starter (see page 181), and are especially delicious when fresh fruits such as blueberries are added as the pancakes are cooking. Compared with the European pancake or *crêpe*, the US version is much thicker and more spongy in texture.

175 g	*plain flour*	*6 oz*
1 tbsp	*baking powder*	*1 tbsp*
1/4 tsp	*salt*	*1/4 tsp*
2 tbsps	*caster sugar*	*2 tbsps*
2	*eggs*	*2*
240 ml	*milk*	*scant 1/2 pint*

a griddle, skillet or heavy frying pan

Sift the flour, baking powder, salt and sugar into a bowl. Lightly beat the eggs with the milk. Without over-stirring, mix the liquid into the dry ingredients to moisten.

Very lightly grease the griddle, skillet or frying pan, heat without smoking, and pour the pancake batter in batches on to the hot griddle or pan. Cook until bubbles form on the surface and the pancake is browned underneath. Turn the pancake over to lightly brown the other side. Serve hot with butter and maple syrup, spice or orange syrup (page 176).

NOTE: To make *Blueberry Pancakes*, add 175–250 g (6–8 oz) of fresh or tinned blueberries, sprinkling the fruit over the pancakes as they are cooking on their first side.

For *Buttermilk Pancakes*, substitute buttermilk for the milk, adding extra liquid if the batter is too thick.

For *Sour Cream Pancakes*, substitute some sour cream for part of the milk, mixing both together well before adding to the eggs.

——FRENCH TOAST——
Makes 4

Americans in the southern states have taken the fairly ordinary French toast or *pain perdu* so popular with children, and turned it into something more special. Americans serve French toast at breakfast, but as usual it comes drenched in maple syrup and butter. I even read that a similar recipe to this is claimed to be the breakfast speciality of the famous Santa Fé railroad.

You can also serve this version as a tasty and easily prepared dessert.

2	*large eggs*	2
3 tbsps	*top of the milk or a milk/cream mixture*	*3 tbsps*
1 tbsp	*sugar*	*1 tbsp*
1/4 tsp	*ground cinnamon*	*1/4 tsp*
	pinch of salt	
1/2	*lemon, grated rind only*	*1/2*
25–50 g	*butter or margarine*	*1–2 oz*
4	*slices of bread*	4

a skillet or frying pan

Beat the eggs, milk (or milk and cream) and sugar in a medium bowl until well blended. Add the cinnamon, salt and grated lemon rind, and beat a little more.

Heat the butter or margarine in the skillet or pan. Meanwhile, dip the bread slices into the egg mixture until coated on both sides, beating the mixture well before each piece is added.

Fry the slices in the pan until browned on both sides, about 2–3 minutes for each side. Serve hot with butter and maple syrup, spice or orange syrup (page 176).

———CHEESE BLINTZES———
Makes about 8

Blintzes are filled pancakes (similar to French *crêpes*), which can be either savoury or sweet and may be served for brunch or as a dessert. They are an important part of Jewish cooking.

———The batter———

2	*eggs*	2
240 ml	*milk*	*scant ¹/2 pint*
3 tbsps	*water*	*3 tbsps*
100 g	*plain flour*	*4 oz*
¹/4 tsp	*salt*	*¹/4 tsp*
	butter or oil for frying	

———The filling———

500 g	*cottage cheese*	*1 lb*
1	*egg yolk*	*1*
15 g	*butter, melted*	*large knob*
2 tbsps	*sugar (optional)*	*2 tbsps*
¹/2 tsp	*ground cinnamon (optional)*	*¹/2 tsp*
¹/4 tsp	*salt (optional)*	*¹/4 tsp*
1	*lemon, grated rind only*	*1*

a 25 cm (10¹/2 inch) skillet or heavy frying pan

Beat together the eggs, milk and water. Sift the flour and salt and beat the egg mixture into the flour until a smooth batter is made. Heat the skillet or pan and lightly grease with butter or oil. Add about 3 tablespoons of batter, swirling the pan to coat the entire surface. Cook until the bottom of the pancake is lightly browned, then, without turning the pancake, remove from the pan on to a large tray. Continue to cook the pancakes on one side only and lay them out separately.

Meanwhile put the cottage cheese, egg yolk and melted butter in a bowl. If sweet blintzes are required, add the sugar and cinnamon but not the salt. If savoury blintzes are preferred, add only the salt. Add the grated lemon rind and mix together very lightly with a fork. Do not overmix or the filling will become too thin.

Put a large spoonful of filling in the centre of the browned side of the pancake. Fold two opposite edges into the centre lapping over each other, then the other two flaps to form square parcels. Repeat until all the pancakes are filled and folded.

Heat some butter or oil in the skillet or pan and cook the parcels, turning once until browned on both sides. Serve hot.

——CALAS——
Makes 16–18

In bygone days, these rice cakes were sold in the streets of New Orleans by black women vendors whose familiar cry of '*Belles calas; calas toutes chaudes*' announced the arrival of these hot breakfast favourites. Traditionally, preparations for making calas begin the day before with a yeast mixture, but the more modern baking powder version cuts down on cooking time. Some recipes recommend mashing or mincing the rice first. Calas also makes a tasty dessert and is a good way of using up left-over rice.

3	*eggs*	*3*
100 g	*sugar*	*4 oz*
175 g	*flour*	*6 oz*
2 tsps	*baking powder*	*2 tsps*
½ tsp	*grated nutmeg*	*½ tsp*
¼ tsp	*vanilla essence*	*¼ tsp*
275 g	*cooked rice*	*9 oz*
	fat or oil for frying	

——To serve——

icing sugar
cream (optional)

a skillet or large frying pan

Beat together the eggs and sugar. Sift the flour, baking powder and nutmeg and gradually add to the egg mixture. Stir in the vanilla and cooked rice.

Heat the fat or oil in the skillet or pan and drop spoonfuls of the rice mixture into the hot fat. When browned on one side, turn over to brown the other. Drain on absorbent paper, and while still hot sift over the icing sugar.

NOTE: For a dessert, serve with fresh cream.

——SPICE SYRUP——
Makes about 300 ml (1/2 pint)

175 g	*sugar*	*6 oz*
50 g	*butter or margarine*	*2 oz*
3 tbsps	*water*	*3 tbsps*
1/2 tsp	*ground cinnamon*	*1/2 tsp*
1/4 tsp	*grated nutmeg*	*1/4 tsp*

Place all the ingredients in a small saucepan and bring very slowly to the boil to dissolve the sugar completely. Simmer gently for 5–10 minutes until the syrup has thickened. Serve hot with pancakes (page 172), French toast (page 173) or waffles (page 171).

——HOT ORANGE SYRUP——
Makes about 300 ml (1/2 pint)

2	*fresh oranges, grated peel of one, juice of both to yield about 120 ml (scant 1/4 pint)*	*2*
100 g	*sugar*	*4 oz*
50 g	*butter or margarine*	*2 oz*
1 tbsp	*lemon juice (i.e. juice of 1/2 a small lemon)*	*1 tbsp*

Put all the ingredients into a small saucepan and heat gently to completely dissolve all the sugar, then boil the syrup for about 5 minutes. Serve hot with pancakes (page 172), French toast (page 173) or waffles (page 171).

BREADS
AND
QUICK BREADS

American home-made breads offer a surprisingly interesting variety of loaves, from foreign creations like pumpernickel to the sourdough breads of the west coast, the cornbreads of the South and steamed Boston brown bread. Quick breads and rolls are just as interesting, from squaw breads and hush puppies to the fun-to-make bagels and pretzels.

——STEAMED BOSTON BROWN BREAD——
Makes 1 large loaf or 4 small

This unusual steamed bread is a favourite accompaniment to that other New England speciality – baked beans (page 125). What makes it even more unusual is that it may be steamed in tin cans, for example former baked bean tins. It also used to be known as 'rye-an'-injun', referring to the rye flour and cornmeal or Indian flour used in the recipe.

100 g	*wholewheat flour*	*4 oz*
100 g	*cornmeal*	*4 oz*
100 g	*rye flour*	*4 oz*
1 tsp	*salt*	*1 tsp*
1 tsp	*bicarbonate of soda*	*1 tsp*
180 ml	*treacle*	*generous 1/4 pint*
360 ml	*soured milk or buttermilk*	*generous 1/2 pint*
75 g	*raisins or sultanas (optional)*	*3 oz*

a 20 cm (8 inch) round baking tin or four 500 g (1 lb) clean, straight-sided tins (e.g. baked bean tins), greased; grease-proof or waxed paper

Sift the flours, if necessary, into a large bowl with the salt and soda. Add the treacle and soured milk or buttermilk and mix well to a smooth batter. Fold in the raisins or sultanas if desired.

Spoon the batter into the greased tin or tins until they are half full. Tie a piece of greaseproof or waxed paper over the tin or tins, securing with string.

Put the tin or tins in a large pan and fill with water to come half-way up the sides of the tins. Cover the pan and steam the bread gently for 2–2½ hours until firm to the touch. Turn the bread out on to a cooling rack. Serve with butter and baked beans (page 125).

——PUMPERNICKEL BREAD——
Makes 2 × 500 g (1 lb) loaves

Many explanations have been offered as to the origin of the name 'pumpernickel'. As none struck us as undeniably true, we will give you the one that amused us the most. The story goes that the great Napoleon was not impressed with his first taste of this bread and remarked that it was only '*bon pour Nickel*' (good for Nickel) – Nickel being his horse, or so the tale goes. We are inclined to believe it more likely that he would have said '*pain pour Nickel*' (bread for Nickel). However, right or wrong, whatever he did or did not say, we disagree with his sentiment and find this a very tasty home-made bread.

20 g	dried yeast	6 tsps
360 ml	lukewarm water	generous ½ pint
1 tsp	sugar	1 tsp
300 ml	warm milk	½ pint
120 ml	treacle	scant ¼ pint
3 tbsps	butter, melted	3 tbsps
3 tbsps	caraway seeds	3 tbsps
2 tsps	salt	2 tsps
350 g	rye flour	12 oz
300 g	wholewheat flour	10 oz
250–300 g	plain flour, sifted	8–10 oz

2 × 500 g (1 lb) loaf tins or 1 × 1 kg (2 lb) loaf tin, greased

Dissolve the yeast in the warm water with the sugar and leave for 10–15 minutes until bubbly.

Combine the warm milk, treacle, melted butter, 2 tablespoons of the caraway seeds and the salt. Add the yeast liquid and stir in the rye and wholewheat flours. Add sufficient sifted plain flour to make a moderately stiff dough.

Turn the dough on to a lightly floured surface and knead until smooth and elastic. Place the dough in a large greased bowl, turn once to grease the top, cover and leave to double in size – about 1½ hours in a warm place.

Remove the dough from the bowl, punch down and knead again lightly. Shape into two small loaves or one large one, and put in the greased loaf tins. Cover the loaves with greased polythene bags and leave in a warm place to double in size.

Preheat the oven to 190°C, 375°F, gas mark 5.

Make about three slashes in the tops of the loaves with a razor or sharp knife, taking care not to deflate the risen dough. Carefully brush the tops of the loaves with water or a water and salt solution, and sprinkle with the remaining 1 tablespoon of caraway seeds.

Bake the loaves in the preheated oven – 30–35 minutes for small loaves or 45–50 minutes for a large one. When the loaves are fully cooked, they will sound hollow when the undersurface is lightly tapped with your knuckles. Leave the loaves to cool on a wire rack.

——ANADAMA BREAD——
Makes 1 large or 2 small loaves

The fascinating name of this bread gives rise to many different explanations as to its origin. The two most popular stories concern a farmer's wife called Anna. The first version portrays her as a very lazy woman, whose desperate husband had to resort to making his own bread by throwing together flour and cornmeal while muttering to himself 'Anna, damn her!' The second story has Anna as a very good cook who leaves her rivals in awe at her damn good bread! Regardless of its origin, it's not disputed that this really is 'damn good bread'.

2 tsps	dried yeast	2 tsps
	or	
15 g	fresh yeast	1/2 oz
1 tsp	sugar	1 tsp
240 ml	lukewarm water	scant 1/2 pint
25 g	butter	1 oz
3 tbsps	treacle	3 tbsps
350–400 g	plain flour	12–14 oz
75 g	cornmeal	3 oz
1 1/2 tsps	salt	1 1/2 tsps

1 × 500 g (1 lb) round loaf tin or 2 × 250 g (8 oz) small loaf tins, greased

Dissolve the yeast and sugar in the lukewarm water. Leave in a warm place for about 10–15 minutes until frothy.

Melt the butter and leave to cool before adding the treacle. Sift together in a large bowl most of the flour, all the cornmeal and the salt. Make a well in the centre and add the yeast mixture and the butter and treacle. Mix well, adding more flour as necessary to make a stiff dough. Turn out on to a lightly floured surface and knead the dough until smooth and elastic – about 5–10 minutes. Place the dough in a large greased bowl, turn once to grease the surface, and cover. Leave in a warm place until doubled in size – about 1–2 hours.

Punch down the dough and knead lightly. Shape into two small round loaves or one large one, put in the greased loaf pans, and cover with greased paper or cling-film. Leave to double in size – approximately 1 hour in a warm place.

Preheat the oven to 190°C, 375°F, gas mark 5.

Brush the top of the dough lightly with water (or water and salt) and bake in the preheated oven – 30 minutes for small loaves and 45 minutes for a large loaf. When fully cooked, the loaves will sound hollow when tapped underneath with the knuckles. Cool on a wire rack.

——BASIC SOURDOUGH STARTER——

A certain mystique has built up around the sourdough starter, which makes the whole business seem far more fragile than it really is. After all, the ancient Egyptians had no problems in the days when pre-packaged yeasts were unknown!

Once you have got your starter pot going, providing you use it on a fairly frequent basis, the starter will remain alive and active while stored in the refrigerator. The pot is kept going by always replacing whatever you have taken out.

There are several different methods of preparing a sourdough starter. The most basic of all uses just plain flour and water left in a warm place until it has attracted the natural yeasts in the atmosphere and begins to ferment. However, our medical expert is apprehensive about attracting other unwelcome bacteria, too, so we recommend the following version as a safer method.

250 g	*plain flour*	*8 oz*
1 tsp	*salt*	*1 tsp*
3 tbsps	*sugar*	*3 tbsps*
1 tbsp	*dried yeast*	*1 tbsp*
480 ml	*lukewarm water*	*generous ³⁄₄ pint*

Sift the flour, salt and sugar into a large mixing bowl, add the dry yeast, and gradually stir in the lukewarm water until the mixture resembles a smooth batter. Cover the bowl with a towel or cheesecloth and leave in a warm place (about 85°F/30°C) to sour. Stir the mixture several times a day.

During fermentation the starter will progress from a stringy mixture to a smooth batter. In between stirring of the starter, a liquid layer may begin to form on the surface. This mildly alcoholic liquid is known as 'hooch', after an Alaskan tribe of Indians who came from Hooch-in-Noo and who did a roaring trade with the gold miners, selling a very powerful potion brewed from this sourdough liquid!

Stir the 'hooch' back into the mixture at each stirring. In 2–3 days' time the sourdough starter will be ready. Store in a heavy plastic container with a hole punched in the lid to allow gases to escape. Once the mixture has settled down in the refrigerator, a layer of 'hooch' will form, which should be incorporated back into the starter before using it for cooking.

——SOURDOUGH BREAD——
Makes 3 × 500 g (1 lb) loaves; 1 × 500 g (1 lb) loaf and
4 miniature loaves; or 12 rolls

This is the bread for which San Francisco is famous. Its great popularity began back in the days of the frantic gold rush west, when hopeful miners arrived in hordes to make their fortunes panning for gold. With them they brought their sourdough starters from which they baked their own bread, and, before long, 'sourdoughs' became the traditional nickname for these miners.

This particular recipe makes the strongest 'sour' flavoured bread by using what is known as the 'long sponge method' – i.e. it takes about two days to ferment.

240 ml	sourdough starter (page 181)	scant ½ pint
480 ml	lukewarm water	generous ¾ pint
¾ kg	plain flour (bread flour is best)	1½ lb
480 ml	scalded milk, cooled	generous ¾ pint
120 ml	sour cream	scant ¼ pint
1 tbsp	butter, melted	1 tbsp
2 tbsps	sugar	2 tbsps
2 tsps	salt	2 tsps
500 g	plain flour	1 lb

3 × 500 g (1 lb) loaf tins or baking trays or 4 miniature loaf pans, greased

To start the sponge, put the sourdough starter, lukewarm water, ¾ kg (1½ lb) of flour and the cooled milk into a large bowl. Cover with a plate and leave in a warm place for 24–36 hours, depending on how sour you wish the bread to taste. In the first 8 hours the mixture should more than double in size, then it will collapse down to more like its original size. If it is fermenting properly you will be able to see it bubbling away; if not, then the temperature is too high or too cold, and the natural yeasts are unable to function.

When fermentation time is over, add the sour cream, melted butter, sugar and salt, and stir to combine. Gradually add a further 500 g (1 lb) of sifted flour to make a firm dough. Turn out on to a lightly floured surface and knead for 5–10 minutes until smooth and elastic.

Divide the dough, shape into loaves, mini-loaves or rolls, and put in the greased baking tins or trays. Brush the tops with a salt and water solution or with a little milk, cover the tins or trays with greased plastic, and leave until double in size – about 1–2 hours.

Preheat the oven to 200°C, 400°F, gas mark 6.

Bake the bread or rolls in the preheated oven – 40–50 minutes for the loaves, 25–30 minutes for the mini-loaves and 20 minutes for the rolls. Leave to cool on wire racks.

NOTE: The bread has a more distinctively sour taste when eaten cold than when eaten hot. It is a moist as opposed to a dry bread.

———SOURDOUGH FRENCH BREAD———
Makes 2 × 40 cm (16 inch) loaves

This is another popular San Franciscan sourdough bread. Because of the enthusiastic way the yeasts expand, it is not possible to create genuine French bread loaves without using special French bread tins to contain the shape – as we soon discovered when our doughs spread out along the flat baking trays giving a wide rather than a rounded shaped loaf. Once we invested in the right equipment, we were quickly able to create a true French bread shape.

240 ml	*lukewarm water*	*scant 1/2 pint*
2 tsps	*sugar*	*2 tsps*
2 tsps	*dried yeast*	*2 tsps*
	or	
15 g	*fresh yeast*	*1/2 oz*
240 ml	*sourdough starter (page 181)*	*scant 1/2 pint*
350 g	*plain flour, sifted*	*12 oz*
4 tbsps	*sour cream*	*4 tbsps*
1 1/2 tsps	*salt*	*1 1/2 tsps*
1/2 tsp	*bicarbonate of soda*	*1/2 tsp*
175–250 g	*plain flour*	*6–8 oz*

a double loaf French bread baking tin, greased; an oven-proof dish

Put the lukewarm water and sugar in a bowl and sprinkle over the dried yeast. Leave in a warm place for 10–15 minutes until frothy. Alternatively, crumble the fresh yeast into the water and sugar and immediately proceed with the recipe.

Add the sourdough starter to the yeast mixture with the first quantity of sifted flour, the sour cream, salt and soda. Mix until well combined, though at this stage the dough will be very wet and rough in texture. Cover the bowl with a large plate or a clean tea towel. Leave in a warm place until the dough has doubled in size – about 1–2 hours.

Sift half the remaining flour into the bowl and stir into the yeast mixture. Mix well until the dough has been reduced to its original size. Sift the rest of the flour on to a work surface and knead the dough in the flour until it has all been absorbed. Continue kneading until the dough has become very smooth and is no longer sticky to the touch. Add more flour if necessary to achieve the right consistency. Divide the dough into two portions and, on a lightly floured surface, gently roll it in the palms on your hands, pushing it back and forward into an elongated shape a little shorter than the length of the baking tin, otherwise as the dough rises it will tip over the edge of the tin. Cover the tins with greased polythene and leave to double in size – about 1–2 hours.

Preheat the oven to 200°C, 400°F, gas mark 6.

Boil some water and put it in a large ovenproof dish which is then placed near the bottom of the oven just before baking commences. Remove the covers from the risen dough, very carefully brush the surface of the dough with a salt and water solution, and gently slash across the top of the loaves with a razor or sharp knife – making about three diagonal slashes, and taking care not to deflate the risen dough.

Bake the loaves in the preheated oven for 35–40 minutes until browned and thoroughly cooked. Cool on a wire rack.

——CORNBREAD——
Serves 6–8

The American Indian is credited with having taught the settlers how to use cornmeal to make different kinds of breads and 'cakes'. To this day, cornbread and cornsticks are still very popular, especially in the southern states. A friend of ours unearthed this delightful version in an old book of community recipes which she discovered in a neglected attic:

Aunt Sally's Cornbread

two aiggs; buttah, big as two persimmons; jes' a little salt; three cups o' cawn meal; none o' you yaller meal, on'y fit foh chickens, but fine white meal made o' flint cawn, like you git in ole Kaintuck; one cup o' white flowah; three heapin' teaspoonfuls o' bakin' powdah.

Beat yo' aiggs up light, melt you' buttah and throw it in along wid de salt. Poah in you' milk – it mus' be fraish and sweet, honey. Now stir in de cawn meal good and hahd, an' las' of all de flowah wid de yeas' powdah mixed in. Poah it into a shaller pan, and pop it inter de oven. Ef you'all's lucky 'nuff to hab a gas stove dis yeah cawn bread'll be done brown in no time. In an' ole wood stove it takes a powahful sight o' bakin'. Ef you don't do it jes laik I tell yo' and on a gas range, deres wher you drops yo' wate-milyon.

It is hard to guess at what exactly Aunt Sally meant by 'there is where you drop your watermelon' – perhaps it's indicating the 'trash can' or the heaviness of the end product. This is our version:

150 g	cornmeal	5 oz
100 g	plain flour	4 oz
2 tsps	baking powder	2 tsps
1/2 tsp	salt	1/2 tsp
2	large eggs	2
240 ml	milk	scant 1/2 pint
2 tbsps	corn oil or melted dripping	2 tbsps

a 22 cm (10 inch) skillet or cake tin, greased

Preheat the oven to 220°C, 425°F, gas mark 7.
Sift the cornmeal, flour, baking powder and salt into a medium bowl. Lightly beat the eggs and milk together. Add the oil or

melted dripping to the dry ingredients with the egg and milk mixture, and mix together until a smooth batter is formed.

Pour into the greased skillet or cake tin and bake in the preheated oven for 20–25 minutes until risen and golden brown. To serve, cut the bread into wedges or slices and serve with butter. Americans also like to eat maple or pancake syrup on their cornbread.

——CORNSTICKS——

Cornsticks are made with cornbread batter as given above, but are baked in special cornstick pans which are shaped and imprinted like miniature corn cobs. Bake as above for 15–20 minutes.

——CORN PONE, HOECAKE AND ASHCAKE——

These are also variations on the cornbread theme, but are formed into flattened cakes. In bygone days the Indians, and subsequently the settlers and pioneers, cooked these cakes over an open fire, and in the case of ashcake, as the name suggests, actually in the ashes of the fire. Hoecake is named after the 'hoe' pan on which they were cooked.

——IRISH SODA BREAD——
Makes 1 loaf

500 g	*plain flour*	1 lb
1 tsp	*salt*	1 tsp
2 tsps	*bicarbonate of soda*	2 tsps
25 g	*butter or lard*	1 oz
240 ml	*buttermilk, soured milk*	scant 1/2 pint
	or plain milk	

a baking tray, greased

Preheat the oven to 200°C, 400°F, gas mark 6.

Sift the flour, salt and soda into a large bowl. Rub in the butter or lard, using the fingertips. Make a well in the centre of the flour and pour in the buttermilk or other milk. Mix into a rough dough, adding a little more liquid if necessary.

Turn the dough out on to a lightly floured surface and knead lightly, but not for long. Shape the dough into a flattish round loaf, about 20 cm (8 inches) in size. Cut a cross over the surface of the dough, and place on the greased baking tray.

Bake in the preheated oven for 35 minutes until the bread is browned and risen. Serve warm with butter.

NOTE: A tea-time loaf may be made by adding 1–2 tablespoons of sugar and 100 g (4 oz) of raisins to the dry ingredients.

——PARKER HOUSE ROLLS——
Makes about 2 dozen

These dinner rolls were named after a well-known Boston inn called the Parker House.

15 g	dried yeast	*4 tsps*
	or	
30 g	fresh yeast	*1 oz*
60 ml	lukewarm water	*3 tbsps*
2 tbsps	sugar	*2 tbsps*
420 ml	milk	scant *3/4 pint*
50 g	butter	*2 oz*
1 kg	plain flour	*2 lbs*
2 tsps	salt	*2 tsps*
1	egg, lightly beaten	*1*
	milk, melted butter or beaten egg to glaze	

baking trays, greased; an 8 cm (3 inch) round cutter

Dissolve the dried yeast in the water with 1 tablespoon of the sugar. Leave in a warm place until frothy – about 10–15 minutes. If using fresh yeast, crumble it into the water, add 1 tablespoon of sugar and stir to dissolve. Put the milk, the rest of the sugar and the butter in a small saucepan and heat to dissolve the butter. Leave until lukewarm.

Sift the flour and salt into a large bowl and make a well in the centre. Add the egg and the yeast mixture to the lukewarm milk and pour into the centre of the flour. Stir until the flour and liquid are combined into a firm dough. Knead the dough on a lightly floured surface until it is smooth and elastic, then cover with greased plastic and leave in a warm place to double in size – about 1–2 hours.

Knock the dough back to its original size, then roll it out on a lightly floured surface until it is 1 cm (½ inch) thick. Using the round cutter, cut out circles of dough. With a sharp knife, cut a slit – but not completely through the dough – off the centre of the rounds from one side to the other. Brush the surface of the dough with milk or beaten egg and fold the smaller section on top of the larger.

Seal the edges together and place the rolls fairly close together on greased baking trays. Brush the tops with milk, melted butter or beaten egg, cover the trays with greased plastic, and leave the rolls to double in size.

Meanwhile preheat the oven to 220°C, 425°F, gas mark 7.

Bake the rolls in the preheated oven for 12–15 minutes until golden brown. Cool on a wire rack.

——BAGELS——
Makes 12–16

Bagels were brought to America by the European Jews and are extremely popular today, particularly in New York City where entire shops and bakeries are devoted to the bagel. These outlets specialize in all varieties of bagels, from those topped with sesame seeds or onion dice to pumpernickel bagels. Traditionally they are served with cream cheese and 'lox' (salted salmon), but nowadays any sandwich filling may be used.

Characteristically the bagel is a chewy, doughnut-shaped roll. Although some people add fat to their dough, we have found that to obtain the right degree of 'chewiness' the fat should be omitted. The bagel is great fun to make, and even more fun to eat!

15 g	*dried yeast*	*4 tsps*
	or	
25 g	*fresh yeast*	*1 oz*
2 tbsps	*sugar*	*2 tbsps*
300–350 ml	*lukewarm water*	*about ½ pint*
1	*egg, lightly beaten*	*1*

350–500 g	plain flour	12 oz–1 lb
1 tsp	salt	1 tsp
4½ litres	water	8 pints
1	egg yolk, lightly beaten	1
1 tsp	water	1 tsp

baking sheets, greased

Dissolve the yeast and 1 tablespoon of the sugar in the lukewarm water and set aside in a warm place until frothy – about 15 minutes. Add the lightly beaten egg. Sift 350 g (12 oz) of the flour with the salt into a large bowl, make a well in the centre, and add the yeast mixture. Combine to form a soft dough, adding more flour as necessary.

Turn the dough out on to a lightly floured surface and knead until smooth and elastic – about 10 minutes. Put in a greased bowl, turning once to grease the top. Cover the bowl (e.g. with greased cling-film) and leave in a warm place to double in size – about 1–2 hours.

Punch the dough down and knead back to its original size. Divide the dough into 12–16 pieces and shape each into a round ball. Using a floured finger, push a hole through the middle of the roll and gently enlarge it until it resembles a doughnut. Put the bagels on the greased baking sheets, cover with greased cling-film or put inside a greased polythene bag, and leave to rise for 15–20 minutes.

Meanwhile, preheat the oven to 190°C, 375°F, gas mark 5.

In a large pan bring the 4½ litres (8 pints) of water to the boil with the remaining tablespoon of sugar. Lower the heat, add 4 bagels at a time and cook for 7 minutes, turning once. (At this stage the bagels will increase considerably in size, so there is no need to leave the rolls to rise for longer than the 15–20 minutes stated earlier.) Drain the bagels from the pan and put them back on the greased sheets. Lightly beat the egg yolk with the teaspoon of water and brush over the tops of the bagels. Bake in the preheated oven for 30–35 minutes until golden brown and hollow when tapped with the knuckles on their bases.

NOTE: For *Seeded Bagels*: After brushing with egg glaze, sprinkle the tops with poppy seeds, sesame seeds or caraway seeds.

For *Salted Bagels*: Sprinkle the glazed rolls with coarse or sea salt.
For *Onion Bagels*: Add 1 tablespoon of instant minced onion to the dry ingredients before the yeast is added. For the topping, soak 1 tablespoon of minced onion in water, squeeze dry and add to the egg glaze before baking.
For *Pumpernickel Bagels*: Use the basic pumpernickel dough (page 178) but omit the butter and proceed as above.
For *Sourdough Bagels*: Use 240 ml (scant ½ pint) of sourdough starter (page 181), 2 eggs, 250–300 g (8–10 oz) of flour, 1 teaspoon of salt and 1 tablespoon of sugar, and proceed as above.

——PRETZELS——
Makes 18–20

There are two kinds of pretzels available in America – the thin, dry cracker-like snacks or the thicker, more bread-like rolls. The latter (given below) are particularly popular in New York City, especially with street vendors – the smell of toasting pretzels and roasted chestnuts is a familiar part of New York street life. Although pretzels are odd-shaped rolls, they are usually eaten as a snack, without butter or any other filling or topping. Pretzels originate in Germany and are an important Jewish food.

2 tsps	*dried yeast*	2 tsps
	or	
15 g	*fresh yeast*	½ oz
240 ml	*lukewarm water*	scant ½ pint
1 tsp	*sugar*	1 tsp
500 g	*plain flour*	1 lb
1 tsp	*salt*	1 tsp
2 litres	*hot water*	3½ pints
6–8 tbsps	*bicarbonate of soda*	6–8 tbsps
1	*egg, to glaze*	1
	coarse or sea salt	

baking sheets or trays, greased

Sprinkle the dried yeast into a small bowl with the lukewarm water and sugar added. Stir to combine, then leave in a warm place until frothy – about 10–15 minutes. If using fresh yeast, cream with water, add the sugar and proceed with the recipe.

Sift the flour and salt, make a well in the centre and add the yeast mixture. Mix until it forms a ball of dough, then knead on a floured surface until smooth – about 10 minutes. Grease a large bowl and put in the dough, turning once to grease the surface. Cover with greased cling-film and leave in a warm place to double in size – about 1–2 hours.

Knock the dough back and knead lightly. To make the pretzels, pull off small balls of dough – about 25 g (1 oz) in weight or the size of a golf ball. Roll out each ball, using the palms of both hands, to form an even-sized rope about 36–40 cm (14–16 inches) long.

Lift the left-hand end into a loop to finish just beyond the centre of the rope. Tuck the end underneath, pressing lightly to seal. Bring the other end over the first loop to a point half-way down the first loop and tuck the end in underneath, pressing lightly to seal. Put the pretzels on a greased baking sheet, cover with greased cling-film or place the sheet inside a large greased plastic bag, and leave to rise for about 20 minutes. (There is no need to leave them much longer than this, as the pretzels rise considerably once put in the hot soda water.)

Preheat the oven to 220°C, 425°F, gas mark 7.

In a large saucepan bring the hot water to the boil. Add the soda – how much you use will determine how strong the distinctive soda taste will be. Using a greased fish slice or spatula, remove 2 or 3 pretzels from the baking sheet and add, one by one, to the soda water. Boil the pretzels for 10 seconds on each side, then drain from the pan and return to the greased baking sheet. Continue until all the pretzels have been partly boiled in the soda water.

Lightly beat the egg with a little water and brush the glaze over the surface of the pretzels. Sprinkle the tops with coarse salt and bake in the preheated oven for 10 minutes until golden brown. Serve while still warm.

——SQUAW BREAD——
Makes 12–14

Many Indian tribes prepared 'breads' like this, for example, the Navajo, Osage, Yavapai. They are more like deep-fried scones than bread and are very easily prepared, making good emergency stand-ins when the bread cupboard is suddenly bare. In fact, they are tastier than one might imagine.

100 g	plain flour	4 oz
1/2 tsp	salt	1/2 tsp
1 tsp	baking powder	1 tsp
1 tbsp	melted lard or fat	1 tbsp
3 tbsps	water	3 tbsps
	oil or fat for deep-frying	

a large skillet or heavy frying pan; a 5–8 cm (2–3 inch) round cutter

Sift the flour, salt and baking powder into a medium bowl. Add the melted lard or fat and water and mix into a soft dough. Roll out on a lightly floured surface and cut into rounds with the cutter.

Heat the oil or fat in the skillet or frying pan and deep-fry the 'breads' for 1–2 minutes on each side until lightly browned, turning once. Drain on absorbent kitchen paper and serve warm with mutton stew, as do the Pueblo Indians of the south-west, or with ham or cheese. They may also be served with jams, jellies, honey or golden syrup.

NOTE: You can also make these breads with small pieces of yeast bread dough – for example, if you are baking a batch of bread and can spare some of the dough.

In some recipes, ground seeds such as sunflower seeds can be added for extra flavour.

——HUSH PUPPIES——
Makes about 20–25

This favourite southern states recipe originated with hunting parties where the fishermen fried their batter-coated catches of catfish, trout, etc. over an open fire. The smell of the frying fish so tantalized the hunters' dogs that they had to be pacified somehow. These puffed cakes made from the batter which coated the hunters' fish were cooked in the same pan as the fish and then thrown to the dogs with the words 'Hush, puppies'.

For our taste the hush puppy needs extra ingredients to improve its flavour, for example, more onion, diced green pepper, grated cheese, etc. The authentic recipe uses cornmeal alone, but to suit our palates the modern adaptation of mixing plain flour and cornmeal is more palatable.

100 g	*cornmeal*	*4 oz*
100 g	*plain flour*	*4 oz*
2 tsps	*baking powder*	*2 tsps*
½ heaped tsp	*salt*	*½ heaped tsp*
1	*egg, lightly beaten*	*1*
180 ml	*milk or buttermilk (or milk with 1 tsp lemon juice added)*	*generous ¼ pint*
1	*small onion, peeled and diced*	*1*
	cayenne pepper or a few drops of tabasco sauce to taste	
	fat for deep-frying, preferably used previously to fry fish	

a deep-fat frying pan

Sift the cornmeal, flour, baking powder and salt into a bowl. Mix the egg with the milk or buttermilk and add to the dry ingredients to make a smooth batter. Finally, fold in the diced onion and season to taste with cayenne or tabasco.

Heat the fat in the frying pan until hot and drop the batter by tablespoons into the fat. When crisp, golden and puffed – about 1–2 minutes – turn to brown the other side. Lift from the pan with a slotted or perforated spoon and serve hot with fried fish.

——POPOVERS——
Makes about 12

The only difference between the ingredients of popovers and those of the traditional English Yorkshire pudding is the addition of a small amount of fat, i.e. oil or melted butter. Yet many Americans are surprised to discover that the two recipes are almost identical. In America, popovers are frequently eaten at breakfast with butter, although they are also served like Yorkshire pudding with roast beef.

Webster's American dictionary defines the popover as a kind of muffin, and muffins to Americans mean something eaten at breakfast.

100 g	*plain flour*	4 oz
1/4 tsp	*salt*	1/4 tsp
240 ml	*milk*	scant 1/2 pint
2	*medium eggs*	2
1 tbsp	*corn oil or melted butter*	1 tbsp
	or margarine	
	extra oil	

a deep cup-cake baking tray or muffin tray

Preheat the oven to 190°C, 375°F, gas mark 5.

Sift the flour and salt into a bowl. In a jug, measure the milk, add the eggs and oil and beat lightly to combine. Gradually add this liquid to the flour and beat until smooth.

Heat the baking tray or muffin tray in the preheated oven, then brush the base and sides of the cups with oil and pour the batter into the cups until nearly full. Bake in the preheated oven for 35–40 minutes until the popovers are puffed and browned.

NOTE: For *Cheese Popovers* add 25 g (1 oz) of grated cheese to the batter before cooking.

——POTATO PANCAKES – LATKES——
Makes approximately 1 dozen

These pancakes came to America with the German and Jewish immigrants. They are the traditional fare served on Chanukkah, the Jewish 'Festival of Lights', and the usual accompaniment to sauerbraten (page 80).

4	*medium potatoes, peeled*	4
1	*medium onion, peeled*	1
2	*eggs, beaten*	2
1 tsp	*salt*	1 tsp
1/4 tsp	*freshly ground pepper*	1/4 tsp
3 tbsps	*plain flour or matzo meal*	3 tbsps
	pinch baking powder	
120 ml	*oil*	scant 1/4 pint

a skillet or frying pan

Grate the potatoes and onion into a bowl. Add the eggs, salt and pepper. Combine the flour and baking powder and lightly stir into the potato mixture.

Heat 2 tablespoons of oil in a skillet or frying pan and drop the potato mixture in by the tablespoon. Cook over a medium heat until brown and crisp, turning once. Repeat, using more oil, until all the mixture is used.

These pancakes may be served with meats (for example, sauerbraten) or with 'apple sauce' – apple purée – and sour cream as they are for Chanukkah.

——BUTTERMILK BISCUITS (SCONES)——
Makes 9–10

Biscuits, or what we know in Britain as scones, are especially popular in the southern states. Unlike the British scone, American biscuits are invariably served for breakfast and not with butter and jam as an afternoon tea treat. Out of curiosity I once ordered a breakfast of buttermilk biscuits with a white sauce made with ham or bacon, and hashed browns (page 130). Unfortunately, like the cat, it nearly killed me! It was not a meal for those of faint appetite.

If you are a fan of British scones, you will love the flavour of these biscuits.

300 g	*plain flour*	*10 oz*
1/2 tsp	*salt*	*1/2 tsp*
1/2 tsp	*bicarbonate of soda*	*1/2 tsp*
1/2 tsp	*cream of tartar*	*1/2 tsp*
1 tbsp	*sugar*	*1 tbsp*
50 g	*butter or margarine*	*2 oz*
240 ml	*buttermilk (or milk with 1 tbsp lemon juice added)*	*scant 1/2 pint*
	milk or beaten egg to glaze	

baking trays, greased; an 8 cm (3 inch) plain round cutter

Preheat the oven to 220°C, 425°F, gas mark 7.

Sift the flour, salt, bicarbonate of soda and cream of tartar into a large bowl. Add the sugar. Rub in the butter or margarine, using the fingertips, until it is absorbed. Stir in the buttermilk to make a rough dough. *Do not overmix* or you will spoil the biscuit's texture. Pat the dough down on a lightly floured surface, or gently roll out to 2 cm (¾ inch) thickness. Using the cutter, cut 9–10 rounds and place them on the greased baking trays. Brush the surface with milk or beaten egg. Bake on the top shelf of the preheated oven for 10–12 minutes until risen and browned. Serve while still warm.

——PANNETONE——
Serves 6–8

This is the traditional Italian Christmas bread which originated in Milan and is now popular in many parts of the USA and South America – in Argentina it is often served with glasses of champagne.

2 tsps	*dried yeast*	2 tsps
	or	
15 g	*fresh yeast*	½ oz
120 ml	*lukewarm water*	scant ¼ pint
50 g	*sugar*	2 oz
350 g	*plain flour*	12 oz
6	*egg yolks, lightly beaten*	6
2 tsps	*vanilla essence*	2 tsps
½ tsp	*salt*	½ tsp
1	*lemon, grated rind only*	1
100 g	*butter, melted*	4 oz
40 g	*currants*	1½ oz
50 g	*raisins*	2 oz
100 g	*sultanas*	4 oz
40 g	*mixed peel*	1½ oz
	extra melted butter	

a 20 cm (8 inch) round cake tin or ring mould, greased

Sprinkle the yeast over the lukewarm water with 1 teaspoon of the sugar added. Stir to dissolve the yeast, then leave in a warm place until frothy – about 15 minutes.

Sift all but 50 g (2 oz) of the flour into a large bowl, make a well in the centre and add the yeast mixture, the rest of the sugar, the egg yolks, vanilla, salt, lemon rind and warm melted butter. Mix into a dough, then turn out on to a floured surface and knead until smooth and satiny, adding the remaining flour as necessary until the dough is no longer sticky. Put in a greased bowl, turn once to grease the surface, and cover with greased plastic. Leave in a warm place until double in size – about 1–2 hours.

Punch down the dough and knead lightly, then work in the fruits and mixed peel. Put the pannetone in the greased cake tin or mould, cover again, and leave to rise for 1 hour.

Preheat the oven to 180°C, 350°F, gas mark 4.

Brush the top of the bread with melted butter, and bake for 35–40 minutes until the pannetone is a rich dark golden brown. Characteristically this bread should have a crisp crust, which is achieved by frequent brushing with melted butter during the cooking time.

——APPLE SAUCE BREAD——
Makes 1

175 g	*plain flour*	*6 oz*
1 1/2 tsps	*baking powder*	*1 1/2 tsps*
1 tsp	*salt*	*1 tsp*
1 tsp	*ground cinnamon*	*1 tsp*
50 g	*quick or old-fashioned porridge oats, uncooked*	*2 oz*
250 g	*sugar*	*8 oz*
250 g	*apple sauce or apple purée*	*8 oz*
1	*egg, lightly beaten*	*1*
75 g	*raisins*	*3 oz*
50 g	*walnuts, pecans, or mixed nuts, chopped*	*2 oz*
90 ml	*vegetable oil or melted fat*	*5 tbsps*

a 20 × 10 × 5 cm (8 × 4 × 2 inch) loaf pan, greased and lightly floured

Preheat the oven to 180°C, 350°F, gas mark 4.

Sift together the flour, baking powder, salt and cinnamon. Mix in the oats, sugar, apple sauce, egg, raisins, nuts and vegetable oil, stirring until well combined.

Pour the batter into the greased and floured loaf pan and bake in the preheated oven for 55–60 minutes. Serve as a tea-bread with butter, jam or honey, or as a cake.

NOTE: Tinned apple sauce may be used.

——BANANA BREAD——
Makes 1 × 500 g (1 lb) loaf

250 g	plain flour	8 oz
2 tsps	baking powder	2 tsps
1/4 tsp	salt	1/4 tsp
50 g	lard and margarine mixed together	2 oz
100 g	sugar	4 oz
2	eggs	2
3	medium bananas, mashed	3

a 500 g (1 lb) loaf tin, greased

Preheat the oven to 180°C, 350°F, gas mark 4.

Sift the flour, baking powder and salt together. In a bowl, cream the fat and sugar until soft. Add the eggs one at a time and beat until the mixture is smooth. Gradually stir in the sifted dry ingredients and finally blend in the mashed bananas.

Spoon the batter into the greased loaf tin and bake in the preheated oven for 1 hour. Test for readiness by inserting a skewer into the centre and if it comes out clean, the loaf is fully cooked. Turn out on to a wire rack to cool.

NOTE: This bread is delicious served warm with butter as a tea-time treat. It may also be toasted.

——PRUNE BREAD——
Makes 1 × 500 g (1 lb) loaf

250 g	cooked and pitted prunes, chopped	8 oz
120 ml	prune juice	scant 1/4 pint
2	eggs, lightly beaten	2

50 g	butter, melted	2 oz
175 g	plain flour	6 oz
50 g	brown (wholewheat) flour	2 oz
2 tsps	baking powder	2 tsps
	large pinch salt	
100 g	soft brown sugar	4 oz

a 500 g (1 lb) loaf tin, greased

Preheat the oven to 190°C, 375°F, gas mark 5.

Prepare the prunes, reserving 120 ml (scant ¼ pint) of juice. Beat the eggs and prune juice with the melted butter. Sift the flours, baking powder and salt. Stir in the sugar.

Gradually add the flour mixture to the egg mixture to make a smooth batter. Stir in the chopped prunes. Spoon into the prepared loaf tin, smoothing over the top. Bake in the preheated oven for about 50 minutes, until a skewer inserted in the centre comes out clean. Serve with butter and jams. When not so fresh, toast slices of the bread and serve hot.

——ZUCCHINI OR COURGETTES BREAD——

Makes 1 large or 2 small loaves

3–4	zucchini or courgettes, washed and grated or puréed	3–4
3	eggs	3
240 ml	cooking oil	scant ½ pint
500 g	sugar	1 lb
350 g	plain flour, sifted	12 oz
½ tsp	baking powder	½ tsp
1 tsp	bicarbonate of soda	1 tsp
1 tsp	salt	1 tsp
3 tsps	ground cinnamon	3 tsps
1 tsp	grated nutmeg	1 tsp
50 g	nuts, chopped	2 oz
1 tsp	grated lemon peel	1 tsp

1 large or 2 small loaf tins, greased

Preheat the oven to 160°C, 325°F, gas mark 3.

Combine the grated or puréed zucchini (peel and all) with the eggs, oil and sugar in a large bowl. Sift together the flour, baking powder, soda, salt and spices, and beat into the egg mixture until well combined. Finally, fold in the nuts and lemon peel. Pour the batter into the greased tin or tins and bake in the preheated oven for 1 hour. Allow to cool for 5 minutes then turn out on to a cooling rack.

NOTE: This is a very moist loaf. If a less moist loaf is preferred, grate the zucchini (*do not* purée), sprinkle with salt and leave for at least 20 minutes to extract some of the moisture. Rinse and gently pat dry with absorbent paper.

——RAISED DOUGHNUTS——
Makes 9–10

The Dutch are believed to be the first people to introduce their 'olykoeks' (oily cakes) to America. They are also popular with the Pennsylvania Dutch, who call them 'fastnachts' as they are traditionally served on Fastnacht Day (Shrove Tuesday) – the last day of feasting before Lent. Since their introduction, doughnuts have become almost an American national obsession, even eaten at breakfast.

2 tsps	*dried yeast*	2 tsps
	or	
15 g	*fresh yeast*	1/2 oz
2 tbsps	*lukewarm water*	2 tbsps
1/2 tsp	*sugar*	1/2 tsp
120 ml	*milk*	scant 1/4 pint
500 g	*plain flour*	1 lb
	large pinch salt	
1/4 tsp	*grated nutmeg*	1/4 tsp
75 g	*sugar*	3 oz
1	*egg, lightly beaten*	1
25 g	*butter, melted*	1 oz
	fat for deep-frying	

———To coat———

water icing (see below) or
icing sugar

a deep-fat frying pan; a doughnut cutter or two plain round
cutters, 8 cm and 1 cm each (3 inches and ½–1 inch)

Dissolve the yeast in the lukewarm water with the ½ tsp of sugar
and leave in a warm place until frothy – about 10–15 minutes.
Scald the milk and leave to cool to lukewarm. Sift the flour, salt
and nutmeg into a large bowl, mix in the 75 g (3 oz) of sugar, and
make a well in the centre.

Mix together the milk, egg and melted butter with the yeast
mixture. Add the liquid to the flour and mix until a ball of dough
forms. Turn out on to a floured surface and knead until smooth –
about 10 minutes. Grease a large bowl, put in the dough and turn
once to grease the surface. Cover the bowl (e.g. with greased
cling-film or plastic) and leave in a warm place to double in size
(prove) – about 1–2 hours.

Knock back the dough and knead lightly. Press the dough out
flat and roll until it is 1 cm/½ inch thick. As the yeast dough is very
elastic, this is less difficult to do if the surface is only very lightly
floured, if at all.

Cut out the doughnuts and lay on greased greaseproof paper
on baking trays. Cover the trays and leave to rise in a warm place
for about 1 hour. (The centres may make miniature doughnuts, or
can be re-rolled with the rest of the trimmings.)

When risen, heat the fat in the frying pan until hot but not
smoking and deep-fry the doughnuts until golden brown on both
sides. If this is done at too high a temperature, the doughnuts will
brown very quickly but the dough inside will still be uncooked. It
should take at least 1 minute for each side to become golden
brown. Drain on absorbent paper. Coat with water icing when
cold, or sprinkle with sifted icing sugar while still warm.

———WATER ICING———

Sift 250 g (8 oz) of icing sugar into a bowl. Add 2–3 tablespoons of
cold water or fruit juice (e.g. lemon or orange). Mix until smooth
enough to spread.

For *Chocolate Water Icing*, add 50 g (2 oz) of melted chocolate to the above icing.

──────DANISH PASTRIES──────
Makes 2 dozen

These beautiful pastries have been enthusiastically adopted from the Danes by Americans, and 'Danish and coffee' has become a common breakfast special, so much so that even fast-food outlets offer a variety of these pastries on their menus.

──────For the basic dough──────

120 ml	lukewarm water	scant ¼ pint
100 g	caster sugar	4 oz
15 g	dried yeast	4 tsps
	or	
25 g	fresh yeast	1 oz
600–750 g	plain flour	1¼–1½ lb
120 ml	milk	scant ¼ pint
500 g + 1 tbsp	unsalted butter	1 lb + 1 tbsp
2	eggs, beaten	2
1 tsp	salt	1 tsp
¼ tsp	ground cardamom (optional)	¼ tsp
1½ tsps	vanilla essence	1½ tsps

──────A selection of fillings and toppings──────

Choose two or more, each one of which is sufficient for 1 dozen pastries.

──────Almond paste──────

75 g	almonds, finely ground	3 oz
100 g	caster sugar	4 oz
1	egg white, beaten	1

──────Glacé icing──────

1	egg white	1
175 g	icing sugar	6 oz
	pinch of salt	

1 tsp	*lemon juice*	1 tsp
	———*Apricot jam*———	
125 g	*apricot jam*	5 oz
	———*Spiced butter*———	
25 g	*butter*	1 oz
25 g	*caster sugar*	1 oz
1 tsp	*ground cinnamon*	1 tsp
	———*Frangipane filling*———	
40 g	*butter*	1½ oz
6 tbsps	*almond paste (see page 202)*	6 tbsps
1 tsp	*flour*	1 tsp
2 tsps	*chopped almonds*	2 tsps
	———*Extras*———	
1	*egg, beaten*	1
3 tbsps	*currants*	3 tbsps
3 tbsps	*mixed peel*	3 tbsps

baking sheets or trays, greased

Mix the lukewarm water and 1 teaspoon of the sugar in a bowl and sprinkle over the yeast. Stir briefly and leave in a warm place until frothy – about 15 minutes.

Sift 500 g (1 lb) of the flour into a large bowl, stir in the remaining sugar and make a well in the centre. Add the yeast mixture, the milk, 1 tablespoon of softened butter, the eggs, salt, cardamom and vanilla. Mix together until a dough forms. Turn out on to a floured surface and knead thoroughly for 10 minutes until the dough is smooth and satiny. Sprinkle the dough with more of the flour, cover with aluminium foil and refrigerate for at least 30 minutes.

Meanwhile, remove the 500 g (1 lb) of butter from the refrigerator. The butter must be cold but not too hard, as it has to be rolled flat between sheets of floured greaseproof or waxed paper. Roll the butter out to a rectangle, 20 × 30 × ½ cm (8 × 12 × ¼ inches) in size. Cut the rectangle in half. If the butter becomes too soft to roll, return it to the refrigerator for a few minutes longer.

Sprinkle the work surface well with more of the flour and roll the chilled dough out to a rectangle, 23 × 46 × ¼ cm (9 × 18 ×

⅛th inches) in size. Put one rectangle of butter on the centre of the dough, fold one flap over it, sealing the edges, then place the second half of the butter on top and fold over the remaining flap of dough, again sealing in the butter. Dust with flour, wrap in aluminium foil, and refrigerate for 20 minutes. Roll out the dough on a floured surface to a rectangle 20 × 46 (8 × 18 inches) in size. Fold both the narrow ends towards the centre, then fold in half, making four layers. Wrap in foil again and chill for a further 20 minutes.

Repeat this procedure twice more, chilling the dough each time. Do not roll too vigorously or too thinly or the butter will break through the surface. If this happens, dust the break with flour. Chill the dough finally for at least 4 hours before using; preferably chill overnight.

───── To prepare the fillings ─────

Almond Paste: Mix together the ground almonds and sugar and add sufficient egg white to make a thick paste.
Glacé Icing: Beat the egg white until frothy and gradually add the sugar, then finally add the salt and lemon juice. Continue beating until the mixture is light and fluffy and forms soft peaks.
Apricot Jam: Press the apricot jam through a sieve, then put in a small pan and cook over a low heat, stirring constantly, until it has reduced slightly.
Spiced Butter: Soften the butter and work in the sugar and cinnamon.
Frangipane Filling: Cream the butter until light and fluffy. Beat in the almond paste a little at a time, then add the flour and stir in the chopped almonds.

───── To assemble the pastries ─────

There are several different shapes of Danish pastries – envelopes, crescents, pinwheels, cocks' combs, etc.

───── *Envelopes* ─────

Roll out half the dough into a rectangle 20 × 50 cm (8 × 20 inches), trim the edges, then cut into squares 10 × 10 cm (4 × 4 inches). Fold each corner in to meet in the centre and press down to seal the points.

Place half a tablespoon of apricot jam in the centre, brush the pastry with beaten egg and sprinkle with caster sugar. Leave on a greased baking sheet or tray to rise for 20 minutes.

Meanwhile, preheat the oven to 200°C, 400°F, gas mark 6. Bake the pastries in the preheated oven for 10 minutes, then reduce the heat to 180°C, 350°F, gas mark 4 and cook for a further 15 minutes until the pastries are a light golden colour. Cool on a wire rack.

——Crescents——

Roll out half the dough into a square 25 × 25 cm (10 × 10 inches) and cut into 4 equal squares. Cut each square diagonally into 2 triangles and place a teaspoon of almond paste at the base of each triangle. Roll up from the base and shape into a crescent. Put them on the greased sheets or trays and leave to rise for 20 minutes. Bake as for envelopes, above.

While still hot, coat the surface with glacé icing.

——Fruit pinwheels——

Roll out half the dough into an oblong 20 × 30 cm (8 × 12 inches). Spread with spiced butter and scatter over currants and mixed peel. Cut the oblong in half lengthwise and roll up each piece from the narrow end to form a thick roll. Cut into 3 cm (1 inch) slices and place cut side down on the greased baking sheets or trays. Leave to rise for 20 minutes, then bake as for envelopes, above.

——Cocks' combs——

Roll out one quarter of the dough into a rectangle 25 × 40 cm (10 × 15 inches) and trim the edges. Spread a thin layer of frangipane lengthwise over half of the dough. Fold the other half over and seal the edges. Cut into strips 5 cm (2½ inches) wide. Make three equidistant cuts three-quarters of the way into each strip and bend the strips slightly into crescent shapes. Put on the greased sheets or trays, brush with egg and sprinkle with caster sugar. Leave to rise for 20 minutes and bake as for envelopes, above.

FINGER FOOD

——HAMBURGERS——

The hamburger took its name not from its meat content but from the German city of Hamburg. The Germans, who brought the minced meat filling with them to America, are believed to have taken the idea from the Russians who in turn adopted it from the Tartars. This nomadic tribe are believed to have begun the custom of eating small pieces of meat scraped away from the bone, but the Tartars ate their meat raw – hence the name of the modern-day speciality, Steak Tartare (or *à la tartare*).

However, it was an American who first devised the idea of serving a hamburger inside a bun, thus establishing the American claim to the invention of the hamburger as we know it today.

The first hamburger is believed to have been eaten at the St Louis World's Fair in 1904, and once launched it was not long before the first major hamburger chain opened for business in 1921. Half a century later a proliferation of hamburger outlets had sprung up all over America and spread abroad into Europe and Australia. No American town is complete without a fast-food eatery serving hamburgers, French fries (chips) and milk shakes, the best known of which are MacDonalds, Burger King and Wendys. MacDonalds, the biggest of these chains, has, by the mid 1980s, over 6,800 franchised premises in all fifty American states, including Hawaii and Alaska, as well as a further 1,800 in thirty-nine countries worldwide. One of the best-known British chains is Wimpy, named after the cartoon character who appears with Pop-Eye the Sailorman and who consumes as many hamburgers as Pop-Eye does tins of spinach!

A Salisbury steak (named after nutritionist Dr J. H. Salisbury) is a hamburger without a bun and re-shaped like a steak.

To make a genuine American hamburger: Use only top quality minced beef – hamburger meat on sale in American supermarkets is usually minced chuck, sirloin or top round beef (we would use rump or 'best' mince), and as a result of using such good quality meat, Americans as a rule find it unnecessary to add anything more to the meat mixture.

To prepare, shape the beef into round patties, weighing from 100 g (4 oz) to 250 g (8 oz) each. Heat a skillet or heavy frying pan, sprinkle with salt (there is no need to use oil or fat – the salt stops the hamburger from sticking to the pan *and* seasons the meat at the same time), and cook over a fairly high heat to darkly brown the beef, turning once. If a medium or well-done burger is preferred, turn the heat down and allow the burger to cook more slowly.

Meanwhile, toast one large round hamburger roll or bun for each meat patty and serve the cooked hamburger inside the toasted roll, with optional extras to top it such as sliced onion or dill pickles (page 277), relishes, mustards or ketchup.

———Variations———

Cheeseburger: Once the hamburger is almost completely cooked, put it inside the roll and top with slices of cheese (processed cheese is a popular (though insipid) American preference – I prefer Cheddar cheese). Pop the cheeseburger under a hot grill to melt the cheese.

Pizzaburger: Top the prepared hamburger with a tablespoon of pizza tomato sauce and a slice of mozzarella cheese. Toast under a hot grill to melt the cheese.

Chiliburger: Before mixing the meat mixture, add 1 finely chopped clove of garlic and 1–2 teaspoons of chili powder, then proceed as for ordinary hamburgers. Alternatively, serve the burgers with a chili sauce.

NOTE: For added flavour, a little Worcestershire sauce may be added to the minced beef. For economy, fresh breadcrumbs may be added in the proportions of 25–50 g (1–2 oz) of breadcrumbs to 350 g (12 oz) of meat.

——HOT DOGS——

This uniquely American snack, which is well known worldwide, has an interesting background. It is believed that the frankfurter – a long, smoked and spiced sausage made of beef – was first produced in Frankfurt, Germany, in the mid 1800s. A little later, an American of German extraction called Charles Feltman hit upon the idea of putting a hot frankfurter inside a Wiener (or Vienna) roll. Thus the hot dog began at New York's Coney Island, which is still regarded as 'the spiritual home of the hot dog'.

But it wasn't until 1906 that the snack received its unusual name. *New York Journal* sports cartoonist 'Tad' Dorgan, who had bought a 'red hot' at a ballpark, immortalized the sausage-in-a-roll when he pictured the frankfurter as a dachshund inside an elongated roll and titled it 'Hot Dog'.

During the First World War, America's only hot dog chain began business selling hot dogs for a nickel (5 cents). 'Nathan's Famous' now has dozens of outlets in the USA, and once even served their famous hot dogs to King George VI and Queen Elizabeth when they visited US President Franklin D. Roosevelt.

Hot dogs are also known in America as 'weenies', derived from the Wiener rolls used to encase the frankfurter.

Frankfurters may be prepared in four different ways: they can be grilled, barbecued, boiled or fried. As the meat is already cooked, the sausage requires only to be heated through. The long finger roll characteristically used is normally not toasted. Serve hot with sauerkraut (page 276), mustard, or green relish (hot dog relish, page 280) – the latter, though, is scorned by real aficionados.

——BARBECUES——

The barbecue is a universally popular outdoor activity; national parks in America are invariably well equipped with fireplace areas and the customary red cedar-wood tables with benches attached. The origin of the word 'barbecue', according to *Webster's New World Dictionary of the American Language*, is from the Spanish word *barbacoa*, meaning the framework of sticks, like a modern grill, over which meat was cooked. Another imaginative explanation of its origin suggests that the word derives from the French expression *barbe à queue* (beard to tail), referring to the original method of cooking the entire animal from its head to its tail.

This was usually accomplished by digging a deep pit, partially filling it with hot coals, topping with sand, leaves or other material, and then laying over the wrapped carcass. Once covered completely, the meat was able to roast gently in its own juices for the best part of the day until it was ready for eating.

A similar method is still employed in Hawaii for their popular festival, now a top tourist attraction, the *luau*, where whole pigs are covered in banana leaves and roasted in pits with bananas and yams to accompany the meat. In Mexico this method of barbecuing whole lambs is still popular, the meat being wrapped in agave leaves.

However, to most Americans a barbecue is usually a less time-consuming, less ambitious affair, which is usually achieved by the use of modern barbecue grills and charcoal brickettes. Many barbecue aficionados like to impart the special flavour of hickory wood to improve the taste of their steaks, barbecued spare ribs (page 92) hamburgers (page 207) and hot dogs (page 208).

——SPICY BARBECUE SAUCE——
Sufficient for 1 1/2 kg (3 lb) chicken or ribs

1	small onion, peeled	1
1	small green pepper (or half a large one), de-seeded	1
2–3	cloves garlic, peeled	2–3
25 g	butter or oil	1 oz
1	lemon, juice only, to yield about 3 tbsps	1
3 tbsps	chili sauce	3 tbsps
120 ml	tomato ketchup	scant 1/4 pint
1 tbsp	tomato paste	1 tbsp
120 ml	water	scant 1/4 pint
1 tsp	made mustard	1 tsp
3 tbsps	Worcestershire sauce	3 tbsps

Mince together or finely chop the onion, green pepper and garlic. Heat the butter in a medium pan and sauté the vegetables for about 3 minutes. Add the remaining ingredients, bring to the boil, then cover the pan and simmer gently for about 10 minutes, by which time the sauce will have thickened.

Use to marinate and baste chicken, ribs, steaks or hamburgers.

NOTE: 1–2 tablespoons of chili powder may be substituted for the chili sauce. Fry the powder for 1–2 minutes after the vegetables have been sautéed for 2 minutes. Add extra liquid, for example 3 tablespoons of water or stock with the rest of the ingredients.

Water or stock may also be substituted for the Worcestershire sauce if a less spicy sauce is preferred.

——PIZZA——
Makes 2 large pizzas

Pizzas have become so popular that they rival the hamburger and hot dog as the favourite snack in the USA. The now traditional pizza is a giant 46 cm (18 inch) pie which divides into 8 triangular-shaped slices – one of which is sufficient for a light lunch. The American pizza has a thickish rim of dough around the outside and a topping which is usually no more than puréed tomatoes, a sprinkling of herbs and grated mozzarella cheese. For added flavour a tomato sauce stewed with onions may be used in place of the puréed tomatoes. Cheddar cheese may be substituted for the expensive, less easily available mozzarella, as may cheeses like Bel Paese. Deep pan pizzas – popular in places like Chicago – have a thicker bread-like crust and are usually served straight from the pan.

240 ml	lukewarm water	scant 1/2 pint
1/2 tsp	sugar	1/2 tsp
2 tsps	dried yeast	2 tsps
	or	
15 g	fresh yeast	1/2 oz
600 g	plain flour	1 1/4 lb
1/2 tsp	salt	1/2 tsp
2 tbsps	oil, e.g. olive or cooking	2 tbsps

794 g	*tin tomatoes*	28 oz
1/2 tsp	*dried oregano*	1/2 tsp
1/2 tsp	*salt*	1/2 tsp
	freshly ground pepper	
250 g	*mozzarella cheese, grated*	8 oz

2 × 30 cm (12 inch) round baking trays or pizza pans
(*Note*: Smaller round trays may be used, making more pizzas)

Mix together the water and sugar in a small bowl or jug and sprinkle over the yeast. Stir until dissolved and leave in a warm place until frothy – about 15 minutes.

Sift together the flour and salt. Make a well in the centre and add the yeast mixture and the oil. Stir until a soft dough forms, then knead on a floured surface for about 10 minutes until it is smooth and elastic. Put the dough in a greased bowl, turn once to grease the top, cover with greased polythene or cling-film and leave to double in size – about 1–2 hours.

Knock back the dough to its original size. Experts in pizza-making in America press the dough into a round then toss it around on their two fists until it expands to the correct size and characteristic shape. The rest of us have to wrestle with rolling out an elastic dough, which is more easily achieved if the surface is hardly floured, if at all.

Divide the dough into two (or more if smaller pizzas are being made). Roll into flattish rounds large enough to fit the baking trays, leaving a slight crust around the outside edge of the dough. Press the dough into the pan.

Purée the tomatoes in a blender or press through a sieve. Spoon the mixture evenly over the pizzas, covering the surface of the dough to within 3 cm (1 inch) of the edge. Sprinkle the tomatoes with oregano, salt and pepper to taste, and cover the sauce with the grated mozzarella cheese. Leave the pizzas to rise for about 20 minutes.

Meanwhile preheat the oven to 200°C, 400°F, gas mark 6, before baking the pizzas for 20 minutes until the dough is browned and the top bubbly.

——SANDWICHES——

The idea of putting a filling between two slices of bread was first conceived by an Englishman, John Montague, the fourth Earl of Sandwich, who gave the snack its name. As with many other foreign inventions, Americans whole-heartedly adopted the sandwich and expanded the idea way beyond its beginnings.

All kinds of fillings – hot, cold, sweet, and savoury – are used to fill many different kinds of breads and rolls, pitta bread ('sandwich pockets'), bagels and thick, crusty Italian bread loaves. The latter are known as heroes, submarines, grinders or po' boys (page 213). Hamburgers (page 206) and hot dogs (page 208) are other examples of the American development of the original sandwich idea, as are club (below), Reuben and western sandwiches (page 213).

American sandwiches are seldom served without the usual garnishes of lettuce, tomatoes, a helping of coleslaw (page 141) and a long, thick slice of dill pickle (page 277) – thus making it virtually impossible to get a light snack when eating out.

Sandwich menus can be a baffling, lengthy list of all the various combinations, some of the more popular ones being pastrami, corned beef, meat loaf, bologna (pronounced 'baloney'), ham, tuna and egg salads, cream cheese (sometimes with grape jelly), other cheeses, and even peanut butter – the latter is undoubtedly the all-time favourite sandwich filling in school lunch boxes throughout the USA, especially when combined with grape jelly!

——CLUB SANDWICH——

American food expert James Beard insists that the triple-decker sandwich so often passed off as a club sandwich is not authentic, as in his opinion the genuine article is made with only two pieces of buttered toast.

Whether two or three pieces of toast are used, it is generally agreed that the filling for a club sandwich must be made with slices of cooked chicken breast, lettuce leaves, mayonnaise, crisply grilled bacon slices, peeled and sliced tomato and a sprinkling of salt.

——REUBEN SANDWICH——

This sandwich is accredited by some to a Nebraskan grocer called Reuben Kay. His concoction was such a success that it won the National Sandwich Idea Contest one year and has been an American favourite ever since. Miniature Reubens or 'Reuben Juniors' are often served as cocktail snacks, as they can be prepared well ahead of schedule and toasted at the last minute.

A Reuben consists of two or three layers of rye bread or pumpernickel bread (page 178), filled with slices of corned beef, slices of Swiss cheese and a layer of sauerkraut (page 276), and dressed with either Thousand Islands (page 150) or Russian dressing or mustard.

——WESTERN (OR DENVER) SANDWICH——

This is made with a filling of an egg omelette, flavoured with bacon or ham, chopped onion and chopped green pepper and seasoned to taste. The omelette is served inside a bread or bun sandwich, either plain or toasted.

HEROES, SUBMARINES, GRINDERS AND ——PO' BOYS——

In our experience, these are entirely American developments of the sandwich. It doesn't take much imagination to understand how they got their quaint names. Only heroes with hearty appetites should take on a hero! We are inclined to believe that submarines are so called because of the shape of the loaves. And grinders? Well, without a strong set of teeth the chewing of one would be impossible. Po' boys are the southern states version of a hero, and, as the name suggests, were originally a cheap luncheon speciality, eaten by rich and poor alike. Six-foot long heroes can be ordered in New York City for parties.

To make a hero (submarine, grinder or po' boy), fresh, crusty Italian bread should be used (this is a shorter, fatter version of French bread). Small Italian loaves are produced in America especially for making into heroes – one loaf is used for each hero. Normal size Italian bread loaves should be cut into 2–3 pieces (or

3–4 for French bread) and lightly buttered if desired, though Americans do not as a rule butter their sandwiches.

Never use ordinary, soft, sliced bread, as this just would not make a hero or anything remotely resembling it.

To make a *cold hero*, fill the prepared loaves with sliced pastrami, salami, bologna, ham, meat loaf (page 88), cold turkey or chicken, even tuna fish. Top the sliced meat with slices of cheese, preferably Italian or Swiss cheese, then cover with layers of salad ingredients, choosing any from the following:

lettuce	chopped celery
sliced onions	green pepper rings
tomatoes	sliced pickles, e.g. dill
hard-boiled eggs	pickles (page 277)

Top with mayonnaise or other favoured salad dressing.

To make a *hot hero*, prepare the bread as above and fill with one of the following:

hot Italian meatballs and tomato sauce (page 154)
hot sausages and peppers with their sauce (page 97)
eggplant parmigiana (page 132)
veal cutlet parmigiana (a grilled cutlet with parmigiana sauce)
hot meat loaf and tomato sauce (page 88)

The most famous po' boy down south is known as 'La Médiatrice' or the mediator. It is traditionally filled with sautéed and seasoned oysters, and gained its nickname from the way that many a wayward husband would offer his angry wife 'La Médiatrice' to placate her after a late night on the town!

DIPS

——GUACAMOLE——

The Maya Indians of Mexico's Yucatan state are believed to have been the first to eat mashed avocados as a sauce, a custom which gradually spread throughout Mexico. Today Mexicans still serve guacamole as a sauce over all kinds of dishes. It is also served as a salad and as a dip with 'tostadas' – triangular or square tortillas fried in hot fat – the latter being the way most people outside Mexico know this recipe.

2 tbsps	onion, peeled and minced	2 tbsps
1	clove garlic, peeled and crushed	1
1	large tomato	1
2 tbsps	lemon juice	2 tbsps
2	small chilis, fresh, bottled or pickled	2
	or	
1/4–1/2 tsp	chili powder	1/4–1/2 tsp
2	large avocados	2
3/4–1 tsp	salt	3/4–1 tsp
	fresh coriander leaves (Chinese parsley) (optional)	

Mince the onion (for such a small quantity, a garlic press will work quite well). Crush or mince the garlic. Skin the tomato, remove the seeds and mince or finely chop the flesh.

Put the onion, garlic, tomatoes and lemon juice in a medium bowl. Finely chop or mince the chilis and add to the bowl. Cut the avocados in half and remove the stones. Scoop out the avocado flesh and mash (you can mash it to a smooth paste if preferred or leave the flesh slightly lumpy to give a rougher texture to the dish). Season with salt to taste. If available you can add a few finely chopped coriander leaves, a popular addition in Mexico.

If serving as a party dip, accompany with crisps, tortilla chips (tostadas), and a selection of thinly sliced strips of raw vegetables or sprigs of cauliflower. Try serving the guacamole as a sauce over Mexican dishes like tacos.

CHILI CON QUESO – CHILI WITH ——CHEESE DIP——
Serves 6–8

This is a Mexican dip popular among Californians. It is a delicious mixture and unusual in that it is normally served hot.

15 g	butter	*large knob*
1	small onion, peeled and finely chopped	*1*
1	clove garlic, peeled and finely chopped or crushed	*1*
1 tbsp	green chili, finely chopped	*1 tbsp*
250 g	tinned tomatoes, puréed or finely chopped	*8 oz*
¼ tsp	salt	*¼ tsp*
250 g	cheese, grated (e.g. Cheddar), or cream cheese	*8 oz*
3 tbsps	double cream	*3 tbsps*

————To serve————

*tostadas (tortilla chips) or
potato chips or crisps
raw vegetables, thinly
sliced (e.g. carrots, celery,
cucumber or sprigs of
cauliflower)*

Heat the butter in a medium pan, add the onion and garlic and sauté for 3–4 minutes. Add the chili, tomatoes and salt, cover and simmer gently for 15 minutes.

Add the grated cheese (or cream cheese) and cook only long enough to completely melt the cheese. Remove from the heat and stir in the cream. Serve while still hot as suggested. The dip will thicken as it cools and is quite solid when fully cold.

NOTE: We used Mexican *jalapeño* chilis which are quite hot. If a milder chili is used, increase the quantity of chopped chili used, unless a less spicy dip is preferred.

————PARTY DIPS————

The most common dips in the USA are based on sour cream. However, many other dressings, for example Louis (page 147), Thousand Islands (page 150) and Green Goddess (page 151) lend themselves to dips, especially if combined with mayonnaise or sour cream. Cream cheese is also a good base for dips and can be blended with sour cream. Serve dips with sliced raw vegetables (for example carrots, celery, green pepper, courgettes, cucumber and cauliflower or broccoli sprigs), and with potato crisps and tostadas (Mexican tortilla chips).

———Additions for dips———

Bacon and Spring Onion: Crumble or finely dice some grilled bacon and finely slice a few spring onions. Add to the dip base and season to taste with salt and pepper.

Clam Dip: A popular dip on American supermarket shelves. Add minced clams to the dip base and season to taste with salt and pepper. (Try chopped mussels or cockles as an alternative to clams.)

Curry Dip: Sauté some chopped onion in a little butter and add curry powder to taste (about ¼–½ teaspoon for each 100 g (4 oz) of sour cream base). Fry for a few minutes before adding chopped fresh parsley and salt to taste. Mix with the dip base and chill before serving.

Packaged Dry Soups: Onion soup mix is by far the most popular of these easy-to-make dips. Stir the soup powder into the dip base (sour cream is usually used for this dip) until the desired strength of flavour is achieved.

CAKES AND COOKIES

——ANGEL FOOD CAKE——
Serves 6

This very delicate cake is almost like a soufflé. The height of the cake depends on the whisking of the egg whites, the best results being achieved when the egg whites are at room temperature and beaten stiff in a copper bowl with a balloon whisk. These days, however, most of us have neither the time nor the energy to dedicate to this whisking, unlike in the past when the reputation of a good American cook was often made by her angel food cake.

The cake tins must be absolutely free of grease, as the cake must cling to the sides of the tin as it rises. Once cooked, the cake is immediately inverted to 'hang' until cooled. Special angel food cake pans are obtainable which have little legs on the edge of the tin, so that once inverted, the tin is lifted at least 3 cm (1 inch) off the surface. Failing this, round tins can be supported on cups or jars, and ring moulds can be placed over the neck of a bottle.

125 g	cake flour (or plain or self-raising flour plus ½ tbsp cornflour), sifted	4 oz
12	egg whites (large), at room temperature	12
1 tsp	cream of tartar	1 tsp
1 tbsp	lemon juice	1 tbsp
1½ tsps	vanilla essence	1½ tsps
250 g	caster sugar	8 oz
½ tsp	salt	½ tsp

a 25 cm/10 inch cake pan or ring mould, *ungreased*

Preheat the oven to 180°C, 350°F, gas mark 4.

To achieve the lightest textured cake, sift the cake flour at least five times to incorporate as much air as possible and aid in the rising process, holding the flour sifter as high as practicable above the bowl.

Beat the egg whites, by hand if possible, until foamy. Add the cream of tartar, lemon juice and vanilla and continue beating. When the bubbles are of a uniform size, add the sugar, a few tablespoons at a time. Beat until all the sugar is dissolved and the egg whites are glossy and form stiff peaks.

Sift the flour and salt over the egg whites and very gently fold into the mixture, taking care not to overmix or the cake will be tough. When all the flour is incorporated, turn the batter into the ungreased cake pan or ring and bake in the preheated oven for 45–50 minutes until the cake springs back when gently touched. Invert and hang the pan as described above, and leave until cool.

To remove the cake from the pan, pull it away from the sides with a fork. The cake may be served either plain or iced. When serving, break apart with a fork, as cutting with a knife makes the cake stick together.

——DEVIL'S FOOD CAKE——
Serves 8–10

Some say this cake (sometimes called red devil's cake when made with cocoa powder, or fudge cake) was invented as an impish alternative to the white, light-textured angel food cake (see previous recipe). Others believe devil's food cake, loaded as it is with calories, presents the eater with unbearable temptation. There is only one answer to that: give in and enjoy this superb cake.

250 g	*self-raising flour*	8 oz
1 tsp	*bicarbonate of soda*	1 tsp
1/4 tsp	*salt*	1/4 tsp
100 g	*chocolate drops or cooking chocolate*	4 oz
240 ml	*milk*	scant 1/2 pint

3	*eggs*	3
250 g	*sugar*	8 oz
100 g	*butter*	4 oz
1 tsp	*vanilla essence*	1 tsp

2 × 18 cm (7 inch) cake pans

Preheat the oven to 180°C, 350°F, gas mark 4.

Grease and flour the cake pans and line the bases with greased greaseproof paper or waxed paper.

Sift the flour, soda and salt into a medium bowl. Dissolve the chocolate in a medium pan with the milk. Meanwhile, beat one of the eggs in a bowl with 125 g (4 oz) of the sugar. Gradually beat in the chocolate milk, then return the mixture to the pan and to the heat. Cook, stirring constantly, until the custard has thickened. Remove from the heat.

Beat the butter with the remaining 125 g (4 oz) of the sugar until well blended. Beat in the two remaining eggs. Alternately beat in the flour and chocolate custard to make a smooth, loose batter. Add the vanilla.

Pour the batter into the prepared cake pans and bake on the shelf above the centre of the preheated oven for 30–35 minutes until the top is springy to the touch. Turn out of the pans on to cooling racks. When cold, sandwich together the two cakes with butter cream, jam or icing, or fresh fruit and whipped cream. Coat the top and sides with chocolate 'frosting' (page 230).

——MARBLE CAKE——
Serves 8–10

250 g	*plain flour*	8 oz
2 tsps	*baking powder*	2 tsps
1/2 tsp	*salt*	1/2 tsp
250 g	*sugar*	8 oz
100 g	*butter*	4 oz
4	*eggs, separated*	4
180 ml	*milk*	generous 1/4 pint
1 tsp	*vanilla essence*	1 tsp
40 g	*semi-sweet chocolate*	1 1/2 oz

| 3 tbsps | water | 3 tbsps |
| 1/2 tsp | baking soda | 1/2 tsp |

a cake mould or Bundt pan,* greased, or 2 × 18 cm (7 inch) cake tins, greased

Preheat the oven to 180°C, 350°F, gas mark 4

Sift the flour, baking powder and salt together. Beat the sugar and butter until light, then beat in the egg yolks. Alternately add the flour mixture and the milk to make a loose batter. Stir in the vanilla.

Divide the batter into two portions, leaving the larger of the two plain. In a bowl, melt the chocolate with the water over a pan of simmering water. Add the baking soda. Mix the chocolate into the smaller portion of batter. Whisk the egg whites until stiff, then divide evenly between the two batters and gently fold in with a metal spoon. Alternate layers of batter in the pan or tins and shake gently to level the surface. Bake in the preheated oven for 30–35 minutes for the mould (Bundt) and 25–30 minutes for the cake tins, until the surface of the cake is springy to the touch. Cool on a wire rack, before drizzling plain or chocolate water icing (pages 201–2) over the mould (Bundt), or coating the sandwiched cakes with chocolate or white 'frosting' (page 230).

——PINEAPPLE UPSIDE-DOWN CAKE——
Serves 8–10

Cooking this cake in a skillet makes this recipe unusual.

50 g	butter	2 oz
100 g	brown sugar	4 oz
8	pineapple slices or rings (i.e. a 500 g (1 lb) tin)	8
7	glacé cherries	7
	or	
14	pecan or walnut halves	14
3	eggs, separated	3

* NOTE: A Bundt mould is an attractive round mould with a hole in the centre, which may be filled with fresh fruits like strawberries or even scoops of ice-cream to make a special cake or dessert.

100 g	*sugar*	4 oz
1/2 tsp	*vanilla essence*	1/2 tsp
3 tbsps	*pineapple juice or syrup*	3 tbsps
100 g	*plain flour*	4 oz
1 tsp	*baking powder*	1 tsp

a 25 cm (10½ inch) skillet

Preheat the oven to 180°C, 350°F, gas mark 4

Dissolve the butter and sugar together in the skillet over a gentle heat. Remove from the heat and place 6 of the pineapple slices or rings around the edges of the skillet, and the seventh in the centre. Cut the last ring into 6 wedges and put a wedge between each of the 6 outside rings. Place a glacé cherry or 2 pecan halves in the centre of each pineapple slice.

Beat the egg yolks and sugar in a medium bowl until light and creamy. Beat in the vanilla and pineapple juice or syrup. Sift the flour and baking powder together and fold into the batter, but do not beat. Finally, beat the egg whites until stiff and carefully fold them into the mixture. Pour over the pineapple slices and bake in the preheated oven for 20–25 minutes until golden brown. Cool slightly, then loosen the sides of the cake with a knife, invert a serving plate over the skillet, and turn the skillet upside down so that the pineapple appears on top of the cake.

Serve the cake hot with custard or cream as a dessert, or cold as a cake.

NOTE: This recipe can be adapted to different fruits, for example apple, apricot, peach and prune.

———LADY BALTIMORE CAKE———
Serves 8–10

This cake achieved widespread fame after it appeared in Owen Wister's novel *Lady Baltimore*. Wister reputedly first tasted the cake in Charleston, Carolina, and enjoyed it so much that he incorporated it into his book. Not surprisingly, it wasn't long before a second cake was created to use up the egg yolks left over from a Lady Baltimore cake – and naturally it was called 'Lord Baltimore cake'.

———For the filling———

75 g	small figs, chopped	3 oz
75 g	raisins	3 oz
3 tbsps	brandy (i.e. 1 miniature)	3 tbsps
1/4 tsp	almond essence	1/4 tsp
50 g	nuts, chopped (e.g. pecans, walnuts)	2 oz

———For the cake———

350 g	cake flour (or plain flour plus 1 1/2 tbsps cornflour)	12 oz
1 tbsp	baking powder	1 tbsp
1/4 tsp	salt	1/4 tsp
250 g	butter	8 oz
350 g	sugar	12 oz
240 ml	milk	scant 1/2 pint
1/2 tsp	vanilla essence	1/2 tsp
4	egg whites	4

———To decorate———

1 quantity	white mountain or boiled icing (page 231)	1 quantity
12–16	pecan or walnut halves fig slices (optional)	12–16

3 × 20 cm (8 inch) cake pans, greased and base lined

The day before, put the chopped figs and raisins in a small bowl with the brandy and almond essence. Cover with a plate and leave overnight to marinate. The following day, add the chopped nuts.

Preheat the oven to 180°C, 350°F, gas mark 4.

Sift the flour, baking powder and salt. Cream the butter until light and soft, add 250 g (8 oz) of the sugar, and beat until well blended. Add the flour and milk alternately to make a soft batter, then stir in the vanilla.

Beat the egg whites until stiff and beat in half of the remaining sugar until glossy. Beat in the remaining sugar. Carefully fold the meringue into the batter and divide the mixture among the three prepared cake pans. Smooth over the surfaces and bake in the preheated oven for 25–30 minutes until the sides of the cakes are coming away from the edges of the pans. Leave the sponges to cool slightly in their pans before turning out to cool on a wire rack.

Prepare the icing as directed on page 231. Fold about one third to one half of the icing into the marinated fruits mixture and spread this mixture over the top of two of the sponges. Sandwich the three sponges together. Coat the top and sides with the remaining plain icing, roughing the surface into peaks. Decorate the edge of the cake with pecan or walnut halves and fig slices, if desired.

——CARROT CAKE——
Makes about 24

Carrot cake is an example of one of the newer recipes to become popular in America, especially in New York. It is believed to have its origins in Jewish cooking, although the now popular cream cheese topping, which usually coats it, seems to be one hundred per cent American in origin.

4	*large eggs*	4
250 g	*sugar*	*8 oz*
240 ml	*oil*	*scant 1/2 pint*
250 g	*plain flour*	*8 oz*
2 tsps	*baking powder*	*2 tsps*
1 tsp	*bicarbonate of soda*	*1 tsp*
2 tsps	*ground cinnamon*	*2 tsps*
1/2 tsp	*salt*	*1/2 tsp*
250 g	*carrots, peeled and grated*	*8 oz*
50 g	*pecans or walnuts, chopped*	*2 oz*

——For the icing——

cream cheese icing (page 230)

a deep 32 × 22 cm (13 × 9 inch) baking tray (or two smaller ones), greased and base lined

Preheat the oven to 180°C, 350°F, gas mark 4.

Beat the eggs until frothy. Beat in the sugar and, when well combined, gradually beat in the oil. Sift the flour, baking powder, soda, cinnamon and salt together and gradually beat into the egg mixture. Finally, fold in the grated carrots and the chopped nuts.

Spread the mixture evenly into the baking tray and bake in the preheated oven for 30–35 minutes until the top is lightly browned and the cake is springy to the touch. Leave to cool slightly in the tin before turning out on to a cooling rack. Chill before spreading the top with cream cheese icing. Serve cut into squares.

NOTE: Once thoroughly chilled, this is a flavoursome, moist cake.

——BOSTON CREAM PIE——
Serves 6–8

Who knows how a cake comes to be called a pie? One credible explanation is that originally the vanilla cream filling was used in a pie before it gradually became adopted as a cake filling.

75 g	*plain flour*	*3 oz*
1 tsp	*baking powder*	*1 tsp*
	pinch of salt	
3	*eggs*	*3*
50 g	*sugar*	*2 oz*

——For the filling——

240 ml	*single cream or a mixture of cream and milk*	*scant ½ pint*
2 tbsps	*flour*	*2 tbsps*
	pinch of salt	
25 g	*sugar*	*1 oz*
1	*egg, lightly beaten*	*1*
1 tsp	*vanilla essence*	*1 tsp*

——Topping——

1 quantity	*chocolate icing (page 230)*	*1 quantity*

2 × 18 cm (7 inch) cake pans, greased and lightly floured, or greased and base-lined with greased greaseproof paper

Preheat the oven to 190°C, 375°F, gas mark 5.

Sift the flour, baking powder and salt into a small bowl. Beat the eggs lightly, add the sugar, and beat with an electric whisk until light in colour, thick, and the whisk leaves a trail in the mixture. (Alternatively, place the mixture in a bowl over a pan of simmering water and whisk until thickened.)

Add the sifted flour all at once and carefully fold into the egg mixture with a metal spoon. Divide the batter between the two prepared cake tins and smooth over the surface. Bake in the preheated oven for about 15 minutes, until golden. Remove from the oven and leave to cool slightly in the pans (the sponges will shrink from the sides of the pans). Remove from the pans and leave to cool on a rack.

Meanwhile prepare the filling: heat the cream or milk and cream mixture in a medium pan. Sift the flour, salt and sugar into a bowl and pour over the hot cream or milk mixture, stirring. Pour a little of this mixture into the lightly beaten egg and combine the egg with the remaining cream or milk mixture. Return to the pan and, stirring constantly, cook until thickened. Simmer gently for about 5 minutes, then add the vanilla and pour back into the bowl. Cover tightly (e.g. with cling-film) and leave to chill.

When the cakes and filling are cold, prepare the icing as detailed on page 230. To assemble, sandwich the two sponges with the vanilla cream filling and top with chocolate icing.

——BUTTER POUND CAKE——
Makes 2 × 20 cm (8 inch) cakes

Pound cake is another example of how Americans have not lost their love for old-fashioned recipes. Many varieties of pound cake line the supermarket and delicatessen shelves, and butter pound cake is one of the most popular. To enjoy its special flavour it must be made with real butter. As its name suggests, it is made with one pound of each of its main ingredients.

500 g	*unsalted butter*	*1 lb*
500 g	*sugar*	*1 lb*

500 g	eggs (8 large)	1 lb
500 g	plain flour	1 lb
1 tsp	salt	1 tsp
2 tsps	grated nutmeg	2 tsps
4 tsps	baking powder	4 tsps

2 × 20 cm (8 inch) cake tins, greased and base lined

Preheat the oven to 180°C, 350°F, gas mark 4.

Cream the butter well, add the sugar, and continue beating until light and creamy. Add 6 of the eggs, one at a time, beating after each addition. Sift together the flour, salt, nutmeg and baking powder, and gradually add to the butter mixture.

Finally, beat in the last 2 eggs. Spoon the mixture into the two prepared tins, smooth over the tops, and bake in the preheated oven for 50–55 minutes until the tops are browned and a knife comes out cleanly when inserted into the centre of each cake. Turn out on to a wire rack to cool.

——CRUMB CAKES——

Many different kinds of cakes – sponges, pound cakes (see previous recipe), Danish-style ring cakes – can be made into crumb cakes, just by adding the topping before baking.

50 g	plain or self-raising flour	2 oz
25 g	butter	1 oz
1–2 tbsps	sugar	1–2 tbsps
	chosen cake batter for a 20–25 cm (8–10 inch) cake	

First prepare the topping: sift the flour then rub in the butter until the mixture resembles coarse, not fine, breadcrumbs. Mix in the sugar.

Prepare the cake batter and spoon into the prepared cake tin. Smooth the surface and sprinkle over the crumb topping. Bake as normal until the topping is lightly browned.

────ELECTION DAY YEAST CAKE────
Makes one 23 cm (9 inch) cake

This unusual yeast cake which originated in New England was traditionally made for sale on election or town meeting days.

100 g	raisins	*4 oz*
50 g	mixed peel	*2 oz*
50 g	nuts, chopped	*2 oz*
3 tbsps	brandy	*3 tbsps*
240 ml	milk	*scant ½ pint*
15 g	dried yeast	*4 tsps*
	or	
25 g	fresh yeast	*1 oz*
1 tbsp	sugar	*1 tbsp*
500 g	plain flour	*1 lb*
175 g	butter	*6 oz*
100 g	white sugar	*4 oz*
100 g	brown sugar	*4 oz*
2	eggs	*2*
1 tsp	lemon juice	*1 tsp*
1 tsp	ground cinnamon	*1 tsp*
1 tsp	grated nutmeg	*1 tsp*
¼ tsp	ground cloves	*¼ tsp*
¼ tsp	ground allspice	*¼ tsp*
1 tsp	salt	*1 tsp*

a 23 cm (9 inch) cake tin or tube pan, greased and base lined

Combine the raisins, peel and nuts with the brandy and leave to soak overnight.

The following day, scald the milk and allow it to cool to lukewarm. Add the yeast, sugar and 200 g (6 oz) of the flour. Beat well, cover and leave in a warm place until very bubbly – approximately 45 minutes.

Cream the butter and sugars until light, add the eggs one at a time, beating well, and stir in the lemon juice and then the yeast mixture.

Sift the remaining 300 g (10 oz) of flour with the spices and the salt. Stir the flour and the soaked fruit mixtures alternately into the yeast batter, beating well between additions. The mixture will be very stiff.

Spoon into the greased tin or pan, cover with buttered paper or cling-film, and leave in a warm place to rise until the cake tin is full – about 1–2 hours.

Meanwhile, preheat the oven to 180°C, 350°F, gas mark 4.

Bake the cake in the preheated oven for 50–55 minutes. The cake is fully cooked when a skewer inserted in the centre comes out clean. Leave the cake to cool for a few minutes in the pan before turning out on to a cooling rack.

——BROWNIES——
Makes about 16

The immense popularity of brownies in the United States was one of the very first things to surprise us in America. This is a good recipe for letting children practise their 'cooking'.

75 g	*unsweetened chocolate*	*3 oz*
75 g	*butter or margarine*	*3 oz*
3	*large eggs*	*3*
1 1/2 tbsps	*milk*	*1 1/2 tbsps*
250 g	*sugar*	*8 oz*
75 g	*plain flour*	*3 oz*
1/4 tsp	*salt*	*1/4 tsp*
1/2 tsp	*baking powder*	*1/2 tsp*
1/2 tsp	*vanilla essence*	*1/2 tsp*
50–75 g	*chopped nuts (optional)*	*2–3 oz*

a 20 cm × 20 cm (8 × 8 inch) deep baking tray or dish, greased

Preheat the oven to 160°C, 325°F, gas mark 3.

Melt the chocolate and the butter or margarine in a bowl over a pan of simmering water. Put the eggs and milk in a large mixing bowl and beat lightly. Add the sugar and beat a little more. Stir in the chocolate and butter mixture.

Sift the flour, salt and baking powder into the mixture and beat until well blended. Stir in the vanilla and finally fold in the chopped nuts. Pour the mixture into the greased baking tray or dish and bake in the preheated oven for 30–35 minutes until risen and springy in texture. Turn out on to a cooling rack, and when cold cut into 5 cm (2 inch) squares.

NOTE: If desired, the surface of the uncut brownies may be coated in melted chocolate or with chocolate icing (see below).

——CREAM CHEESE FROSTING OR ICING——
For 1 large cake

175 g	cream cheese, softened	6 oz
1/2 tsp	vanilla essence	1/2 tsp
350 g	icing sugar	12 oz
1–2 tbsps	milk	1–2 tbsps

In a medium bowl, beat the cheese until smooth. Add the vanilla and gradually beat in the icing sugar. If necessary, add the milk to make a softer icing. Spread over the cake.

NOTE: This icing is very popular on carrot cake (page 224).

——CHOCOLATE FROSTING OR ICING——
For 1 cake

50 g	plain chocolate	2 oz
50 g	butter or margarine	2 oz
3 tbsps	milk	3 tbsps
1 tsp	vanilla essence	1 tsp
250 g	icing sugar	8 oz

Melt the chocolate and the butter or margarine in a bowl with the milk over a pan of simmering water. Beat until the chocolate is well blended into the milk. Remove from the heat and stir in the vanilla. Gradually sift in the icing sugar, beating until smooth.

As the frosting cools, it will thicken and harden. For a smooth surface to the cake, put it on a rack over a tray and pour over the frosting while still hot. For a spreading consistency, leave to cool slightly.

——MAPLE BUTTER FROSTING OR ICING——
For a 23 cm (9 inch) two-layer cake

75 g	butter, softened	3 oz
500 g	icing sugar	1 lb
5 tbsps	maple syrup	5 tbsps

Beat the butter until creamy. Gradually add the sugar until well combined. At high speed, whisk in the maple syrup and beat until light and fluffy. Ice the cake.

——BOILED WHITE FROSTING OR ICING——

3/4 kg	sugar	1 1/2 lb
1/4 tsp	cream of tartar	1/4 tsp
180 ml	water	generous 1/4 pint
3	egg whites	3
1 tsp	vanilla essence	1 tsp

Dissolve the sugar and cream of tartar in the water, then bring to the boil and cook until the syrup reaches the firm ball stage (242°F on the sugar thermometer). Meanwhile, beat the egg whites until stiff but not dry. Pour the syrup in a steady stream into the egg whites, beating constantly – an electric beater makes this task much easier. Add the vanilla essence and continue to beat the frosting until it is stiff enough to spread over the cake.

TOLL HOUSE OR CHOCOLATE CHIP ——COOKIES——
Makes 30–35

Toll House cookies, as the chocolate chip cookie was first known, were developed by adding chocolate chips to a butter drop cookie dough. Chopped nuts and later peanut butter chips provided newer variations. The name is believed to have originated with the Toll House Inn in Massachusetts, and whoever invented these cookies really started something! Americans are addicted to their chocolate chip cookies, which come in many different varieties and sizes up to the jumbo 'addicts' cookie. In New York, there were several chains in our time which specialized in varieties of

the Toll House cookie, for example 'Absolutely the Best Chocolate Chip Cookies', which had eight branches in the city, and
'David's Cookie Kitchen' which produced sensational cookies.

100 g	*butter or margarine*	*4 oz*
100 g	*sugar*	*4 oz*
100 g	*plain flour*	*4 oz*
1/2 tsp	*bicarbonate of soda*	*1/2 tsp*
1/4 tsp	*salt*	*1/4 tsp*
1/2 tsp	*vanilla essence*	*1/2 tsp*
I	*large egg, lightly beaten*	*I*
100 g	*chocolate drops*	*4 oz*
50–75 g	*chopped nuts, e.g. pecans, walnuts (optional)*	*2–3 oz*

baking trays, greased

Preheat the oven to 190°C, 375°F, gas mark 5.

Cream the butter or margarine with the sugar. Sift the flour,
soda and salt into a bowl. Beat the vanilla into the butter mixture,
then alternately add the flour mix and lightly beaten egg until a
stiff dough is made. Finally, fold in the chocolate chips and the
chopped nuts, if desired. Using a teaspoon, scoop balls of dough
on to the greased trays. If a crisper cookie is preferred, flatten the
balls with a palette knife (this is best achieved by dipping the knife
into a small bowl of hot water to prevent the knife from sticking to
the cookie dough).

The traditional American cookie is, however, usually raised in
shape. Bake the cookies in the preheated oven for 8–10 minutes
and cool on a wire rack.

NOTE: *Butter Drop Cookies* are made by using butter and not
margarine, and by omitting the chocolate chips and the nuts. Drop
small balls of dough on to the baking trays and bake as described
above.
'M and M' or Smartie cookies can be made using this cookie dough.
Omit the chocolate chips and nuts, and press 'M and M' candies
(recently launched in Britain) or Smarties into the surface of the
prepared cookies before baking.

——VANILLA SUGAR COOKIES——
Makes about 70–80

500 g	*plain flour*	*1 lb*
1½ tsps	*baking powder*	*1½ tsps*
½ tsp	*salt*	*½ tsp*
175 g	*butter or fat*	*6 oz*
350 g	*sugar*	*12 oz*
1	*whole egg*	*1*
1	*egg yolk*	*1*
2 tbsps	*milk*	*2 tbsps*
1 tsp	*vanilla essence*	*1 tsp*
	extra sugar	

baking trays; biscuit cutters

Sift together the flour, baking powder and salt. In a large bowl beat the butter until creamy, then add the sugar and beat until well combined. Add the egg and egg yolk and then the dry ingredients alternately with the milk and vanilla essence. Mix until a firm dough results. Cover the dough with greaseproof paper or place inside a plastic bag and chill for several hours or overnight.

Preheat the oven to 190°C, 375°F, gas mark 5.

When chilled, cut the dough into 3–4 pieces and roll each piece on a lightly floured surface to ½ cm (¼ inch) thick. Cut out the cookies with round, fluted or shaped cutters. Put the cookies on the trays, sprinkle the surfaces with extra sugar, and bake in the preheated oven for 8–10 minutes until lightly browned. Cool on a wire rack. When completely cold these are crisp delicious cookies.

NOTE: Completely by accident I discovered that this cookie dough makes a delicious 'pastry' crust for single-crust sweet pies. Roll the dough out to line the pie dish and prick the base and sides with a fork. Bake in an oven preheated to 190°C, 375°F, gas mark 5 for 5 minutes before adding the filling if it requires cooking; or cook for 10–15 minutes until browned, allow to cool, then add the filling if it does not require baking.

——SNICKERDOODLES——
Makes 40–45

Everyone in New England seems to have their own way of making snickerdoodles. This recipe will give you crisp cookies the taste of which is as irresistible as the name!

100 g	*butter or margarine*	*4 oz*
100 g	*sugar*	*4 oz*
1	*egg*	*1*
1/2 tsp	*vanilla essence*	*1/2 tsp*
250 g	*plain flour*	*8 oz*
1 tsp	*cream of tartar*	*1 tsp*
1/2 tsp	*bicarbonate of soda*	*1/2 tsp*
	pinch of salt	
1 tbsp	*sugar*	*1 tbsp*
1 tsp	*ground cinnamon*	*1 tsp*
baking trays		

Preheat the oven to 200°C, 400°F, gas mark 6.

In a large bowl, cream the butter or margarine with the sugar until light and soft. Beat in the egg and the vanilla. Gradually sift in the flour, cream of tartar, soda and salt and blend until a firm biscuit dough results.

In a small bowl, put the 1 tablespoon of sugar and the cinnamon and mix well together.

Using a teaspoon, scoop out small amounts of dough and roll in the palms of the hands into a ball. Press the ball into the cinnamon sugar, then turn it over and press lightly to coat the other side, too. Lay the cookies on the baking tray or sheet and flatten to about 5 cm (2 inches) in diameter. Bake the cookies on the centre shelf of the preheated oven for 8–10 minutes until browned. Cool on a wire rack.

——SAND TARTS——
Makes about 7 dozen

These 'tarts' are the traditional Christmas cookies made by the Pennsylvania Dutch people. They should be extremely thin –

paper-thin in fact. They probably get their name from the topping of sugar, cinnamon and chopped nuts. Although they take some time to make, they are well worth the effort.

125 g	*butter*	*4 oz*
250 g	*sugar*	*8 oz*
1	*egg, lightly beaten*	*1*
250 g	*plain flour*	*8 oz*

——For the topping——

1	*egg white*	*1*
1 tsp	*water*	*1 tsp*
1/2 tsp	*ground cinnamon*	*1/2 tsp*
50 g	*sugar*	*2 oz*
40 g	*nuts, finely chopped, e.g. walnuts, almonds or pecans*	*1 1/2 oz*

5–8 cm (2–3 inch) round cutter; baking sheets, greased

Cream the butter until light and soft. Add the sugar and beat until well blended. Add the lightly beaten egg and gradually stir in the sifted flour, mixing well. Cover and chill the mixture overnight in the refrigerator.

The following day, preheat the oven to 180°C, 350°F, gas mark 4. Cut the dough into four pieces and, on a lightly floured surface, roll out the pieces of dough as thin as possible. Cut out the 'tarts' with the round cutter and lay on the baking or cookie sheets. Brush the tops of the cookies with the egg white lightly beaten with the water. Mix together the cinnamon and sugar and sprinkle a little over each cookie, then top with a few finely chopped nuts. Bake in the preheated oven for 8–10 minutes. Cool on a wire rack.

——OATMEAL COOKIES——
Makes about 60

250 g	*brown sugar, firmly packed*	*8 oz*

250 g	fat, margarine or butter, softened	8 oz
175 g	plain flour	6 oz
1 tsp	baking powder	1 tsp
1/2 tsp	salt	1/2 tsp
1	egg	1
1/2 tsp	vanilla essence	1/2 tsp
100 g	quick porridge oats or oatmeal	4 oz

baking trays

Preheat the oven to 180°C, 350°F, gas mark 4.

Cream together the sugar and softened fat. Sift together the flour, baking powder and salt. Beat the egg and vanilla into the creamed sugar mixture, then gradually add the flour until a soft dough forms. Finally, stir in the oats or oatmeal.

Drop spoonfuls of the mixture on to the baking trays and bake for about 12 minutes until lightly browned. Remove the cookies to a cooling rack, and cool until crisp.

NOTE: Sometimes these cookies are made using rolled oats instead of the quick porridge or oatmeal.

——SHAPED GINGER COOKIES——
Makes about 40

America is *the* place to buy cookie cutters, which are sold in a bewildering range of shapes and sizes, from animals of all kinds to special festive shapes and those capable of imprinting detailed designs on to the cookie dough. This particular cookie dough is very suitable for the latter as it makes flat and crunchy cookies.

100 g	margarine and lard, blended	4 oz
100 g	soft brown sugar	4 oz
1 tsp	ground ginger	1 tsp
1 tsp	ground cinnamon	1 tsp
1/2 tsp	salt	1/2 tsp
1	egg	1

| 6 tbsps | treacle | 6 tbsps |
| 350 g | plain flour, sifted | 12 oz |

baking trays, greased; shaped biscuit cutters

Cream the margarine and lard with the sugar, ginger, cinnamon and salt until soft. Beat in the egg and treacle. Finally, gradually blend in the sifted flour to make a softish dough. Chill for several hours.

Preheat the oven to 190°C, 375°F, gas mark 5.

Roll out the dough on a well-floured surface to ½–1 cm (¼–½ inch) thick and cut into the desired shapes. Place the cookies on greased baking trays and bake in the preheated oven for about 8 minutes until beginning to brown. Cool on a wire rack.

NOTE: If a strong ginger flavour is preferred, double the quantity of ground ginger used in the recipe.

DESSERTS AND PIES

——MAPLE MOUSSE——
Serves 6–8

This frozen cream dessert provides a superb, very sweet ending to a dinner party. It is also very simple, if rather expensive, to prepare, and can be made long in advance of special occasions.

240 ml	maple syrup	scant 1/2 pint
4	eggs, separated	4
480 ml	double cream, whipped	generous 3/4 pint

——To decorate——

240 ml	double cream, whipped	scant 1/2 pint
	chocolate ivy leaves or rose petals	
	fresh strawberries or cherries	

a 1 3/4 litre (3 pint) fluted mould or 6–8 individual moulds

Combine the maple syrup and the egg yolks in a double boiler or a bowl over a pan of simmering water. Cook, stirring constantly, for 10 minutes until thick. Remove from the heat and leave to cool.

Beat the egg whites until stiff but *not* dry – if you overbeat the whites at this stage the mousse may separate out during freezing. Fold the whipped cream into the egg whites.

Beat the syrup and egg custard until light and frothy and stir in the egg white mixture. Pour the mousse into the mould or moulds and freeze until solid.

To unmould, quickly dip the mould into a bowl of hot water to loosen the sides, and invert the mousse on to a serving plate. Pipe whipped cream down the corners of the mousse, over the top and around the base. Decorate with chocolate ivy leaves or rose petals, and fresh strawberries or cherries.

NOTE: To make *Chocolate Ivy Leaves*, collect fresh ivy leaves, wash them clean and wipe dry. Spread melted chocolate over the leaves and when set, peel away the leaves. Chocolate rose petals are made in the same manner.

——BAKED CHEESECAKE——
Serves 10–12

New York City is famous for its baked cheesecakes, which are so rich, delicious and utterly addictive that we had to persevere through a few disappointing attempts before we could re-create the mouth-watering slices we had sampled in restaurants or from our favourite delicatessens. At last we hit on the right ingredients and the right method. One word of warning – your cheesecake will only be as tasty as the cream cheese it contains, so don't stint by buying cheaper, less tasty cheese or the flavour will suffer accordingly. This cheesecake freezes well.

25 g	crushed biscuit crumbs, e.g. digestives	1 oz
3/4 kg	good quality cream cheese	1 1/2 lb
120 ml	double cream	scant 1/4 pint
4	eggs	4
250 g	sugar	8 oz
1 tsp	vanilla essence	1 tsp
1	small lemon, grated rind of whole, juice of half (optional)	1

a 20 cm (8 inch) deep-sided cake tin (*not* one with a removable base); a metal or ovenproof pan or dish

Preheat the oven to 150°C, 300°F, gas mark 2.

Butter the base and sides of the cake tin well. Sprinkle the biscuit crumbs over the base and turn the tin around on its sides to coat them also.

Beat the cream cheese, cream, eggs, sugar and vanilla together. Add the lemon rind and juice if desired. Pour the mixture into the cake tin and put the tin in a pan or dish of shallow water. Bake in the preheated oven for 2 hours, then turn off the heat and leave the cheesecake inside the oven for a further 1 hour.

Remove the cake from the oven and from the pan of water and leave it in the cake tin to chill. Do not be tempted to take the cheesecake out of its tin before it is completely cold and set, or it will break up. When chilled, remove the cheesecake on to a serving dish.

NOTE: The top of the chilled cheesecake may be covered with a thickened fruit syrup made with fresh or tinned blueberries (page 274) cherries, strawberries, apricots, etc.

GELATINE CHEESECAKE WITH ——PINEAPPLE——
Serves 8–10

Recipes for unbaked cheesecakes, sometimes also called refrigerator, blender or icebox cakes, abound in American cookbooks, especially in the vast number of community cookbooks produced as fund-raising ventures.

——Biscuit crust——

175 g	*digestive biscuits crushed*	*6 oz*
75 g	*butter, melted*	*3 oz*
1 tbsp	*sugar*	*1 tbsp*

——The filling——

15 g	*powdered gelatine*	*4 tsps*
6 tbsps	*pineapple juice (e.g. from the tinned pineapple)*	*6 tbsps*
2	*eggs, separated*	*2*
100 g	*sugar*	*4 oz*
500 g	*cottage cheese*	*1 lb*
1	*small lemon, rind and juice*	*1*
350 g	*crushed pineapple, drained*	*12 oz*

a 23 cm (9 inch), deep-sided pie dish

First prepare the crust. Mix together the crushed biscuits, melted butter and sugar. Press the mixture into the base and around the sides of the pie dish. Chill in the refrigerator until set.

Meanwhile, dissolve the gelatine in the pineapple juice in a bowl over a pan of simmering water. Beat together the egg yolks and sugar until light and creamy. Sieve the cottage cheese, or purée in a blender with the lemon rind and juice until smooth. Add the sieved cheese, lemon rind and juice to the egg yolk mixture (or add the puréed cheese mixture). Beat until well blended. Stir in the crushed pineapple and the strained gelatine. Finally, whisk the egg whites until stiff and carefully fold into the pineapple mixture. Turn the cheesecake mixture into the prepared crust and chill until set. Serve plain or with cream.

——BLUEBERRY OR FRUIT BAKED ALASKA——
Serves 6

America's third president, Thomas Jefferson, is thought to have served a dish similar to the modern day baked Alaska at a White House dinner. Jefferson, who had learned to make ice-cream while in France as the first US Minister to France, was renowned for his interest in new foods, new techniques and new methods of farming. He discovered waffles and waffle irons in Holland, and macaroni in Italy. He also, against the Italian laws, smuggled out of the country two bags of superior grained rice to be re-planted in South Carolina.

Jefferson's baked Alaska was made not with sponge cake but with crisp pastry.

——Sponge——

75 g	*butter*	3 oz
75 g	*caster sugar*	3 oz
1	*large egg*	1
1	*egg yolk*	1
1 tsp	*lemon juice*	1 tsp
75 g	*plain flour*	3 oz
1½ tsps	*baking powder*	1½ tsps

pinch salt

——Filling——

500 g	*blueberries (or other fresh berries, e.g. blackberries or raspberries*	*1 lb*
3 tbsps	*sugar (or more to taste)*	*3 tbsps*
3 tbsps	*brandy*	*3 tbsps*
600 ml	*vanilla ice-cream (page 267)*	*1 pint*

——Topping——

2	*egg whites*	*2*
2 tbsps	*caster sugar*	*2 tbsps*

a 20–23 cm (8–9 inch) sponge tin, greased and base lined

Preheat the oven to 190°C, 375°F, gas mark 5.

Beat the butter in a bowl until creamy. Add the sugar and continue beating until light and fluffy. Beat in the whole egg and egg yolk and the lemon juice.

Sift together the flour, baking powder and salt. Fold into the butter mixture and spoon into the prepared tin. Smooth over the surface, and bake in the preheated oven for 20–25 minutes until the centre springs back when gently touched. Turn out on to a cooling rack and leave until completely cold.

To prepare the blueberries or other berries, wash them and put them into a saucepan with the sugar and brandy. Cook gently for 5–10 minutes then leave to cool completely.

When it is time to serve the dessert, preheat the oven to 230°C, 450°F, gas mark 8. Put the sponge on an ovenproof dish, prick the sponge with a fork or toothpick, and pour over the liquid from the fruit, allowing it to soak in. Pile the berries on top of the sponge.

Whisk the egg whites until stiff but not dry, add the sugar, and beat until the sugar is dissolved and the mixture is stiff and glossy. Heap the ice cream on top of the berries and cover the dessert completely with the meringue. Bake in the preheated oven for 3–4 minutes until the top is beginning to brown. Serve immediately.

——STRAWBERRY SHORTCAKE——
Serves 6

The basic mixture in this cake is really a scone (or biscuit as Americans call it) mixture.

250 g	*plain flour, sifted*	8 oz
2 tsps	*baking powder*	2 tsps
1/4 tsp	*salt*	1/4 tsp
50 g	*sugar*	2 oz
75 g	*butter*	3 oz
180 ml	*cream*	generous 1/4 pint
1	*egg, beaten*	1

——Filling——

500 g	*strawberries, hulled*	1 lb
300 ml	*whipping cream*	1/2 pint

2 × 23 cm (9 inch) pans, greased

Preheat the oven to 220°C, 425°F, gas mark 7.

Sift together the flour, baking powder, salt and sugar. Cut in the butter with a pastry cutter or rub in with the fingertips until the mixture resembles fine breadcrumbs. Add the cream and the egg and mix only enough to moisten the dry ingredients. Do not overhandle or the dough will become tough.

Spread the dough evenly into the two greased pans and bake in the preheated oven for 15–20 minutes or until a knife comes out clean. Cool slightly, then turn out of the pans.

While still warm, put one half of the shortcake on a serving plate, cover with halved strawberries and half the whipped cream. Put the remaining shortcake on top, cover with the rest of the cream, and arrange whole strawberries on top. Serve lukewarm.

——APPLE PANDOWDY——
Serves 6–8

There ought to be a good explanation for this dish's fascinating name, but we could find no agreement on its name, origin and ingredients. It seems to be popular in New England, and our version below is as near as we could get to the traditional dish. The topping is sponge-like, but a pastry crust may be substituted.

1 kg	*cooking apples*	*2 lb*
6 tbsps	*treacle*	*6 tbsps*
1/2 tsp	*ground cinnamon*	*1/2 tsp*
1/4 tsp	*grated nutmeg*	*1/4 tsp*
175 g	*plain flour*	*6 oz*
1/4 tsp	*salt*	*1/4 tsp*
2 tsps	*baking powder*	*2 tsps*
100 g	*sugar*	*4 oz*
100 g	*butter, melted*	*4 oz*
180 ml	*milk*	*generous 1/4 pint*

a 1¼ litre (2 pint) ovenproof, deep-sided dish, buttered

Preheat the oven to 180°C, 350°F, gas mark 4.

Peel, quarter and core the apples and thinly slice them into a bowl. Add the treacle, cinnamon and nutmeg and toss gently to coat the apple slices evenly. Spoon the mixture into the buttered dish.

Sift the flour, salt, and baking powder into a bowl and stir in the sugar. Make a well in the centre and add the melted butter and the milk. Stir to make a smooth batter, then spread the mixture evenly over the apple slices. Bake in the preheated oven for 40–45 minutes, until the sponge topping has risen and is browned.

To serve, you may invert the pudding or serve as it is. It is delicious with cream or custard.

——INDIAN PUDDING——
Serves 6

This simple recipe is almost as commonplace now as it was hundreds of years ago when it helped the first settlers fight off starvation. Naturally, certain improvements have been added as people became more affluent and more varied products were available, for example white sugar began to replace the treacle, and extra ingredients like raisins, sultanas, currants and grated orange peel became optional additions.

The recipe we give below is the original version which relies solely on treacle for its sweetening. However, if you have a sweet tooth you may add the optional two tablespoons of sugar to the boiling cornmeal mixture.

Indian pudding is another of those recipes which has caused a great deal of dispute in its time, but the following ingredients are the ones most experts agree are essential for it to be genuine.

1 litre	*milk*	*1³/₄ pints*
15 g	*butter*	*large knob*
6 tbsps	*cornmeal*	*6 tbsps*
¹/₄ tsp	*salt*	*¹/₄ tsp*
2 tbsps	*sugar (optional)*	*2 tbsps*
1	*large egg*	*1*
6 tbsps	*treacle*	*6 tbsps*
¹/₂ tsp	*ground cinnamon*	*¹/₂ tsp*
¹/₂ tsp	*ground ginger*	*¹/₂ tsp*
¹/₄ tsp	*grated nutmeg*	*¹/₄ tsp*

a 1¹/₄ litre (2 pint) ovenproof dish, greased

Preheat the oven to 150°C, 300°F, gas mark 2.

Heat the milk in a large saucepan and add the butter to melt it. Slowly add the cornmeal, stirring constantly to keep the mixture smooth. Add the salt (and sugar if desired) and bring to the boil, stirring until thick.

Put the egg, treacle, cinnamon, ginger and nutmeg in a bowl and beat until well blended. Pour the egg mixture over the cornmeal and stir to combine well. Turn the pudding into the greased baking dish and bake in the preheated oven for 1³/₄–2 hours until the pudding is set and a knife comes out cleanly.

Americans serve this dessert with cream, hot custard, brandy or rum butter or vanilla ice-cream (page 267).

——MEXICAN FLAN——
Serves 6

The Mexican influence is felt strongly in America's border states – California, Arizona, New Mexico and Texas. This popular dessert, with its confusing title, is actually the Mexican equivalent of a *crème caramel*, and nothing like a flan as we know it.

100 g	sugar	4 oz
2 tbsps	water	2 tbsps
1 1/4 litres	milk	2 pints
6	egg yolks	6
2	whole eggs	2
175 g	sugar	6 oz
2 tsps	vanilla essence	2 tsps
1/4 tsp	salt	1/4 tsp

a 1 3/4 litre (3 pint) mould; a pan or ovenproof dish for water

To make the caramel, preheat the mould either in a low oven or by standing it in hot water. In a small pan combine the 100 g (4 oz) of sugar and the water, and stir over a low heat until all the sugar is dissolved. Heat the syrup to boiling and continue to boil until it caramelizes to a rich golden brown. Pour the caramel into the mould and coat the bottom and sides evenly. Set aside to cool.

Preheat the oven to 180°C, 350°F, gas mark 4.

Scald the milk and leave to cool slightly. Lightly beat the egg yolks and whole eggs, gradually add the 175 g (6 oz) of sugar, and beat until thick and creamy. Add the milk slowly, beating continuously. Add the vanilla and salt and mix well.

Strain the custard into the mould, and place the mould in the pan or ovenproof dish with hot water to come half-way up the sides of the mould. Bake in the preheated oven for 1 hour or until a knife inserted into the centre comes out clean. Chill well.

To unmould, run a knife around the edge of the custard, place a serving dish upside down over the mould and invert it quickly. Serve with cream.

CHOCOLATE CREAM PUDDING
Serves 4–6

50 g	semi-sweet chocolate	2 oz
480 ml	top of the milk or milk and cream mixed together	generous 3/4 pint
2 tbsps	cornflour	2 tbsps
1–2 tbsps	sugar	1–2 tbsps
1/4 tsp	salt	1/4 tsp

3 tbsps	*milk*	*3 tbsps*
2	*eggs, lightly beaten*	2
1 tsp	*vanilla essence*	*1 tsp*

a 1½ litre (2½–3 pint) mould or bowl, greased

Gently heat the chocolate and milk (or milk and cream mixture) in a medium pan. Stir well to blend the melted chocolate into the milk. Mix the cornflour, sugar and salt in a small bowl and add the tablespoons of milk, stirring until blended.

Pour a little of the hot chocolate milk into the cornflour mixture, then stir the cornflour mixture into the chocolate milk. Return to the heat and, stirring constantly, bring to the boil until thickened.

Remove from the heat, pour a little of the chocolate sauce into the lightly beaten eggs, and add the egg mixture to the chocolate sauce. Return to the heat and heat gently until bubbling and thick. Finally, stir in the vanilla.

Pour the chocolate pudding into the greased mould (or bowl) and chill until set.

NOTE: For *Chocolate Cream Pie*, pour the chocolate filling into a pre-cooked pastry-lined pie dish or 23 cm (9 inch) pie shell and chill. Decorate with whirls of whipped cream and grated chocolate.

——FUNNEL CAKES——

My first experience of this Pennsylvania Dutch speciality came as we explored New York's 9th Avenue Food Fair – an annual event where food, novelty stalls and millions of interested visitors replace the usual traffic down a two-mile stretch of the Avenue. Enormous containers of hot fat were used to deep-fry these attractive spiral cakes until bronzed and crisp. Once drained, the funnel cakes were then dredged in sifted icing sugar – millions of calories in one handful!

To make funnel cakes, prepare a batter as given in the pancakes recipe on page 172, but using 1 teaspoon of baking powder in place of 1 tablespoon. The batter should be able to be easily poured – add extra milk if necessary.

Heat some oil or fat in a deep-fat frying pan until hot but not smoking. Meanwhile pour the batter into a funnel, keeping your finger on the hole (or use a jug with a narrow lip). Use a finger to regulate the batter as it is poured in a spiral into the hot fat. Deep fry, turning once to brown the other side if necessary. Drain on kitchen paper before sifting over some icing sugar.

NOTE: The cakes may also be made into cobweb patterns by criss-crossing the funnel over the fat.

———PECAN PIE———
Serves 6–8

Pecan pie is a truly national American dish and is one of the desserts traditionally served at Thanksgiving. The pecan closely resembles the walnut in looks, though it has a flavour entirely its own. It grows prolifically in America (for example, the 1978 crop was over 250 million pounds and worth over 144 million dollars). Texas and Georgia are famous for their pecans, and of course, for their pecan pies, a popular end to a barbecued meal.

100 g	*shortcrust pastry (page 263)*	*4 oz*
	or 1 × 23 cm (9 inch) unbaked deep-dish pie shell	
3	*eggs*	*3*
180 ml	*corn or maple syrup*	*generous ¼ pint*
175 g	*sugar*	*6 oz*
50 g	*butter, melted*	*2 oz*
1 tsp	*vanilla essence*	*1 tsp*
¼ tsp	*salt*	*¼ tsp*
75 g	*pecan halves (walnuts may be substituted if necessary)*	*3 oz*

a 20–23 cm (8–9 inch) deep-dish pie dish

Prepare the shortcrust pastry and leave to rest for 15 minutes. Roll out the pastry on a lightly floured surface and line the pie dish. Leave to rest for a further 15 minutes.
   Preheat the oven to 230°C, 450°F, gas mark 8.

Beat the eggs until frothy, add the syrup and sugar, and beat until well blended. Stir in the melted butter, vanilla and salt.

Lay the pecans in the base of the pastry shell and pour over the egg mixture. Bake the pie in the preheated oven for 10 minutes, then reduce the temperature to 180°C, 350°F, gas mark 4 and continue to bake for a further 40–50 minutes until the top is well browned and the centre is cooked. Leave to cool. When cold, this pie will have a crunchy hard surface and is delicious served with cream.

——PUMPKIN PIE——
Serves 6–8

This pie is the traditional dessert to complete a Thanksgiving dinner and has become more American than apple pie! The American pumpkin, unlike the grey-skinned Australian vegetable, is orange and thick skinned and is almost exclusively used in sweet dishes and seldom as a savoury vegetable. However, the Australian pumpkin may be substituted quite successfully.

100 g	*shortcrust pastry (page 263)*	*4 oz*
	or 1 × 23 cm (9 inch) unbaked deep-dish pie shell	
500 g	*pumpkin purée*	*1 lb*
240 ml	*evaporated milk*	*scant 1/2 pint*
2	*eggs*	*2*
3 tbsps	*maple syrup*	*3 tbsps*
175 g	*soft brown sugar*	*6 oz*
1 tsp	*ground cinnamon*	*1 tsp*
1/2 tsp	*ground ginger*	*1/2 tsp*
1/2 tsp	*grated nutmeg*	*1/2 tsp*
1/4 tsp	*mixed spice*	*1/4 tsp*

a 20–23 cm (8–9 inch) deep-dish pie dish

Prepare the shortcrust pastry and leave to rest for 15 minutes. Preheat the oven to 220°C, 425°F, gas mark 7.

Roll out the pastry on a lightly floured surface and line the pie dish. Leave the pastry to rest a further 15 minutes.

Meanwhile put all the remaining ingredients into a large bowl and beat until smooth and well blended. Pour the mixture into the prepared pie shell and bake on the centre shelf of the preheated oven for 10 minutes. Reduce the temperature to 180°C, 350°F, gas mark 4, and bake the pie for a further 40–50 minutes until the pie is set. You may test for readiness by piercing the centre with a skewer – if it comes out clean, the pie is set. However, this will spoil the smooth appearance of the pie top. We find it satisfactory to give the pie a gentle shake to see if the centre is no longer wobbly like a jelly and is therefore set. Chill and serve cold with cream.

——SHOO-FLY PIE——
Serves 6–8

This pie is the best known in a long line of scrumptious pies for which the Pennsylvania Dutch are famous. The name originates from the way that flies, attracted to the sweetness of the treacle, had to be shooed away. Somewhat to our surprise it appears that the locals these days are unenthusiastic about this unusual pie, yet still produce vast quantities of them – mainly to please the tourists.

100 g	*shortcrust pastry (page 263)*	*4 oz*
	or 1 × 23 cm (9 inch) unbaked deep-dish pie shell	

——Topping——

100 g	*plain flour*	*4 oz*
1/2 tsp	*ground cinnamon*	*1/2 tsp*
1/4 tsp	*grated nutmeg*	*1/4 tsp*
50 g	*butter or margarine*	*2 oz*
50 g	*soft brown sugar*	*2 oz*

——Filling——

6 tbsps	*treacle*	*6 tbsps*

120 ml	*boiling water*	scant 1/4 pint
1	*large egg*	1
1/2 tsp	*baking powder*	1/2 tsp

a 20–23 cm (8–9 inch) deep-dish pie dish

Prepare the pastry and leave to rest for 15 minutes. Roll out the pastry on a lightly floured surface and line the pie dish. Leave to rest a further 15 minutes.

Preheat the oven to 220°C, 425°F, gas mark 7.

To prepare the topping, sift the flour, cinnamon and nutmeg into a bowl. Rub in the butter or margarine until the mixture resembles fine breadcrumbs. Stir in the soft brown sugar to distribute evenly.

To prepare the filling, mix the treacle with the boiling water. Lightly beat the egg in a bowl, add the baking powder, and then gradually stir in the treacle mixture. Beat until well combined and pour into the pie shell.

Sprinkle the topping evenly over the entire surface of the treacle mixture. Bake immediately in the preheated oven for 10 minutes, then reduce the heat to 180°C, 350°F, gas mark 4, and bake for a further 25 minutes until the filling is set and the top is browned. Serve hot or cold.

——PENNSYLVANIA DUTCH CUSTARD PIE——
Serves 6–8

There are different types of custard pie in America, but it is the brown sugar and ground cinnamon which makes this one a speciality of the Pennsylvania Dutch. White sugar and grated nutmeg may be substituted, but it could no longer be considered typically Pennsylvania Dutch.

100 g	*shortcrust pastry (page 263)*	4 oz
	or 1 × 23 cm (9 inch) unbaked deep-dish pie shell	
360 ml	*milk*	generous 1/2 pint
240 ml	*single cream*	scant 1/2 pint

4	eggs	4
175 g	brown sugar	6 oz
1 tsp	flour	1 tsp
1/4 tsp	salt	1/4 tsp
1 tsp	vanilla essence	1 tsp
1/2 tsp	ground cinnamon	1/2 tsp

a 20–23 cm (8–9 inch) deep-dish pie dish

Prepare the pastry and leave to rest for 15 minutes. Scald the milk and cream in a small pan, then cover and leave to cool. Roll out the pastry on a lightly floured surface to line the pie dish and leave to rest for a further 15 minutes.

Preheat the oven to 200°C, 400°F, gas mark 6.

Bake the pie crust for 5 minutes on the top shelf of the preheated oven. Meanwhile, beat the eggs lightly and add the brown sugar, flour, salt and vanilla. Add the cooled milk and cream, beating well.

Remove the pie shell from the oven and pour in the custard mixture. Dust the top lightly with cinnamon and bake for 25–30 minutes, taking care not to overcook the pie as the eggs may separate out. Remove from the oven as soon as the centre is firm when gently shaken, or when a knife inserted in the centre comes out clean. Serve cold.

——DEEP-DISH APPLE PIE——
Serves 6

'As American as apple pie' is a common if somewhat odd expression which would be more accurate if applied to pumpkin or pecan pies. What's odd about it is that apple pie isn't American at all, but one of those recipes brought to America by the early English settlers. In fact, as far as food historians can determine, the apple (in contrast to the pumpkin or pecan) is not even a native crop of America. The first apples were only grown in the USA when seeds were brought over with the pilgrim settlers.

However, combining apple pie and Cheddar cheese in the same mouthful is uniquely American – or more specifically, peculiarly New England. In the early days apple pie and Cheddar cheese was often served for breakfast (see page 160).

Another interesting way of combining the cheese and apple flavours is to make a cheese pastry by adding 75–100 g (3–4 oz) of grated Cheddar to the dry ingredients.

100 g	*shortcrust pastry (page 263)*	*4 oz*
1 kg	*cooking apples*	*2 lb*
1 tbsp	*lemon juice (optional)*	*1 tbsp*
100–150 g	*sugar*	*4–6 oz*
1/2 tsp	*ground cinnamon*	*1/2 tsp*
1/4 tsp	*grated nutmeg*	*1/4 tsp*
25 g	*butter*	*1 oz*

————To serve————

slices of Cheddar cheese (optional)

a 1¼ litre (2 pint) ovenproof, deep-sided pie dish

Prepare the pastry and leave to rest for 15 minutes.

Preheat the oven to 220°C, 425°F, gas mark 7.

Peel, quarter and core the apples and slice them into a bowl. Sprinkle over the lemon juice if the apples are not tart enough in flavour. Add the sugar, cinnamon and nutmeg and toss to coat the slices evenly.

Put the apples in the deep dish and dot with butter. Roll out the pastry on a lightly floured surface to overlap the sides of the dish by about 1 cm (½ inch). Trim the edge and use the trimmings to make a second rim around the pastry. Pinch the edges together, prick the surface of the pie to let out steam, and brush the surface of the pastry with egg glaze or milk. Bake in the preheated oven for 10 minutes before reducing the temperature to 180°C, 350°F, gas mark 4. Bake for a further 25–30 minutes. Serve hot or cold with slices of Cheddar cheese. Alternatively, serve hot or cold with ice-cream, cream or custard.

——BLUEBERRY PIE——
Serves 6–8

Blueberries are native to North America, thriving in the boggy areas of the colder north-east. The larger cultivated berries are less flavoursome than their smaller wild counterparts. I know of at least one British grower producing blueberries for sale in British greengrocers. Wild ones can be picked in boggy areas such as parts of the Scottish countryside.

250 g	*shortcrust pastry (see page 263)*	*8 oz*
	or 2 × 23 cm (9 inch) unbaked deep-dish pie shells	
500–600 g	*blueberries*	*1–1¼ lb*
4 tbsps	*sugar*	*4 tbsps*
2 tbsps	*cornflour*	*2 tbsps*
½	*lemon, juice only*	*½*

——To glaze——

egg glaze

a 20–23 cm (8–9 inch) deep pie dish

Prepare the pastry and leave to rest for 15 minutes.

Preheat the oven to 220°C, 425°F, gas mark 7.

Divide the pastry into two portions and roll one piece out on a lightly floured surface to line the base of the pie dish. Trim the edges and leave to rest for a further 15 minutes.

Wash, drain and pick over the blueberries, discarding any green berries, stalks and leaves. Gently pat dry with kitchen paper.

Mix together the sugar and cornflour and lightly toss the dried berries in the mixture to coat evenly. Sprinkle over the lemon juice and pour the tossed berries into the lined pie dish.

Roll out the second pastry piece to cover the top of the pie, and trim and crimp the edges. Decorate the centre of the pie with pastry leaves and brush the surface of the pie with egg glaze. Gently slash the surface of the pie in about four places for air vents, and bake the pie in the preheated oven for 10 minutes before reducing the temperature to 180°C, 350°F, gas mark 4 to bake for a further 24–30 minutes.

Serve the pie hot or cold with vanilla ice-cream (page 267) or fresh cream.

NOTE: For *Deep-Dish Blueberry Pie*, see deep-dish apple pie on page 252 and use the above blueberry filling with a single pastry crust to top the pie. Bake as above.
For *Blueberry Crumb Pie* see note to cherry crumb pie, page 256.

──KEY LIME PIE──
Serves 6–8

This most famous of American pies originates in the Florida Keys, a strip of islands off the southernmost tip of the state. The Keys were, until Hawaii became a state in 1959, the most southerly point in the United States, and are still famous for their Key limes, the small yellow-skinned fruits which grow so prolifically in what is justly called the 'Sunshine State'.

Traditionally, the pie is made with shortcrust pastry – however, the more modern biscuit crumb base has been adopted by many people who believe it more suitable for chilling in the refrigerator. Opinions vary also on whether the egg whites should be folded into the lime mixture or combined with sugar into a meringue topping. We prefer the former as this gives a lighter texture to the pie, which is rich enough without the extra sugar of the meringue topping.

100 g	*shortcrust pastry (page 263)*	*4 oz*
	or 1 × 23 cm (9 inch) pie shell or biscuit crumb crust (see page 240)	
3	*eggs, separated*	*3*
396 g	*tin condensed milk*	*14 oz*
3	*fresh limes*	*3*

──To decorate──

120 ml	*double cream, whipped*	*scant ¼ pint*

a 20–23 cm (8–9 inch) pie dish

Prepare the shortcrust pastry and leave to rest for 15 minutes. Roll out the pastry on a lightly floured surface and line the pie dish. Leave to rest a further 15 minutes.

Preheat the oven to 200°C, 400°F, gas mark 6.

Bake the pastry 'blind' (see page 258) in the preheated oven for 15 minutes. Remove the cover and bake for a further 5 minutes until lightly browned. Leave to get cold.

Lightly whisk the egg yolks and condensed milk in a medium bowl to blend. Grate the rind of two of the limes into the mixture; grate the rind of the third lime into a small bowl and reserve for decoration. Squeeze the juice from all three limes and, stirring constantly, add to the egg mixture with the lime pulp (but not the pips). The filling will now be thickening.

Finally, whisk the egg whites until stiff and gently fold into the filling. Pour into the cooled pie shell and leave in the refrigerator to chill.

Before serving, either spread the whipped cream over the surface of the pie or pipe in rosettes around the edge. Sprinkle the cream with the reserved grated lime rind.

——CHERRY CRUMB PIE——
Serves 6–8

100 g	*shortcrust pastry (page 263)*	*4 oz*
	or 1 × 23 cm (9 inch) unbaked deep-dish pie shell	
1 kg	*fresh cherries*	*2 lb*
1 tbsp	*cornflour*	*1 tbsp*
250 g	*sugar*	*8 oz*
2 tbsps	*kirsch*	*2 tbsps*
75 g	*flour*	*3 oz*
75 g	*butter*	*3 oz*

a 20–23 cm (8–9 inch) deep-dish pie dish

Prepare the shortcrust pastry and leave to rest for 15 minutes. Roll out the pastry on a lightly floured surface to line the pie dish, trim the edges and leave to rest for a further 15 minutes.

Preheat the oven to 220°C, 425°F, gas mark 7.

Pit the cherries, then slightly mash the cherry flesh to extract some of the juice. Strain the juice into a small pan, add the cornflour and 125 g (4 oz) of the sugar, and, stirring constantly, cook until thickened. Add the kirsch and the cherries and spoon the mixture into the prepared pie shell.

To make the crumb topping, mix the flour with the remaining 125 g (4 oz) of sugar and chop the butter into the mixture with two knives. Rub the butter into the mixture, using fingertips only, until it resembles fine breadcrumbs. Spread evenly over the top of the fruit. Bake the pie in the preheated oven for 10 minutes, then reduce the heat to 180°C, 350°F, gas mark 4, and bake for a further 40 minutes. Allow to cool. Chill before serving with cream or ice-cream.

NOTE: For *Blueberry Crumb Pie*, substitute rinsed blueberries for the cherries, and use 2 *heaped* tablespoons of cornflour to thicken the berries.

——CHOCOLATE FUDGE PIE——
Serves 8–10

100 g	shortcrust pastry (page 263) or 1 × 23 cm (9 inch) pie shell	*4 oz*
100 g	butter	*4 oz*
50 g	plain cooking chocolate	*2 oz*
3	eggs	*3*
3 tbsps	golden syrup	*3 tbsps*
175 g	sugar	*6 oz*
	large pinch salt	
½ tsp	vanilla essence	*½ tsp*

a 20–23 cm (8–9 inch) pie dish

Prepare the pastry and leave to rest for 15 minutes. Roll out on a lightly floured surface to line the pie dish and leave to rest for a further 15 minutes.

Preheat the oven to 200°C, 400°F, gas mark 6. Bake the pastry shell 'blind' (see page 258) for 10 minutes in the preheated oven. Remove from the oven and reduce the temperature to 180°C, 350°F, gas mark 4.

Melt the butter and chocolate in a bowl over a pan of boiling water. Beat the eggs until light, then beat in the syrup, sugar, salt and vanilla. Add the melted chocolate and butter, blend well, and pour the mixture into the pie shell. Bake for 25–30 minutes in the preheated oven, until the top is crusty but the filling is still soft. Leave to chill, during which time the chocolate filling will set to a fudge-like consistency. Serve chilled with cream or vanilla ice-cream (page 267).

——BLACK BOTTOM PIE——
Serves 6–8

100 g	shortcrust pastry (see page 263)	*4 oz*
	or 1 × 23 cm (9 inch) deep-dish pie shell	
50 g	unsweetened chocolate	*2 oz*
1 round tbsp	cornflour	*1 round tbsp*
4	eggs, separated	*4*
100 g	sugar	*4 oz*
360 ml	milk	*generous ½ pint*
120 ml	double cream	*scant ¼ pint*
1 tsp	vanilla essence	*1 tsp*
1–2 tbsps	rum	*1–2 tbsps*
1 tbsp	powdered gelatine	*1 tbsp*
3 tbsps	cold water	*3 tbsps*
2 tbsps	sugar	*2 tbsps*

a 20–23 cm (8–9 inch) deep-dish pie dish

Prepare the pastry and leave to rest for 15 minutes.

Preheat the oven to 200°C, 400°F, gas mark 6.

Roll out the pastry on a lightly floured surface, line the pie dish and leave to rest a further 15 minutes. Cover the pastry with greaseproof paper and place rice or dried beans in the base. Bake 'blind' on the top shelf of the preheated oven for 15 minutes, then remove the cover and the rice or beans and bake uncovered for a further 5 minutes until the pastry is lightly browned. Leave to cool.

Meanwhile, melt the chocolate in a bowl over hot water and leave to cool slightly. Beat the cornflour with the egg yolks for 2–3 minutes until light and creamy. Add the sugar and beat until very light and thick.

Heat the milk and cream to scalding point and slowly pour over the egg mixture, whisking constantly. Add the vanilla and rum, return to the pan and to the heat, and, stirring constantly, bring to the boil until thickened.

Strain the custard through a fine sieve into a large measuring jug. Add 360 ml (generous ½ pint) of the custard to the melted chocolate, beating well to combine thoroughly. Leave to cool slightly.

Dissolve the gelatine in the cold water in a small bowl over a pan of simmering water, and when clear, add to the remaining custard in the measuring jug. Stir the mixture well.

Whisk the egg whites until stiff, add 2 tablespoons of sugar and beat until glossy. Carefully fold the egg whites into the custard and gelatine mix.

To assemble the pie, pour the chocolate custard into the base of the baked pie shell and smooth over the surface. Pile the egg white custard over the top of the chocolate and rough up the surface into little peaks. Leave to set in a cool place for at least 2 hours. Decorate the edge of the pie with swirls of whipped cream and sprinkle with extra grated chocolate, if desired.

——RAISIN AND SOUR CREAM PIE——
Serves 6–8

100 g	*shortcrust pastry (page 263)*	*4 oz*
	or 1 × 23 cm (9 inch) unbaked deep-dish pie shell	
100 g	*raisins*	*4 oz*
120 ml	*water*	*scant ¼ pint*
100 g	*sugar*	*4 oz*
2 heaped tsps	*cornflour*	*2 heaped tsps*
½ tsp	*ground cinnamon*	*½ tsp*
1	*large egg*	*1*
250 g	*sour cream*	*8 oz*

a 20–23 cm (8–9 inch) deep-dish pie dish

Prepare the pastry and leave to rest for 15 minutes.

Preheat the oven to 190°C, 375°F, gas mark 5.

Roll out the pastry on a lightly floured surface and line the pie dish. Leave to rest for a further 15 minutes. Meanwhile, put the raisins and water in a small pan, bring to the boil and simmer for 10 minutes. Mix the sugar, cornflour, and cinnamon in a bowl, then add to the hot raisin mixture. Stir to dissolve all the sugar, then bring to the boil again until thickened. Remove from the heat and leave to cool slightly.

Put the egg and sour cream in the bowl and mix together well with a wire whisk or fork. Gradually stir in the thickened raisin mixture, then pour into the pie shell. Bake in the preheated oven for about 40 minutes. This pie may be served hot or cold, but is more flavoursome cold.

NOTE: *Raisin and Buttermilk Pie* may also be made by substituting buttermilk for the sour cream. To make buttermilk add 2 teaspoons of lemon juice to ordinary milk.

——COCONUT CUSTARD PIE——
Serves 6–8

100 g	shortcrust or sweet shortcrust pastry (page 263) or 1 × 23 cm (9 inch) unbaked pie shell	*4 oz*
4	eggs, separated	*4*
1 tbsp	cornflour	*1 tbsp*
175 g	sugar	*6 oz*
730 ml	milk	*scant 1¼ pint*
100 g	grated or desiccated coconut (loosely packed)	*4 oz*
1½ tsps	vanilla essence	*1½ tsps*
75–100 g	caster sugar (optional)	*3–4 oz*
	extra coconut to decorate	

a 20–23 cm (8–9 inch) ovenproof pie dish

Prepare the pastry and leave to rest for 15 minutes.

Preheat the oven to 200°C, 400°F, gas mark 6.

Roll out the pastry on a lightly floured surface and line the pie dish. Bake blind (see page 258) in the preheated oven for 10 minutes. Remove the cover and bake for a further 5 minutes until lightly browned. Leave to cool.

Meanwhile, beat the egg yolks with the cornflour for 2 minutes, then add the sugar and continue beating until the mixture is light in colour and thick. Heat the milk in a medium pan until nearly boiling, then gradually pour on to the egg yolk mixture, stirring constantly. Return the mixture to the pan, and, over a gentle heat, stir constantly until the custard thickens. Remove from the heat, stir in the coconut and vanilla and leave to cool.

There are two ways in which the pie may now be completed. (1) The stiffly beaten egg whites may be folded into the cooled custard and the mixture then poured into the pie shell. (2) The stiffly beaten egg whites may be made into a meringue topping by adding the optional caster sugar and whisking until stiff and glossy. Pile the meringue over the custard filling in the pie shell and rough over the surface.

Whichever way it is completed, sprinkle the top of the pie with a little extra coconut. Bake on the top shelf of the preheated oven for 10 minutes to brown the top and the coconut. Serve hot or cold.

——CRANBERRY AND APPLE PIE——
Serves 6–8

250 g	*shortcrust pastry (page 263)*	*8 oz*
	or 2 × 23 cm (9 inch) unbaked deep-dish pie shells	
250 g	*sugar*	*8 oz*
40 g	*flour*	*1½ oz*
½ tsp	*ground cinnamon*	*½ tsp*
¼ tsp	*grated nutmeg*	*¼ tsp*
¼ tsp	*ground cloves*	*¼ tsp*

500 g	*tart apples, peeled and*	*1 lb*
	sliced	
250 g	*fresh cranberries*	*8 oz*
120 ml	*maple or pancake syrup*	*scant ¼ pint*
2 tbsps	*butter*	*2 tbsps*

——To glaze——

beaten egg or milk

a 20–23 cm (8–9 inch) deep pie dish

Prepare the pastry and leave to rest for 15 minutes.

Preheat the oven to 220°C, 425°F, gas mark 7.

Divide the pastry into two portions. Roll out one piece to line the pie dish and reserve the second to fit the top of the pie.

Mix together the sugar, flour, cinnamon, nutmeg and cloves. Arrange alternate layers of sliced apples, cranberries and sugar mixture in the pie base, beginning and ending with apples. Pour over the maple or pancake syrup and dot the top of the filling with the butter. Finally, cover the pie with the second pastry piece, seal and flute the edges of the pastry, cut a few slits in the pastry to let out steam, and brush the top of the pie with egg glaze or milk. Bake in the preheated oven for 40–50 minutes.

——BUTTERED POPCORN——
Serves 4

The only popcorn I remember eating in my childhood in Britain was the sugar-coated kind. So it came as some surprise to discover that Americans, normally famous for their sweet-tooth approach to food, prefer savoury, buttered popcorn. For more information on popcorn, see page 120.

2 tbsps	*oil*	*2 tbsps*
50 g	*popcorn kernels*	*2 oz*
	salt to taste	
25–50 g	*butter, melted*	*1–2 oz*

a large pan with a lid

Heat the oil in the pan, add one kernel of popcorn, and when this has 'popped', add the rest of the popcorn. Immediately cover the pan with the lid, lower the heat to medium, and shake the pan gently until all the kernels have stopped popping. Turn into a large serving bowl, sprinkle lightly with salt, then drizzle over the melted butter, tossing to coat evenly. Serve while still hot.

——SHORTCRUST PASTRY——
Makes 200 g (8 oz) or 2 pie crusts

200 g	*plain flour*	8 oz
	pinch of salt	
100 g	*butter (or butter or margarine blended with lard)*	4 oz
	iced water	

Sift the flour and salt into a bowl. Cut the butter or other fats into the flour and rub into the flour, using fingertips only, until the mixture resembles fine breadcrumbs. Add sufficient iced water to mix to a firm but not sticky dough. Do not overhandle or knead the pastry, as this will affect the light texture of the cooked pastry. Cover the dough and leave in a cool place for 15 minutes to rest.

——ROUGH PUFF PASTRY——
Makes 500 g (1 lb)

500 g	*plain flour*	1 lb
	large pinch salt	
350 g	*butter or margarine and fat mixed together*	12 oz
1 tsp	*lemon juice*	1 tsp
about 300 ml	*ice-cold water*	about ½ pint

Sift the flour and salt into a bowl and cut in the butter or other fat with two knives until it is reduced to small pieces. Add the lemon juice and enough ice-cold water to make a fairly soft, elastic dough, taking care not to break up the pieces of fat.

Put the dough on a floured surface and roll out to a rectangle about 45 × 15 cm (18 × 6 inches). Fold the bottom third of pastry up and the top third down over it. Give a quarter turn, seal the edges and roll again to a rectangle and fold as before.

Repeat this rolling/folding process four times in all, by which time the pastry should be smooth and the fat evenly distributed. If possible leave the pastry to rest in a cool place for 15 minutes between the second and third rolling and folding. Cover the pastry with polythene to prevent it hardening, and leave to rest for 20 minutes before using.

ICE-CREAMS

Neither the Americans nor the Italians, both of whom are renowned for their ice-creams, can take full credit for inventing frozen desserts. The Italians adapted the idea from the Chinese, via explorer Marco Polo.

The Italians, French and British brought ice-cream to America, where in time it became elevated to a national dish. As with many other foreign foods, Americans took ice-cream and developed it far beyond its first beginnings. The different flavours and mixtures on sale in modern ice-cream shops are overwhelming – down to such incredible creations as bubble-gum ice-cream (not surprisingly a number one hit with the kids!). However, the old standards such as vanilla, chocolate and strawberry are still usually the leading best-sellers overall. Even supermarket-bought ice-cream offers more flavours than we could get in Britain and Australia.

In 1846 the hand-cranked ice-cream freezer was invented in America, and later still the ice-cream cone provided another American contribution to the history of ice-cream.

Ice-cream sodas (carbonated drinks with ice-cream) and ice-cream sundaes were American improvisations rather than deliberate creations. It is believed that ice-cream was first served with 'soda' as a substitute for the usual cream, which had either gone sour or into short supply. The sundae began as a result of local laws which forbade the serving of ice-cream sodas on Sundays. Enterprising vendors served ice-cream with non-carbonated syrups on top and at first called the dish 'Sunday Soda'.

Modern sundaes range from ordinary ice-cream with lashings

of syrup or sauces like hot fudge (page 274) or butterscotch (page 274), to layered creations topped with whirls of whipped cream, chopped nuts, a cherry and sometimes those children's favourites – chocolate or multi-coloured 'sprinkles' ('hundreds and thousands').

Recent American developments in ice-cream marketing include soft ice-cream (created by Tom Carvel who operates one of America's big ice-cream chains), yoghurt ice-cream (page 273) for diet-conscious Americans, and ice-cream cakes, which have become so popular as birthday or celebration cakes.

HOW TO MAKE ICE-CREAM

Once you have followed the individual recipe instructions and the ice-cream is ready to freeze, make sure you have already turned the fridge freezer or home freezer to its coldest setting.

If you are fortunate enough to own an electric ice-cream machine, making your own ice-creams could not be easier. The light texture of machine-made ice-creams produces a most professional texture which is difficult to match without any machine help. Follow the manufacturers' instructions for electric and hand-cranked machines.

However, hand-made ice-cream, while it may not always match the bought product in lightness of texture, can rival, even exceed, the best of manufactured flavours. Pour the prepared ice-cream mixture into ice-cream trays and freeze until the ice-cream begins to set around the edges. Empty the ice-cream into a chilled bowl and beat to break up the ice crystals that have formed. Return the ice-cream to its tray and to the freezer for a further half an hour until the mixture has begun to set again.

Repeat the process of beating the ice-cream in a chilled bowl to break up the crystals and again return the ice-cream to the freezer until it has completely set. (Beating to break up the ice crystals gives a smoother, lighter textured ice-cream, so repeat the process two or three times if possible.)

Finally, when the ice-cream is fully frozen, return the fridge freezer or home freezer to its normal setting.

NOTE: To make ice-cream easier to serve, remove the container from the freezer 5–10 minutes before serving to thaw slightly.

——EASY VANILLA ICE-CREAM——
Makes 1 litre (1³/4 pints)

2 tsps	unflavoured powdered gelatine	2 tsps
120 ml	milk	scant ¹/4 pint
100 g	sugar	4 oz
	large pinch salt	
2–3 tsps	vanilla essence	2–3 tsps
480 ml	double or whipping cream	generous ³/4 pint
240 ml	single cream	scant ¹/2 pint

an ice-cream machine or trays

Turn the fridge freezer or home freezer to its coldest setting.

Sprinkle the gelatine over the milk in a small bowl and set the bowl over a pan of simmering water until the gelatine is completely dissolved. Strain the mixture into a larger bowl, and stir in the sugar and salt. Leave to get cool. Stir in the vanilla and double and single creams and pour into the container or trays. Freeze as detailed on page 266.

——FRENCH VANILLA ICE-CREAM——
Makes 1 litre (1³/4 pints)

360 ml	single cream or top of the milk or evaporated milk	generous ¹/2 pint
360 ml	whipping or double cream	generous ¹/2 pint
1	vanilla bean pod	1
6	egg yolks	6
100 g	sugar	4 oz
	large pinch salt	
50 g	butter	2 oz

an ice-cream machine or ice-cream trays

Turn the fridge freezer or home freezer to its coldest setting.

Heat the cream (or substitute), the whipping or double cream and the vanilla pod (split lengthwise) in a saucepan. Bring almost to the boil but do not allow to boil. Remove from the heat, cover the pan with a lid or cling-film, and leave at the back of the cooker to infuse for 30 minutes.

Meanwhile beat the egg yolks with the sugar until light in colour, thick and creamy. Add the salt.

Scrape the little black seeds from the inside of the vanilla pod into the cream mixture, then discard the pod. Gradually beat the vanilla cream into the egg yolk mixture, then return to the pan. Cook, stirring constantly, until the custard begins to thicken and become foamy. Beat in the butter until absorbed. Remove from the heat and pour back into the mixing bowl. Cover tightly (e.g. with cling-film) and leave in the refrigerator to chill thoroughly for about 1–2 hours.

When chilled, pour into the ice-cream machine or trays and freeze as detailed on page 266. When completely frozen, return the fridge freezer or home freezer to its normal setting.

NOTE: Vanilla essence may be substituted for the whole vanilla bean, using 2–3 teaspoons and reducing the sugar to 75 g (3 oz). There is no need to leave the vanilla cream to infuse for 30 minutes. Use some of the reserved egg whites to make blueberry or fruit baked Alaska (page 241).

——STRAWBERRY ICE-CREAM——
Makes 1¼ litres (2 pints)

500 g	*strawberries, hulled*	*1 lb*
3–4 tbsps	*sugar*	*3–4 tbsps*
1 litre	*Easy vanilla ice-cream*	*1¾ pints*
	(page 267)	
	a few drops of red	
	colouring (optional)	

PURÉE the strawberries in a blender or mash through a sieve. Measure the purée and add 2 tablespoons of sugar for each 240 ml (scant ½ pint) of purée, stirring to dissolve. Add the strawberry purée to the ice-cream just before freezing. If a darker red colour is preferred, add a few drops of red colouring.

NOTE: Alternatively, the strawberries can be sliced and tossed in the sugar before being folded into the ice-cream when it is frozen but still soft.

———REAL COFFEE ICE-CREAM———
Makes 1 litre (1¾ pints)

Follow the recipe for French vanilla ice-cream (page 267) but substitute 40 g (1½ oz) of whole coffee beans for the vanilla bean pod.

Crush the coffee beans or grind roughly, and add to the cream (or substitute) and whipping or double cream mixture in place of the vanilla pod. Leave the coffee to infuse for 30 minutes, then strain the grains from the cream mixture by pouring through a sieve lined with muslin or cheesecloth.

Continue to follow the remainder of the French vanilla ice-cream recipe, ignoring any references to vanilla.

———CHOCOLATE CHIP MINT ICE-CREAM———
Makes about 1 litre (1¾ pints)

1 tbsp	*powdered gelatine*	*1 tbsp*
120 ml	*cold water*	*scant ¼ pint*
384 ml	*evaporated milk*	*13 fluid oz*
75–100 g	*sugar*	*3–4 oz*
360 ml	*double cream*	*generous ½ pint*
1 tsp	*peppermint essence*	*1 tsp*
4–5	*drops of green food colouring*	*4–5*
175 g	*chocolate mini-chips or drops or coarsely grated good quality block chocolate*	*6 oz*

an ice-cream machine or freezing trays

Turn the fridge freezer or home freezer to its coldest setting.

Sprinkle the gelatine into the cold water and leave to soak for 5 minutes.

Meanwhile heat the evaporated milk in a saucepan. Add the gelatine mixture, remove from the heat, and stir until dissolved. Add the sugar and stir until it has dissolved. Strain the mixture and leave to cool.

Add the double cream, peppermint essence and green

colouring, and stir to blend into a pale green mixture. Do not add the chocolate at this stage.

Pour the ice-cream into trays or containers and freeze according to the instructions on page 266. When it is of the consistency of soft ice-cream, remove from the freezer to a chilled bowl. Fold in the mini-chips or grated chocolate, then return the ice-cream to sealed containers and freeze until solid.

When completely frozen, return the fridge freezer or home freezer to its normal setting.

CHOCOLATE MARSHMALLOW ——ICE-CREAM——
Makes 1 litre (1¾ pints)

100 g	*chocolate drops or block chocolate*	*4 oz*
360 ml	*evaporated milk (i.e. 1 large tin)*	*generous ½ pint*
360 ml	*double cream*	*generous ½ pint*
100 g	*large marshmallows, cut in half*	*4 oz*

an ice-cream machine or ice-cream trays

Turn the fridge freezer or home freezer to its coldest setting.

Melt the chocolate in a bowl over a pan of simmering water. Heat the evaporated milk, then gradually blend it into the melted chocolate. Add the double cream and leave to cool until warm. Then add the marshmallows. (*Note*: the hotter the liquid, the more the mallows will dissolve into the mixture; the cooler the cream, the chunkier the mallows will remain.)

Pour the mixture into the ice-cream machine or trays and freeze as detailed on page 266.

When completely frozen, return the fridge freezer or home freezer to its normal setting.

NOTE: For *Rocky Road Ice Cream* the mallows should be chunky, so add them when the chocolate cream is cooler. When the chocolate mallow mixture is at the soft ice-cream stage, fold in 100 g (4 oz) of chopped nuts (e.g. walnuts, pecans, filberts, mixed nuts).

——BUTTER PECAN ICE-CREAM——
Makes 1 litre (1¾ pints)

4	*egg yolks*	4
100 g	*sugar*	4 oz
50 g	*butter*	2 oz
75 g	*pecans, chopped*	3 oz
360 ml	*single cream or top of the milk*	*generous* ½ *pint*
360 ml	*whipping or double cream*	*generous* ½ *pint*
½ tsp	*vanilla essence*	½ tsp
	pinch of salt	

an ice-cream machine or ice-cream trays; a skillet or frying pan

Turn the fridge freezer or home freezer to its coldest setting.

Beat the egg yolks and sugar until light, thick and creamy. Heat the butter in the skillet or pan, add the pecan pieces, and sauté the nuts very gently for about 5 minutes, taking care not to brown them.

Heat the single cream (or substitute) to almost boiling, then remove from the heat. Stirring constantly, stir into the egg yolk mixture. Return to the pan and to the heat and cook, still stirring constantly, until the custard thickens and coats the back of a spoon. (The custard may be cooked in a double boiler or in a bowl over boiling water to avoid the danger of the eggs curdling.)

Remove from the heat, add the butter and pecans, and stir until the butter is absorbed into the custard. Put the whipping or double cream into a large bowl with the vanilla and salt, and strain in the custard so that the pecan pieces are reserved for adding to the ice-cream later. Once all the liquid has drained from the pecans, cover the custard tightly (e.g. with cling-film) and leave to cool. Also chill the pecan pieces.

Pour the vanilla cream into the ice-cream machine or trays and freeze as detailed on page 266. When the mixture reaches the soft ice-cream stage, fold in the chilled pecan pieces and freeze until solid.

When frozen completely, return the fridge freezer or home freezer to its normal setting.

NOTE: To make *Butter Almond Ice Cream* (another popular flavour in America), substitute almonds for the pecans. Walnuts may also be used in place of the pecans.

——PISTACHIO ICE-CREAM——
Makes 1 litre (1¾ pints)

3	egg yolks	3
100 g	sugar	4 oz
360 ml	milk	generous ½ pint
50 g	butter	2 oz
	large pinch salt	
½ tsp	vanilla essence	½ tsp
½ tsp	almond essence	½ tsp
480 ml	double or whipping cream	generous ¾ pint
6 drops	green food colouring	6 drops
100 g	roasted pistachio nuts in their shells, to yield 50 g (2 oz) shelled nuts	4 oz

an ice-cream machine or ice-cream trays

Turn the fridge freezer or home freezer to its coldest setting.

Beat the egg yolks and sugar in a medium bowl until light and creamy. Heat the milk to scalding point then gradually stir into the egg and sugar mixture. Return the mixture to the pan (or a double boiler) and, stirring constantly, cook until thickening and the mixture coats the back of a wooden spoon. Add the butter and stir until melted. Return the custard to the bowl, cover (e.g. with cling-film), and leave to get cold (if necessary, stir occasionally to prevent a skin forming).

When cold, stir in the salt, vanilla and almond essences, cream and colouring. Pour into the ice-cream containers and freeze as detailed on page 266.

Meanwhile, shell the nuts and rub between thumb and fingers to remove the thin skins. Chop the nuts, or lightly crush in a polythene bag with a rolling pin or mallet.

When the ice-cream is at the 'soft' stage, transfer from the machine or trays to a chilled bowl and stir in the nuts. Return to

ice-cream storage containers and freeze until solid. Return the
fridge freezer or home freezer to its normal setting.

———FROZEN VANILLA YOGHURT———
Makes about 1 litre (1³/4 pints)

Diet-conscious Americans eat many frozen yoghurt products,
such as yoghurt cones and chocolate-coated yoghurt sticks. These
products offer a less fattening alternative to the very sweet,
calorie-laden ice-creams which are so popular in the USA. You
can even buy soft frozen yoghurt from machines, just as you would
soft ice-cream.

1 tbsp	*powdered gelatine*	*1 tbsp*
3 tbsps	*water*	*3 tbsps*
2 tbsps	*honey*	*2 tbsps*
³/4 kg	*vanilla yoghurt*	*24 oz*
360 ml	*double cream*	*generous ¹/2 pint*

an ice-cream machine or ice-cream trays

Turn the fridge freezer or home freezer to its coldest setting.
   Soften the gelatine in the water in a small bowl, then place the
bowl over a pan of simmering water until the gelatine has completely dissolved and is clear. Do not boil. Add the honey and stir
until dissolved. Leave to cool slightly.
   Beat together the vanilla yoghurt and cream in a medium bowl
until well combined. Stir in the gelatine mixture. Pour into the
ice-cream trays or machine, and freeze as detailed on page 266.
   When completely frozen, store in sealed containers and return
the fridge freezer or home freezer to its normal setting.

NOTE: You may substitute plain yoghurt and vanilla essence for
the vanilla yoghurt, but the quantity of sweetening should be
increased, e.g. extra honey or sugar. Other fruit or flavoured
yoghurts may also be used.

——BUTTERSCOTCH SAUCE——
Makes 360 ml (generous ½ pint)

120 ml	corn syrup	scant ¼ pint
175 g	brown sugar	6 oz
	pinch of salt	
25 g	butter	1 oz
5 tbsps	cream or evaporated milk	5 tbsps

Heat the syrup, sugar, salt and butter in a medium pan over a very gentle heat to dissolve the sugar and butter. When completely dissolved, bring to the boil and boil rapidly for about 3 minutes. Remove from the heat, leave to cool slightly, then while still hot stir in the cream or evaporated milk. Serve hot over ice-cream, for example vanilla (page 267).

——HOT FUDGE SAUCE——
Makes about 300 ml (½ pint)

175 g	sugar	6 oz
5 tbsps	water	5 tbsps
25 g	butter	1 oz
75 g	chocolate drops or block chocolate	3 oz
1 tbsp	corn or maple syrup	1 tbsp

Gently dissolve the sugar in the water over a low heat. When completely dissolved, add the butter, chocolate and syrup and continue to heat gently until the butter and chocolate are melted. Bring to the boil and simmer for 3–5 minutes until thickening. Serve hot over ice-cream, for example vanilla (page 267).

——BLUEBERRY SAUCE——
Makes about 1 litre (1¾ pints)

250 g	sugar	8 oz
240 ml	water	scant ½ pint
1	lemon, grated rind and juice	1
¾ kg	fresh or tinned blueberries	1½ lb

| *1 tbsp* | *cornflour* | *1 tbsp* |
| *1 tbsp* | *water* | *1 tbsp* |

Put the sugar and water in a medium saucepan with the lemon rind and juice and bring slowly to the boil. Boil this syrup for 5 minutes.

Meanwhile, wash the blueberries if necessary and pick over the fruit, removing any green berries and the berry stalks. Drain and add to the syrup. Cook for a further 5 minutes.

Dissolve the cornflour in the 1 tablespoon of water, stir in a little of the hot blueberry syrup, then add the mixture to the pan, stirring until thickened. Cook for 1 minute then cool. Chill in the refrigerator.

When chilled serve over vanilla ice-cream (page 267).

NOTE: To thicken the mixture further so that it may be spread as a dessert topping (for example, for cheesecake, page 239), use half the quantity of the above ingredients, except for the cornflour and water, which should remain 1 tablespoon each.

PRESERVES
Pickles, Chutneys, Jellies etc.

——SAUERKRAUT——

This German speciality is often served with hot dogs (page 208) and is an essential ingredient in a Reuben sandwich (page 213). Sauerkraut is also one of the mainstays of Jewish food.

500 g	*hard white cabbage*	*1 lb*
1 tbsp	*coarse (pickling) or sea salt*	*1 tbsp*
1/4 tsp	*caraway seeds*	*1/4 tsp*

NOTE: It is extremely important that all utensils and storage containers should be properly sterilized with boiling water before being used, otherwise you will not achieve the desired results and the cabbage will not keep.

Choose only firm white cabbages (e.g. Dutch) for this recipe. Remove any wilted outer leaves and shred the cabbage very finely into a large bowl. Stir in the salt and caraway seeds and mix together very thoroughly.

Sterilize a large earthenware jar or crock and pack in the prepared cabbage as tightly as possible. Fill to the top of the container and cover first with a clean linen cloth and then with a well-fitting lid. Press the lid down with a heavy weight, for example large tins of fruit or a heavy stone, to exclude as much air as possible.

Leave the container in a warm place for a few days, during which time a brine will have formed which will cover the lid of the container. Every 3 days, remove any scum from the surface and replace the cloth with a clean one. If the level of brine falls below the lid, top it up with extra brine (25 g (1 oz) of salt dissolved in 1¼ litres (2 pints) of water).

The sauerkraut should be left in a warm place for 2–3 weeks to ferment. When fermentation has stopped, it is ready to be used. It will keep for about one more week, but if it is to be stored for longer, it must be processed.

To Process: Drain the cabbage from its brine. Pour the brine into a pan and bring to the boil. Put the cabbage and the hot brine immediately into warm, sterilized preserving jars. Put on the lids, seal, and place in a pan of simmering water (the water should come to within 3 cm (1 inch) of the tops of the jars) for about 25 minutes. Remove the jars from the pan, tighten the seals, and leave to get cold. Label and store.

Processed sauerkraut will keep for at least a year, but once a jar is opened it should be used within a week.

To cook sauerkraut, drain from the brine, put in a pan with only a little water, cover and bring to the boil. Simmer gently for about 10 minutes, then drain and serve with pork dishes, for example smoked pork chops (or bacon chops) and casseroles.

——DILL PICKLES——
Makes about 3 kg (6 lb)

Visitors to the USA will realize how popular dill pickles are from the moment they order their first sandwiches or hamburgers (see page 206) or shop in any American supermarket with its rows of bottles of these baby cucumbers. This is a good recipe for the home gardener looking for ways to use immature cucumbers! French beans can also be bottled this way.

2 kg	*miniature cucumbers, about 8–10 cm (3–4 inches)*	*4 lb*
3–4	*stalks of fresh dill*	*3–4*
1 litre	*water*	*1¾ pints*
480 ml	*cider vinegar*	*generous ¾ pint*
25 g	*pickling or sea salt*	*1 oz*
3–4	*cloves garlic, peeled*	*3–4*
½ tsp	*mustard seed*	*½ tsp*

3 or 4 × 1 kg (2 lb) preserving jars; a preserving pan, water bath or other large pan

Wash and dry the preserving jars and warm them in a low oven.

Scrub the cucumbers, trim the ends, and dry thoroughly. Leave whole or slice lengthwise, if desired, into 4–8 long strips. Wash the dill and separate into pieces.

Heat the water, cider vinegar and pickling salt in a pan until boiling (do *not* use ordinary table salt, which will spoil the colour of the pickles). Bring a preserving pan, water bath, or large pan of water to the boil.

Place one peeled clove of garlic and several pieces of dill in each preserving jar. Add ⅛ teaspoon of mustard seed to each bottle. Pack in the cucumbers as tightly as possible (sliced cucumbers will require 3 jars, whole ones 4). Pour over the hot vinegar solution to almost fill the jars. Lay on the lids and screw caps. Tighten the caps, then release by one quarter turn.

Place the jars on a trivet or a wad of newspaper in the pan or water bath to ensure that the jars do not touch the base. Bring the water back to the boil, then process the jars for 10 minutes for sliced pickles and 15 minutes for whole pickles. Remove the jars on to a board and leave to cool. Check that the lids are completely sealed, then tighten the screw caps, label the jars and store in a cool, dry place.

——CHOW CHOW——
Makes about 4 litres (8 pints)

Nobody knows how this Pennsylvania Dutch mixed pickle got its quaint name. It is traditionally made at the end of the summer growing season and is an excellent way of preserving left-over crops, unripened tomatoes, and smaller cucumbers.

3	small cucumbers	*3*
up to 175 g	salt	*up to 6 oz*
4	onions, peeled	*4*
¾ kg	French beans, topped and tailed	*1½ lb*
4	medium carrots, peeled	*4*
½	head of celery	*½*

2	small sweet peppers (red or green or both), de-seeded	2
1	small, firm head of cabbage	1
1 kg	green tomatoes	2 lb
1	head of cauliflower	1
3/4 kg	butter or broad beans	1 1/2 lb
2 tbsps	celery seed	2 tbsps
4 tbsps	mustard seed	4 tbsps
1/2 tsp	cloves, ground	1/2 tsp
1 tsp	peppercorns	1 tsp
1 tsp	allspice	1 tsp
1 tbsp	turmeric	1 tbsp
1 1/2 litres	white or cider vinegar	2 1/2 pints
240 ml	water	scant 1/2 pint
500 g	sugar	1 lb

a preserving pan or large saucepan; preserving jars

Slice the cucumbers, sprinkle thickly with salt, and leave to stand overnight. The next day, rinse them and drain. Slice the onions, French beans, carrots and celery. Chop the peppers, cabbage and green tomatoes. Separate the cauliflower into florets. Cook the butter or broad beans, green beans, carrots and celery separately until just tender. Drain well.

Combine the spices, vinegar, water and sugar with the cooked and uncooked vegetables in a preserving pan or large saucepan, adding extra water if there is not sufficient liquid. Bring to the boil and simmer for 15 minutes. Pack into sterilized, warm jars, seal and label. Store in a cool place.

——CORN RELISH——
Makes 2 1/4–2 1/2 kg (5–6 lb)

12	ears fresh corn, to yield 1 1/4 kg (3 lb) corn kernels – or frozen or tinned sweetcorn kernels	12

1	large red pepper	*1*
1	large green pepper	*1*
3	large stalks celery, finely chopped	*3*
2	medium onions, peeled and finely chopped	*2*
600 ml	white vinegar	*1 pint*
1 tsp	turmeric	*1 tsp*
1 tbsp	salt	*1 tbsp*
1 tbsp	dry mustard	*1 tbsp*
1 tsp	celery seeds (optional)	*1 tsp*
1/4 tsp	cayenne	*1/4 tsp*
250 g	sugar	*8 oz*

a large preserving pan or heavy saucepan

Strip the corn kernels from the cobs by running a knife or the pointed tip of a potato peeler down the lines of kernels. This will part the kernels, but not the hulls, from the cob. Cut the peppers in half and remove the centre seeds and any white pith. Cut the flesh into small thin strips.

Put the kernels, pepper strips, finely chopped celery and onions in the pan with the vinegar, turmeric, salt, mustard and celery seed, if used, cayenne and sugar. Dissolve the sugar slowly over a gentle heat, then bring to the boil. Reduce the heat and simmer for about 20 minutes until the relish is beginning to thicken. Pour into clean, warm, dry jars, seal with polythene, and store in a cool, dry place. Keep for 1 month before using.

——HOT DOG OR GREEN RELISH——
Makes about 2 1/4 kg (5 lb)

2	large onions, peeled	*2*
1	large green pepper, de-seeded	*1*
1	large red pepper, de-seeded	*1*
4 small or 2 large	cucumbers	*4 small or 2 large*

2 tbsps	salt	2 tbsps
1 dsp	celery salt	1 dsp
1 tbsp	made mustard	1 tbsp
1 tbsp	turmeric	1 tbsp
600 ml	cider or white vinegar	1 pint
500 g	sugar	1 lb

a preserving pan or large saucepan

Mince together or finely chop the onion, green pepper, red pepper and cucumbers, and put in the pan or saucepan with the rest of the ingredients. Heat gently until all the sugar is dissolved, then bring to the boil and simmer for about 15–20 minutes until the relish has thickened.

Pot in warm, sterilized jars, seal, label, and store in a cool, dry place. Serve over hot dogs (page 208), hamburgers (page 206), or with cold meats.

——PICKLED WATERMELON RIND——
Makes about 2½ litres (4 pints)

Huge, juicy watermelons are a common sight in fruit and vegetable shops, in supermarkets, and on farmers' roadside stands during the summer months in the USA. At the height of their season they can be surprisingly cheap, and these pickles ensure that even better value for money is gained from the watermelon by using the normally discarded white rind. Although a favourite throughout the country, they are also part of the Pennsylvania Dutch 'seven sweets (desserts) and seven sours (pickles, salads, etc.)' served at a traditional Pennsylvania Dutch meal. Use a large whole watermelon, approximately 2¼ kg (5 lb) in weight.

1 kg	watermelon rind	2 lb
3 tbsps	salt	3 tbsps
2½ litres	cold water	4 pints
240 ml	white vinegar	scant ½ pint
600 g	sugar	1¼ lb
½ tsp	grated nutmeg	½ tsp
1	cinnamon stick	1
1 dsp	whole allspice	1 dsp

1 tsp	*whole cloves*	*1 tsp*
1	*lemon, thinly sliced*	*1*
2–3	*drops of green food colouring*	*2–3*

a preserving pan or large saucepan; pickling jars

Prepare the rind by cutting away the red pulp of the watermelon. Remove the green skin with a sharp knife, leaving only the white inner rind. Cut this into 3 cm (1 inch) cubes and place in a glass bowl. Add the salt and enough cold water to cover the rind completely – about 1¼ litres (2 pints). Leave to stand for 12 hours or overnight at room temperature.

Drain the rind in a colander and rinse well with cold water until it runs clear. In a preserving pan or large saucepan, put the remaining water with the vinegar, sugar and nutmeg. Tie the cinnamon stick, allspice and cloves in a piece of cheesecloth or muslin and add to the pan.

Heat gently until the sugar is dissolved, then bring to a rolling boil. Add the watermelon rind and simmer gently, uncovered, until the rind is cooked – about 40 minutes. Remove from the heat and remove and discard the cinnamon, allspice and cloves. Add the sliced lemon and the green colouring, stir well, and pour into warm, sterilized jars. Seal, label and store in a cool, dry place. This pickle is best left for at least 2 weeks before sampling.

——SPICED PUMPKIN——
Makes 3 litres (5 pints)

2 kg	*pumpkin, peeled and cut into 3 cm (1 inch) squares*	*4 lb*
1¼ kg	*sugar*	*2½ lb*
480 ml	*white vinegar*	*generous ¾ pint*
1 tbsp	*whole allspice*	*1 tbsp*
2 tbsps	*whole cloves*	*2 tbsps*
3	*sticks of cinnamon*	*3*
1 tsp	*ground ginger (optional)*	*1 tsp*

a preserving pan or large saucepan

Put the prepared pumpkin in a large bowl and cover with the sugar. Leave to stand overnight.

The following day, put the pumpkin, sugar and the liquid which has accumulated into the preserving pan or large saucepan. Add the vinegar, allspice, cloves, cinnamon and ginger, and bring to the boil slowly to dissolve the sugar completely. Cook until the pumpkin is clear and the syrup is thick – approximately 30 minutes. Pack the pumpkin in warm, sterilized jars and pour over the hot syrup. Seal and label the jars, and store in a cool, dry place.

NOTE: This is a delicious way to preserve pumpkin. The pieces should be a little chewy, not soft and mushy.

——CRANBERRY MOULD——
Makes 600 ml (1 pint)

Cranberries are native to North America and were one of the new fruits that the settlers learned to adopt and adapt to their cooking techniques. It wasn't long before their tart flavour made cranberries the natural complement to meats like turkey. Today, ready-made moulds in attractive, thick glass jars can be bought in American supermarkets at Thanksgiving and Christmas. Usually these moulds are jellies, but the home-made mould is more attractive and tastier if the berries are left whole. It is also a tasty accompaniment to lamp chops or a crown roast of lamb.

250 g	*sugar*	*8 oz*
360 ml	*water*	*generous ½ pint*
350 g	*cranberries*	*12 oz*

a 600 ml (1 pint) mould

Dissolve the sugar in the water in a pan over a gentle heat. Bring to the boil and simmer for 10 minutes.

Wash the cranberries and discard any that are unripe. Remove any stalks. Add the berries to the syrup and simmer for 7–8 minutes until all the berries have 'popped' – i.e. burst their skins – and the mixture has thickened. Pour into the mould and chill until set.

To un-mould, dip the mould in hot water to loosen the sides and invert on a serving plate. This mould will keep well for quite a while if covered and stored in the refrigerator.

NOTE: A little grated orange rind will add extra flavour to the mixture.

——GRAPE JELLY——
Makes about 1¼ kg (3 lb)

This is America's best-loved preserve, a must on breakfast toast, the kids' favourite in peanut butter sandwiches, and even a popular addition to cream cheese sandwiches. California and New York states are the chief grape producers in the USA – both also head production of America's growing wine industry.

2 kg	black grapes	4 lb
300 ml	water	½ pint
about 800 g	sugar	about 1¾ lb
40 g	liquid pectin	1½ oz

a preserving pan or large saucepan; a jelly bag or piece of muslin cloth

Strip the grapes from the stalks, wash them, and put them in a large pan with the water. Stew, covered, for 10 minutes, then remove from the heat and mash the grapes (e.g. with a potato masher or large fork). Return the pan to the heat and stew for a further 5 minutes. Strain the grape juice from the pulp through a jelly bag or a piece of muslin, suspended over a bowl. Leave the bag to drip overnight.

The following day, measure the strained juice into the preserving pan or large saucepan. Allow 400 g (14 oz) of sugar for each 600 ml (1 pint) of juice. Add the pectin and, stirring, bring the mixture to the boil. Remove from the heat, add the sugar, then return to the heat. When the sugar is dissolved, bring to a full rolling boil and boil hard for 1 minute.

Remove from the heat and pot the jelly in clean, warm, dry jars; seal, label and store in a cool, dry place.

NOTE: Grapes do not have sufficient pectin of their own to set the jelly without the aid of commercial pectin.

INDEX

MORE ABOUT PENGUINS, PELICANS, PEREGRINES AND PUFFINS

For further information about books available from Penguins please write to Dept EP, Penguin Books Ltd, Harmondsworth, Middlesex UB7 0DA.

In the U.S.A.: For a complete list of books available from Penguins in the United States write to Dept DG, Penguin Books, 299 Murray Hill Parkway, East Rutherford, New Jersey 07073.

In Canada: For a complete list of books available from Penguins in Canada write to Penguin Books Canada Ltd, 2801 John Street, Markham, Ontario L3R 1B4.

In Australia: For a complete list of books available from Penguins in Australia write to the Marketing Department, Penguin Books Australia Ltd, P.O. Box 257, Ringwood, Victoria 3134.

In New Zealand: For a complete list of books available from Penguins in New Zealand write to the Marketing Department, Penguin Books (N.Z.) Ltd, Private Bag, Takapuna, Auckland 9.

In India: For a complete list of books available from Penguins in India write to Penguin Overseas Ltd, 706 Eros Apartments, 56 Nehru Place, New Delhi 110019.

COOKERY AND GARDENING IN PENGUINS

□ *Italian Food* **Elizabeth David** £3.95

'The great book on Italian cooking in English' – Hugh Johnson. 'Certainly the best book we know dealing not only with the food but with the wines of Italy' – *Wine and Food*

□ *An Invitation to Indian Cooking* **Madhur Jaffrey** £2.95

A witty, practical and irresistible handbook on Indian cooking by the presenter of the highly successful BBC television series.

□ *The Pastry Book* **Rosemary Wadey** £2.95

From Beef Wellington to Treacle Tart and Cream-filled Eclairs – here are sweet and savoury recipes for all occasions, plus expert advice that should give you winning results every time.

□ *The Cottage Garden* **Anne Scott-James** £4.95

'Her history is neatly and simply laid out; well-stocked with attractive illustrations' – *The Times*. 'The garden book I have most enjoyed reading in the last few years' – *Observer*

□ *Chinese Food* **Kenneth Lo** £1.95

The popular, step-by-step introduction to the philosophy, practice, menus and delicious recipes of Chinese cooking.

□ *The Cuisine of the Rose* **Mireille Johnston** £5.95

Classic French cooking from Burgundy and Lyonnais, explained with the kind of flair, atmosphere and enthusiasm that only the most exciting cookbooks possess.

COOKERY AND GARDENING
IN PENGUINS

☐ *The Magic Garden* **Shirley Conran**   £3.95

The gardening book for the absolute beginner. 'Whether you have a
window box, a patio, an acre or a cabbage patch . . . you will enjoy
this' – *Daily Express*

☐ *Mediterranean Cookbook* **Arabella Boxer**   £2.95

A gastronomic grand tour of the region: 'The best book on
Mediterranean cookery I have read since Elizabeth David' – *Sunday
Express*

☐ *Favourite Food* **Josceline Dimbleby**   £2.50

These superb recipes, all favourites among Josceline Dimbleby's
family and friends, make up 'an inspiration to anyone who likes to be
really creative in the kitchen' – Delia Smith

☐ *The Chocolate Book* **Helge Rubinstein**   £3.95

Part cookery book, part social history, this sumptuous book offers an
unbeatable selection of recipes – chocolate cakes, ice-creams, pies,
truffles, drinks and savoury dishes galore.

☐ *Good Healthy Food* **Gail Duff**   £2.50

Mushrooms in Sherry, Lamb with Lemon and Tarragon, Strawberry
and Soured Cream Mousse . . . You'll find that all the dishes here are
tempting and delicious to taste, as well as being healthy to eat.

☐ *The Adventurous Gardener* **Christopher Lloyd**   £4.95

Prejudiced, delightful and always stimulating, Christopher Lloyd's
book is essential reading for everyone who loves gardening. 'Get it
and enjoy it' – *Financial Times*

PENGUINS ON HEALTH, SPORT AND KEEPING FIT

☐ **Audrey Eyton's F-Plus**   £1.95

F-Plan menus for women who lunch at work * snack eaters * keen cooks * freezer-owners * busy dieters using convenience foods * overweight children * drinkers and non-drinkers. 'Your short-cut to the most sensational diet of the century' – *Daily Express*

☐ **The F-Plan Calorie Counter and Fibre Chart**
Audrey Eyton   £1.95

An indispensable companion to the F-Plan diet. High-fibre fresh, canned and packaged foods are listed, there's a separate chart for drinks, *plus* a wonderful selection of effortless F-Plan meals.

☐ **The Parents A–Z** **Penelope Leach**   £6.95

From the expert author of *Baby & Child*, this skilled, intelligent and comprehensive guide is by far the best reference book currently available for parents, whether your children are six months, six or sixteen years.

☐ **Woman's Experience of Sex** **Sheila Kitzinger**   £5.95

Fully illustrated with photographs and line drawings, this book explores the riches of women's sexuality at every stage of life. 'A book which any mother could confidently pass on to her daughter – and her partner too' – *Sunday Times*

☐ **Alternative Medicine** **Andrew Stanway**   £3.25

From Acupuncture and Alexander Technique to Macrobiotics and Yoga, Dr Stanway provides an informed and objective guide to thirty-two therapies in alternative medicine.

☐ **Pregnancy** **Dr Jonathan Scher and Carol Dix**   £2.95

Containing the most up-to-date information on pregnancy – the effects of stress, sexual intercourse, drugs, diet, late maternity and genetic disorders – this book is an invaluable and reassuring guide for prospective parents.

PENGUINS ON HEALTH, SPORT AND KEEPING FIT

☐ **Medicines** **Peter Parish**   £4.95

Fifth Edition. The usages, dosages and adverse effects of all medicines obtainable on prescription or over the counter are covered in this reference guide, designed for the ordinary reader and everyone in health care.

☐ **Baby & Child** **Penelope Leach**   £7.95

A fully illustrated, expert and comprehensive handbook on the first five years of life. 'It stands head and shoulders above anything else available at the moment' – Mary Kenny in the *Spectator*

☐ **Vogue Natural Health and Beauty**
   Bronwen Meredith   £7.50

Health foods, yoga, spas, recipes, natural remedies and beauty preparations are all included in this superb, fully illustrated guide and companion to the bestselling *Vogue Body and Beauty Book.*

☐ **Pregnancy and Diet** **Rachel Holme**   £1.95

With suggested foods, a sample diet-plan of menus and advice on nutrition, this guide shows you how to avoid excessive calories but still eat well and healthily during pregnancy.

☐ **The Penguin Bicycle Handbook** **Rob van der Plas**   £4.95

Choosing a bicycle, maintenance, accessories, basic tools, safety, keeping fit – all these subjects and more are covered in this popular, fully illustrated guide to the total bicycle lifestyle.

☐ **Physical Fitness**   £1.25

Containing the 5BX 11-minute-a-day plan for men and the XBX 12-minute-a-day plan for women, this book illustrates the famous programmes originally developed by the Royal Canadian Air Force and now used successfully all over the world.

PENGUIN REFERENCE BOOKS

☐ **The Penguin Map of the World** £2.95

Clear, colourful, crammed with information and fully up-to-date, this is a useful map to stick on your wall at home, at school or in the office.

☐ **The Penguin Map of Europe** £2.95

Covers all land eastwards to the Urals, southwards to North Africa and up to Syria, Iraq and Iran * Scale = 1:5,500,000 * 4-colour artwork * Features main roads, railways, oil and gas pipelines, plus extra information including national flags, currencies and populations.

☐ **The Penguin Map of the British Isles** £2.95

Including the Orkneys, the Shetlands, the Channel Islands and much of Normandy, this excellent map is ideal for planning routes and touring holidays, or as a study aid.

☐ **The Penguin Dictionary of Quotations** £3.95

A treasure-trove of over 12,000 new gems and old favourites, from Aesop and Matthew Arnold to Xenophon and Zola.

☐ **The Penguin Dictionary of Art and Artists** £3.95

Fifth Edition. 'A vast amount of information intelligently presented, carefully detailed, abreast of current thought and scholarship and easy to read' – *The Times Literary Supplement*

☐ **The Penguin Pocket Thesaurus** £2.50

A pocket-sized version of Roget's classic, and an essential companion for all commuters, crossword addicts, students, journalists and the stuck-for-words.

PENGUIN REFERENCE BOOKS

☐ **The Penguin Dictionary of Troublesome Words**   £2.50

A witty, straightforward guide to the pitfalls and hotly disputed issues in standard written English, illustrated with examples and including a glossary of grammatical terms and an appendix on punctuation.

☐ **The Penguin Guide to the Law**   £8.95

This acclaimed reference book is designed for everyday use, and forms the most comprehensive handbook ever published on the law as it affects the individual.

☐ **The Penguin Dictionary of Religions**   £4.95

The rites, beliefs, gods and holy books of all the major religions throughout the world are covered in this book, which is illustrated with charts, maps and line drawings.

☐ **The Penguin Medical Encyclopedia**   £4.95

Covers the body and mind in sickness and in health, including drugs, surgery, history, institutions, medical vocabulary and many other aspects. Second Edition. 'Highly commendable' – *Journal of the Institute of Health Education*

☐ **The Penguin Dictionary of Physical Geography**   £4.95

This book discusses all the main terms used, in over 5,000 entries illustrated with diagrams and meticulously cross-referenced.

☐ **Roget's Thesaurus**   £3.50

Specially adapted for Penguins, Sue Lloyd's acclaimed new version of Roget's original will help you find the right words for your purposes. 'As normal a part of an intelligent household's library as the Bible, Shakespeare or a dictionary' – *Daily Telegraph*

A CHOICE OF PENGUINS

☐ **The Complete Penguin Stereo Record and Cassette Guide**
Greenfield, Layton and March   £7.95

A new edition, now including information on compact discs. 'One of the few indispensables on the record collector's bookshelf' – *Gramophone*

☐ **Selected Letters of Malcolm Lowry**
Edited by Harvey Breit and Margerie Bonner Lowry £5.95

'Lowry emerges from these letters not only as an extremely interesting man, but also a lovable one' – Philip Toynbee

☐ **The First Day on the Somme**
Martin Middlebrook   £3.95

1 July 1916 was the blackest day of slaughter in the history of the British Army. 'The soldiers receive the best service a historian can provide: their story told in their own words' – *Guardian*

☐ **A Better Class of Person** John Osborne   £2.50

The playwright's autobiography, 1929–56. 'Splendidly enjoyable' – John Mortimer. 'One of the best, richest and most bitterly truthful autobiographies that I have ever read' – Melvyn Bragg

☐ **The Winning Streak** Goldsmith and Clutterbuck   £2.95

Marks & Spencer, Saatchi & Saatchi, United Biscuits, GEC . . . The UK's top companies reveal their formulas for success, in an important and stimulating book that no British manager can afford to ignore.

☐ **The First World War** A. J. P. Taylor   £4.95

'He manages in some 200 illustrated pages to say almost everything that is important . . . A special text . . . a remarkable collection of photographs' – *Observer*

A CHOICE OF PENGUINS

☐ *Man and the Natural World* **Keith Thomas**   £4.95

Changing attitudes in England, 1500–1800. 'An encyclopedic study of man's relationship to animals and plants . . . a book to read again and again' – Paul Theroux, *Sunday Times* Books of the Year

☐ *Jean Rhys: Letters 1931–66*
Edited by Francis Wyndham and Diana Melly   £4.95

'Eloquent and invaluable . . . her life emerges, and with it a portrait of an unexpectedly indomitable figure' – Marina Warner in the *Sunday Times*

☐ *The French Revolution* **Christopher Hibbert**   £4.95

'One of the best accounts of the Revolution that I know . . . Mr Hibbert is outstanding' – J. H. Plumb in the *Sunday Telegraph*

☐ *Isak Dinesen* **Judith Thurman**   £4.95

The acclaimed life of Karen Blixen, 'beautiful bride, disappointed wife, radiant lover, bereft and widowed woman, writer, sibyl, Scheherazade, child of Lucifer, Baroness; always a unique human being . . . an assiduously researched and finely narrated biography' – *Books & Bookmen*

☐ *The Amateur Naturalist*
Gerald Durrell with Lee Durrell   £4.95

'Delight . . . on every page . . . packed with authoritative writing, learning without pomposity . . . it represents a real bargain' – *The Times Educational Supplement*. 'What treats are in store for the average British household' – *Daily Express*

☐ *When the Wind Blows* **Raymond Briggs**   £2.95

'A visual parable against nuclear war: all the more chilling for being in the form of a strip cartoon' – *Sunday Times*. 'The most eloquent anti-Bomb statement you are likely to read' – *Daily Mail*